1992

Aristotle's *Poetics*

Perspectives on Classical Political and Social Thought

Citizens and Statesmen: A Study of Aristotle's *Politics* (1992)
  Mary P. Nichols, Fordham University

Love of Glory and the Common Good: Aspects of the Political
Thought of Thucydides (1992)
  Michael Palmer, University of Maine

Marx and Aristotle: Nineteenth-century German Social Theory
and Classical Antiquity (1992)
  edited by George E. McCarthy, Kenyon College

Aristotle's *Poetics*: The Poetry of Philosophy (1992)
  Michael Davis, Sarah Lawrence College

Aristotle's *Poetics*

The Poetry of Philosophy

Michael Davis

Rowman & Littlefield Publishers, Inc.

ROWMAN & LITTLEFIELD PUBLISHERS, INC.

Published in the United States of America
by Rowman & Littlefield Publishers, Inc.
4720 Boston Way, Lanham, Maryland 20706

British Cataloging in Publication Information Available

Library of Congress Cataloging-in-Publication Data

Davis, Michael, 1947–
Aristotle's Poetics : the poetry of philosophy / Michael Davis.
p.   cm. — (Perspectives on classical political and social
thought)
Includes bibliographical references and index.
1. Aristotle. Poetics. 2. Poetics. I. Title. II. Series.
PN1040.A53D38 1992
808.1—dc20   92–7952 CIP

ISBN 0-8476-7741-9 (cloth : alk. paper).
ISBN 0-8476-7742-7 (paper : alk. paper)

Printed in the United States of America

The paper used in this publication meets the minimum requirements of
American National Standard for Information Sciences—Permanence of
Paper for Printed Library Materials, ANSI Z39.48–1984.

For Seth Benardete

Because of wondering, human beings, both now and at first, began to philosophize, wondering from the beginning at the absurdities at hand and then moving forward by small steps also being perplexed by greater ones.

Metaphysics 982b11–15

Contents

Acknowledgments

I am grateful to Sarah Lawrence College and to the Earhart Foundation for grants generously supporting my work on Aristotle's *Poetics*. Seth Benardete, Ronna Burger, and Susan Davis read and commented on earlier versions of this book with great care. It has been much improved by their suggestions.

Introduction

It would be tragic to write a book on Aristotle's *Poetics* unarmed with a sense of humor. Because no Aristotelian text has been so commented on, any new commentary will deserve two responses. On the one hand, its novelties should be met with a suspicion increasing in proportion to their importance, for how could generations of commentators—many rather illustrious—have missed the point? On the other hand, if there is nothing new of importance to say about the *Poetics*, why say it? Either what follows is exotic, in which case it is suspect, or it is ordinary, in which case it is superfluous.

This difficulty is connected to another. While certain terms of the *Poetics* (e.g., *katharsis*, *mimêsis*, *hamartia*, and *peripeteia*) are important and ambiguous enough to have given rise to long traditions of scholarly controversy, the overall intent of the book seems straightforward. Aristotle means to give an account of poetry, emphasizing tragedy. Now, there are a variety of ways in which one might argue that the truth of Aristotle's *Poetics* as a whole goes deeper than it seems. It wouldn't be hard to "deconstruct" a book that uses cognate words to describe the errors of characters in tragedy (*hamartia*, 1453a10), of those criticizing tragedians (*harmartanousin*, 1453a24), and of the poets themselves (*hamartanein*, 1451a20). As a piece of artfully constructed writing—a *poiêma*, the *Poetics* is in some sense subject to its own analysis. Nor would it be difficult to understand the preoccupation of the *Poetics* with tragedy as symptomatic of an illness of Western culture generally, whether in terms of a misguided celebration of the "individual," which reaches its climax in bourgeois capitalism, or in terms of a "phallocentric" affirmation of *logos* or in terms of a "hierarchizing of genres," which is only the overt sign of "class bias" and "conservative politics."[1] Or, Aristotle's rationalizing

of poetry might be understood as the perennial reaction of human beings to their darker side—the Apollinian defense against Dionysian chaos
or the superego's attempt to cancel the id.[2] Or, perhaps Aristotle's el-
evation of plot over character might be taken to reveal Greek rationalism's
imperfect understanding of human subjectivity.[3] Any of these approaches
would lend a certain depth to the *Poetics*. While not denying that it is
about poetry, each in its way would argue that when properly understood
the *Poetics* is about much more—it is about everything. Of course, "properly
understood" means understood in a way other than Aristotle understood
it; in becoming an object to be explained, the *Poetics* would cease to be
an explanation in its own right. We therefore seem once again to be confronted
with a choice. Either we take the "straightforward" intention of the *Poetics*
seriously (Aristotle's intention), or we treat the book as less straightforward but with a borrowed significance symptomatic of some foreign force
altogether beyond Aristotle (e.g., language, history, gender, or eros). The
Poetics may gain in significance as the particularity of its concern is
transcended, but, as Aristotle and his intention are left behind, the explicit subject matter of the book becomes trivialized. The *Poetics* might
as well have been a cookbook.

But perhaps these alternatives are only apparently exhaustive. While
the *Poetics* is about poetry generally and about tragedy in particular (the
commentators have not missed the point), it is also about the fundamental
structure of human action. Now, if reason is what is distinctive to human action, a book about the structure of human action must also be a
book about reason. The *Poetics* can be about both not because Aristotle
has chosen to conceal an exotic discussion underneath an ordinary account of poetry—as though esoteric writing meant hiding one's real intention behind an arbitrary facade—but rather because poetry, action,
and reason are so profoundly connected that a discussion of one necessarily involves the others. The nature of this necessity is an issue important enough to justify yet another commentary on Aristotle's *Poetics*. It forces us to reinterpret the meaning of the book as a whole without
committing the folly of assuming that no one has ever understood anything important about what is probably Aristotle's most frequently read
piece of writing.

Still, if the *Poetics*'s discussion of poetry by way of tragedy is on
another level a discussion of reason by way of human action, why does
Aristotle nowhere make the relation between these two levels explicit?
Is he unaware of the connection? If so, then something else must be
responsible for the uncanny superimposition of one discussion over another. In various ingenious and mutually incompatible ways this is the
assumption of most contemporary modes of interpretation. The cunning

of history, eros, language, or whatever—any cunning but Aristotle's—allows interpreters to do what they cannot in any case resist doing by virtue of an impulse deeply rooted in the nature of thinking itself; it allows them to see that a text means more than it first seems to mean, that its ordinary surface has a depth, a being underlying its seeming. At the same time it powerfully finesses the question of why it should be possible for them to do what they are doing. What deconstructionists, Freudians, Marxists, and historicists share is an understandable desire to both have and eat their cake. A world without knots and puzzles—and so levels of meaning—is uninteresting to them, but the solutions they give these puzzles make the very activity of being puzzled an anomaly. Whenever intelligence gets resolved into some preintelligent foundation, searching for meaning gets squeezed out by what is "found." And those interpreters, who, having noticed that our seeking after the ground—what is hidden beneath—never seems to result in a foundation, conclude that the task of interpretation is unending and that all foundations are therefore merely posited, fail to notice that they have noticed this unendingness of interpretation. They have taken a step back from the world to learn something of it even in their denial that such a step is possible. All meaning is therefore not simply posited. Now, despair of the possibility of interpreting might not be so bad if it meant only that literary criticism would cease. While such a world might be poorer, it would not be bankrupt. However, the possibility of interpretation is intimately connected to the possibility of thought. Intelligence and humanity compel critics to continue questioning, yet their doctrines make the activity absurd. Fortunately intelligence and humanity regularly triumph over doctrine.

The question not to be finessed has two parts. Why should Aristotle have made an inquiry into the nature of human action look like an inquiry into poetry, especially since elsewhere (*Nicomachean Ethics* 1040a1–6) he clearly distinguishes the two? What is the relationship between poetry and action, and what about this relationship requires that it be presented in the indirect way in which Aristotle has presented it? And second, why does the man who also clearly distinguishes elsewhere between the theoretical and the poetic (*Metaphysics* 981b26–82a3) embed a discussion of reason in a discussion of poetry? These—no small questions—amount to asking why the *Poetics* has the form it has or what the relationship is between its form and its content. This is the guiding question of the commentary that follows.

To justify the claim that the *Poetics* is concerned with the structure of human action and reason is an odyssey requiring an interpretation of the book as a whole. As always, *pathei mathos*—the proof of the pudding is in the eating. Still, one ought to offer some preliminary observations by way of inducement to taste the pudding. The stated subject matter of the *Poetics* is *poiêtikê* (the art of poetry) itself and its species (*eidê*). Aristotle argues that tragedy is paradigmatic for poetry (*poiêsis*), and so the book about poetry can be primarily about its most perfect manifestation. At the same time, something important is left implicit. At the end of his discussion of the historical origins of comedy and tragedy, Aristotle remarks that the Dorians lay claim (*antipoiountai*) to both, citing their names as signs.

> And they [claim to call] *poiein* by the name *dran*, but they claim the Athenians call it by the name *prattein*. (1448b1–2)[4]

While this seems scarcely more than a footnote, and granted that *poiein* would ordinarily mean "to do" in the sense of "to make," here Aristotle goes out of his way to invite us to consider *poiein* and *prattein* as synonyms.[5] In this context *poiein* means "to act." Ought we to retranslate the title of the *Poetics* accordingly? *Peri poiêtikê*s would then mean Concerning the Art of Action. Actors and acting would have something to do with action; poetry would somehow be at the center of human life.

Circumstantial evidence favors such a view of the *Poetics*. If all human action seems to aim at some good, and if the existence of instrumental goods points toward a good for the sake of which we choose all the others, and if there is a science of this highest good, and if as Aristotle says this is political science, or *politikê* (*Nicomachean Ethics* 1094a), then one would expect poetry and politics to be closely linked. They are. Aristotle's *Politics* ends with an account of music, and especially poetry, as both the means for educating men to be good citizens and the goal for which the rational animal is educated.

What all of this might mean becomes somewhat clearer in Aristotle's *Nicomachean Ethics*. In Book III, courage or manliness (*andreia*) is said to be the proper mean with regard to the passions fear and confidence. However, since fear can be understood as an anticipation or *prosdokia* of bad things generally, lest courage be thought somehow equivalent to all of virtue, the particular fear with which it deals must be specified. As the most terrible fear is of death, this must be what concerns courage—but not all death. Courage comes into play where it is possible for us to exercise choice. It is therefore most of all concerned with facing death in war.

To make this point Aristotle compares drowning at sea with fighting a battle. The comparison recalls *Iliad* XXI where Achilles fights with a river—called Xanthus by the gods and by us and Scamander by Achilles and the Trojans. Achilles laments the possibility that he might die in this ignominious way; to us who are aware that he is fighting with a god, his fate does not seem so disgraceful. Aristotle knows, of course, that is possible to be courageous in a hurricane but thinks such courage is understood metaphorically. The paradigm is always fighting in battle. The account of the specific moral virtues, therefore, begins with courage because courage is a model for how to deal with all fear understood as *prosdokia* of the bad, and so for how to deal with the bad generally. Aristotle focuses on a situation in which we have a choice so as to provide a model for behaving always as though we had a choice. Accordingly, Achilles is not simply the most courageous but the model for virtue altogether.

The hardest problem for Aristotle's account of courage is that, while the moral virtues are supposed to make us happy, courage is frequently rather unpleasant and can easily make us dead. Why, then, does the brave man risk his life? Aristotle says it is for the sake of the *kalon*—the noble or beautiful. But this *kalon* end is clearly not present in the activity itself. Neither killing nor being killed is by itself beautiful. We must look elsewhere than the dead bodies fouling the Scamander to see Achilles' devotion to the *kalon*. The brave man, presenting an image to himself of his action as completed, contemplates his deed as others will contemplate it, and so reaps the benefits of honor even before it has been granted. The current action becomes *kalon* insofar as it is made complete through reflection or imagination. The brave, therefore, do what they do not because it is good but because they can say "it is good." This is what the *kalon* means; it is impossible without *logos*.

Aristotle calls the highest of the spurious forms of courage political courage; its goal is honor. He uses as examples Hektor and Diomedes worrying about what will be said of them if they do not fight (1116a22–26). But just what is it which differentiates this from acting "for the sake of the *kalon*"? If courage always means courage in war, then it will always manifest itself in a political context. Cities make war; individual men do not. But if courage is a virtue, it ought to be something that transcends any particular *polis*. This is the problem of Achilles. Apart from the *polis* he cannot show his virtue, but once he returns to the fighting his motives are necessarily obscure. Does he do it for Patroklos, for the Greeks, for honor, for immortality? *Andreia* is in principle invisible, for one cannot see it apart from a political context, which is to say apart from the ulterior motives for action that are attributed to the political man.

The most startling thing about the account of courage in the *Nicomachean Ethics* is that Aristotle uses almost exclusively fictional examples—Achilles, Hektor, Diomedes, and so forth. Without poetry there is virtually no possibility of seeing that element that makes courage what it is. The brave man does not risk his life out of a greater fear, or shame, or confidence due to superior experience. And yet from the act itself it is impossible to tell the difference between these spurious forms of courage and the real thing. We need the whole story, and only poetry gives it to us. Poetry lets us see inside men so that we can celebrate their devotion to the *kalon*. It makes visible the reflection that enobles action. This points us back to the earlier account of the metaphorical character of courage in a storm at sea. In a way, *all* courage is metaphorical. Even Achilles is playing a role; he knows his fate and is therefore the paradigm of the courageous man; like all brave men, he wants "to die like Achilles." Poetry makes it possible to experience our action as whole before it is whole. This wholeness then becomes a part of the experience itself. Or rather, because the conjunction does not really occur temporally, poetry constitutes the experience. In the case of courage what would be essentially painful is transformed into something "pleasant."[6] And insofar as courage represents all moral virtue here, poetry would be the necessary condition for moral virtue generally. It is what allows us to experience our lives as wholes.

We can go one step further. All human action is always already an imitation of action—Achilles is living up to his own image of himself; it is therefore poetic. Accordingly, given the beginning of Aristotle's famous definition of tragedy as an "imitation of action" (1449b24), the *Poetics* would seem to be about two things: *poiêsis* understood as poetry—an imitation of action; and *poiêsis* understood as human action—already itself also an imitation of action. Aristotle can combine an analysis of poetry with an analysis of action because in some sense the two are the same thing. That they are the same thing is what it means for human beings to be rational animals. With this in mind, let us begin at the beginning.

Part I

Mimêsis

The most important thing about acting is honesty. If you can fake that, you've got it made.

—George Burns

1

Second Things
(1447a8–18)

[1][7] The *Poetics* may be something deeper than it seems; however, its seeming remains to be explained. Poetry has a power impressive enough to be an object of wonder in its own right. Aristotle's book—not often read as an explanation of ourselves to ourselves—is nevertheless often read. Now, if it is obvious that the *Poetics* is about poetry, it is equally obvious that Aristotle understands poetry as a form of *mimêsis*—imitation or representation. At first glance, *mimêsis* seems to be a stylizing of reality in which the ordinary features of our world are brought into focus by a certain exaggeration, the relationship of the imitation to the object it imitates being something like the relationship of dancing to walking. Imitation always involves selecting something from the continuum of experience, thus giving boundaries to what really has no beginning or end. *Mimêsis* involves a framing of reality that announces that what is contained within the frame is not simply real. Thus the more "real" the imitation the more fraudulent it becomes.[8] If the concern of the *Poetics* is the art of poetry itself, and the heart of poetry is *mimêsis*, then perhaps the concern of the *Poetics* can be understood to be *mimêsis*, not in its various forms or its products but what it really is in itself. According to Aristotle, human beings differ from other animals in being the most imitative. We delight in seeing images because in doing so we "learn and reason about [*sullogizesthai*] what each thing is, i.e., that this man is that" (1448b4–17). That we imitate, therefore, has to do with our uncontrollable urge to see past the surface of things. To have to say "this is that," of course, means "this" does not first appear to be "that," whatever further examination reveals as the truth of the matter. We must put things together. At 1450a4–5 Aristotle defines plot

3

as the "putting together [*sunthesis*] of deeds [*pragmata*]." Shortly after that (1450a38–39), he calls plot "the soul and first principle of tragedy." Tragedy is, of course, an imitation of actions or deeds (1450a16). Putting all of this together, it looks as though the putting together of actions or deeds is the soul and first principle of imitation of actions or deeds. That is, putting together is the soul and first principle of imitation. When Aristotle points to *mimêsis* as our distinctive feature, he may seem to be offering a new definition of human beings potentially at odds with his other definitions—rational animal (*Nicomachean Ethics* 1098a, 1102a–103a, *Politics* 1253a10–15) and political animal (*Politics* 1253a3). However, understanding our nature as mimetic proves to be an interpretation of our nature as rational, which in turn is the same as our nature as political. The *Poetics* is an account of the rationality that is the distinctive feature of human action.

But to represent *mimêsis* as such would be like giving a *logos* of *logos*, or thinking about thought.[9] A representation of representation would involve an initial displacement of our attention in the direction of the object represented. To represent representation one would have to show something being represented. But it is not possible to show an image of an apple without showing an apple. The *Poetics* is primarily about *mimêsis*—this fundamental thing we do that makes us human. However, *mimêsis* defies being looked at directly. In general it is accessible only by way of its product, also called *mimêsis*. But the inquiry into these products insofar as they are understood as imitations looks like an inquiry into poetry. The *Poetics*, an inquiry into the art of poetry itself, is about human action as constituted by the irresistible impulse of reason to *sullogizesthai*—to see this as that. Making this issue thematic in general rather than in a particular context would mean taking a direct look at what can be seen only indirectly. Because this task is impossible, the normal mimetic displacement of our attention toward the object represented must crop up elsewhere. Since all representation must be of some object, in the *Poetics* the representation of *mimêsis* in general shows itself as an inquiry into something particular—poetry, but with a necessary narrowing of the meaning of the term. Poetry is peculiar; while it ranges everywhere imitating all of life, not everything is poetry. Poetry has a specific range. Aristotle tells us that no one would mistake what Empedocles wrote for poetry despite the fact that it is metrical; at the same time, there is no limit to the range of poetry—anything can be its object. Ironically, this strange possibility of displacing the general meaning of *mimêsis* by the queerly particular meaning present in poetry is at the root of the power of poetry—the subject matter of the book as ordinarily understood. Poetry is the poetic object of Aristotle's *Poetics*.

From the second the *Poetics* begins, Aristotle has introduced these issues:

> Concerning both *poiêtikê* [the art of poetry, making, doing] itself and the forms [*eidê*] of it, what particular power each has, and how one should put plots together if the *poiêsis* [poetry, making, doing] is to hold beautifully, and further from how many and from what sort of parts it is, and similarly also concerning whatever else belongs to the same inquiry, let us speak, beginning according to nature first from the first things. (1447a8–13)

Presumably if one possessed the art of carpentry itself, one would be adept in the making of anything out of wood. And, possessing the art of politics itself, one would have the knowledge necessary to function in every political regime. But what is the art of poetry itself? Would the man possessing *poiêtikê autê* be capable of producing every species of poetry?[10] Has there ever been such a poet? And what does Aristotle mean by the *eidê*, the forms or species, of the art of poetry? The sequel suggests that he is referring to the various forms of poetry (e.g., tragedy or epic), but that cannot be the case. The *eidê* must be the forms of the art of poetry.[11] Still, the two are easily confused. How could one articulate the variety within *poiêtikê* other than by articulating the variety it produces? Tragic poets make tragedies, epic poets make epics; while there is one art of poetry "itself," it takes various forms depending on whether it is concerned with epics, tragedies, lyric poems, and so forth. The matter with which the art of poetry deals is peculiar. Carpenters know the nature of wood and so its potential for transformation independent of their knowledge of precisely what the wood is to be transformed into. But what exactly is the matter with which the poet deals? Words? But they are the matter of prose as well. All speech is no more poetry than all bodily movement is dance. More than the other arts, then, *poiêtikê*—the art of poetry or production or making or doing or acting—is invisible in itself apart from its products. There is no hiding a half-constructed bookshelf; a half-written poem need exist nowhere. If, like the art of carpentry, *poiêtikê* is a knowledge that is responsible for a certain manner of dealing with things, then this manner is not really separable from its object as an art, the content of what it deals with.

Aristotle's inquiry into *poiêtikê* begins first from the "first things." "First" is both adverbial, how we begin, and also refers to that with which we begin. Nevertheless, as the making must in some way precede the thing made, although Aristotle may claim to begin with first things, he cannot help beginning with what comes second. The various *eidê* of *poiêtikê* are visible only in the different *poiêseis* of which they are the arts. This primacy of the "second things" is curiously confirmed by Aristotle's language.

Poiêtikê is originally an adjective modifying a feminine noun. However, in adjectives with the *ikê* ending (e.g., *aulêtikê, politikê, rhêtorikê*), the noun—either art (*technê*) or knowledge (*epistêmê*)—has come to be implicit in the adjective; it becomes a substantive—the art or science of the flute, the city, or the orator. As an object in its own right, it appears to be a first thing when in fact it is a second thing. This change is confirmed by the double appearance of *autês*—"itself" in the first instance and "of it" in the second. By referring to *poiêtikê* itself, or the poetic itself, Aristotle transforms what was adjectival, and so dependent for its existence on what it modified, into an independent substance. To speak of the poetic as such or the poetic in itself is to make a second thing into a first thing, a transformation confirmed by the second *autês* that at first seems parallel to the first but in fact is not intensive but only a genitive pronoun, "of it." The apparently parallel structure poetically seduces us into gliding over the real movement of the sentence. *Poiêtikê* has been made an "it"— a first thing—without our even realizing it. It is the purpose of the first sentence of the *Poetics* to call attention to this fact while at the same time concealing it. This is no accident; a book on the art of poetry must be about something that is always about something else without itself being about that something else.

Aristotle glosses his inquiry into the *eidê* of the art of poetry as an inquiry into what power each *eidos* has. *Poiêtikê* itself is visible only in its various species—the arts of tragedy, epic, and so forth. These species are in turn visible only as the powers they have to show themselves as products—poems. Aristotle is therefore concerned with the parts of a poem and how they are to be put together *kalôs*—beautifully or nobly— not as a guide for how to generate poetry but as an analysis of how poetry is generated. The *Poetics* is philosophy of literature masquerading as a writing workshop. It is an analysis or a taking apart of what it means to put things together. It seems to tell us how to put poems together out of certain parts, but in fact the parts will never exist sufficiently apart from one another to allow us to begin with any of them in isolation. They are the results of analysis, not building blocks. One cannot begin with the "parts" of tragedy named by Aristotle in chapter six and discussed in the remainder of the *Poetics* and put them together to make a tragedy. Tragedy is not plot plus character plus diction, etc.; these things are never apart from one another. Only by realizing how they are already necessarily mixed together can they be remixed in a way that is most *kalon*.

Poetry can never be a mixture of elements that are truly "first things." The *Poetics* begins as it does to display the cause of this feature of poetry. By distinguishing the art of poetry and its species from the beautiful products of the art, Aristotle already suggests the distinction within *mimêsis*, later to become thematic, between the act of imitating and the product of imitation (1448b4–17), a distinction that parallels Aristotle's ordinary understanding of the difference between acting and making. Children who mimic their elders practice imitation; artists, who in their imitating paint portraits, produce imitations. We all do the former by nature and take pleasure in inspecting the latter. Once having seen the explicit distinction in *mimêsis* between the act of making poetry and the poetry made, we are able to see Aristotle's beginning in a new light. What comes later is already implied in the word *poiêtikê* itself. Formed ultimately from a verb that means "to do" (*poiein*) and an ending (*ikê*) that transforms the action of the verb into the object of an art, *poiêtikê* must treat action as a product. Furthermore, the verb is itself ambiguous, meaning "to do" both in the sense of "to act" and in the sense of "to produce." Aristotle begins the *Poetics* with the simple distinction between act and product, but each time we try to isolate the act itself, we discover in it a product. *Poiêtikê autê* seems always to hide itself behind a poem.

The first things of *poiêtikê* to which Aristotle, without explanation, now turns are imitations, things in their very natures of something else— that is, second things. The list is peculiar.

> Now epic poetry [*epopoiia*] and the making [*poiêsis*] of tragedy, and further comedy and the art of making dithyrambs [*dithurambopoiêikê*], and most of the art of the flute and of the kithara all happen to be in general [*to sunolon*] imitations. (1447a13–16)

As *epoipoiia* contains the verb *poiein* within it and can mean either the making of epic or epic, Aristotle begins by retaining the ambiguity between activity and product. That the second first thing is the making of tragedy seems at first to resolve this ambiguity by separating *poiein* from the sort of thing made—the first thing is not the poem but the activity of the poet. *Poiêtikê* would then be the art of this activity. And yet the word Aristotle uses to isolate tragedy from its making, *poiêsis*, means something made or produced. What is left then but to get rid of the troublesome verb altogether? Accordingly, Aristotle's next example is simply *kômôidia*—comedy; the word can mean only the poetry itself, not the act of its production. And yet that comedy should serve this purpose is curious, for it is not like other forms of poetry. Just as stand-up comics frequently write their own material—we see them acting, but their action is also their product, perhaps most of all in comedy is the act of making represented. A Sophocles might be too busy for tears while weaving together the strands of the plot of the *Trachiniae*, but it is not so clear that an Aristophanes wouldn't at least smile his way through the composition of the *Birds*. Comic actors frequently begin or end as comic writers; are tragedy and tragic acting similarly bound together?[12] Now, if even expunging the verb *poiein* doesn't allow us to isolate one term of this dyad of action and production so as to get us to a first thing, what about throwing everything into one word so as at least to display the elements side by side? Although *dithurambopoiêtikê*—the art of making dithyrambs—puts everything into the pot, it can refer only to the art of the action, or making dithyrambs, and not to dithyrambic poetry. So the addition of the *ikê* ending makes an object of the activity that is itself intelligible only in terms of the object it produces. This seems to be the feature of poetic *mimêsis* that differentiates it from other imitation—two examples of which follow, *aulêtikê* and *kitharistikê*. The art of the flute means flute playing. It does not involve making flutes. Rather, the knowledge that constitutes the art is determined by the features of an instrument that preexists the act of flute playing. Flautists play the flute and play tunes but in different senses; their art is not the art of the tune. *Aulêtikê* is not the same as *mousikê*.

Mimêsis first means mimicry but also representation, both as an action and as a product. The movement of Aristotle's list reflects this doubleness. The how and the what of imitation are so blurred together in *epopoiia* as to suggest an unself-conscious making akin to mimicry. The "making of tragedy" suggests a clear-cut distinction, and *dithurambopoiêtikê* suggests a conscious bringing together of act and product, or of mimicry and representation, or of how and what, or of unself-conscious making (habit or *sunêtheia*) and analysis of the making *(technê)*. But one might go one step further. *Mimêsis*, already connected to thinking, has proved to have a problematic unity. The *Poetics* means to be an account of this unity. But the unity of *mimêsis* is nothing less than the unity of that being in which reason and impulse mix to form the rational animal.

Aristotle's examples reveal the crucial feature of poetic imitation to be the difficulty in separating its object from its activity. That is borne out in the immediate sequel.

> But they [imitations] differ from one another in three ways—either by imitating in different things, [imitating] different things, or [imitating] differently and not the same way. (1447a16–18)

This seems straightforward enough; it provides a structure for the first three chapters of the *Poetics*—the remainder of chapter one dealing with that in which the imitation takes place, chapter two with what is imitated, and chapter three with how it is imitated. However, there is an ambiguity in the Greek. *To mimeisthai hetera* certainly means to imitate different things, and *to mimeisthai heterôs* means to imitate differently. But the accusative neuter plural of an adjective can also be adverbial.[13] If we were to take *hetera* as equivalent to *heterôs* here, beneath the obvious and sensible surface, Aristotle would be suggesting that what is imitated is somehow the same as how it is imitated. That how something is imitated is always the real object of imitation seems crazy unless imitating the act of imitation itself, collapsing the distinction between product and act, means depicting the peculiarly human element of action. Of course the *Iliad* must have a certain content for it to be a poem at all. But the "wrath of Achilles" is not identical to the sum of the events Achilles undergoes as viewed from the outside. There is no wrath of Achilles unless these events seem significant to Achilles. When we are angry we may rehearse alleged wrongs done to us, but this representation of particular events is meant as paradigmatic. It is not the slap in the face that arouses our wrath, but its significance. Ironically, the presentation to ourselves of the significance of the event involves a representation of the event. Similarly, these events are not what Homer is imitating despite the fact that they are the content of his imitation. Homer's reason for imitating the events lies behind the events themselves. In this sense, his own act of imitation is ultimately what he is imitating.

Insofar as all human action is already an imitation of action, it is in its very nature poetic. This places the beginning of Aristotle's famous definition of tragedy—that tragedy is an imitation of action—in a new light. The *Poetics* is about *poiêsis* understood as poetry, or imitation of action, and *poiêsis* understood as action, which is also imitation of action. It is the distinctive feature of human action that whenever we choose what to do we imagine an action for ourselves as though we were inspecting it from the outside. Intentions are nothing more than imagined actions—internalizings of the external. All action is therefore imitation of action; it is poetic.

But what does this perplexing formulation mean? The issue is really the same as arises, say, for Freudian psychology. Why are we inclined to try to understand ourselves in terms of what happened to us when we were very young? The events of our youth seem to be formative because pure; they are so remote as even to be sometimes thought of as prenatal. These events are meant on the one hand to be experiences and thus real but on the other hand to be perfect types or forms and thus formative. The power of Freudian psychology for us has to do with its attempt to understand experience in terms of a more purified experience—that is, with its attempt to understand experience poetically. But, of course, if all experience is of this kind, then there never could have been a primal experience. My current behavior might be understood as Oedipal, but the initial Oedipal reaction cannot be understood as Oedipal. That is the reason why it is characterized by way of a poetic reference (i.e., by reference to the behavior of an adult). The grown man is understood in terms of a primordial event experienced as a child that is, in turn, only intelligible in terms of a myth about a grown man. In what sense, then, can we ever discuss first reactions? On the one hand, we cannot understand our experience by way of some primal experience because what determines our experience and makes it what it is cannot be one of our experiences. On the other hand, we do not seem to be able to understand our experience in any other way. It may be that to say that the first things for us are always imitations (i.e., second things) is paradoxical, but it is a paradox not easily resolved.

2

In What
(1447a18–b29)

The second-hand character of the first things of *poiêtikê* becomes clearer in Aristotle's account of differences in that in which imitations are made.

> For just as some who make images imitate many things with [or by] colors and figures—some through art and some through habit [*sunêtheia*], and others through the voice [*phônê*], so also with respect to the arts mentioned, all make the imitation in rhythm and speech [*logos*] and harmony, but these either apart or mixed together. (1447a18–23)

This is a puzzling passage. One thinks at first that Aristotle means to distinguish between imitations in visual images and imitations in sound— thus demonstrating how the *eidê* of imitation can be differentiated by the medium in which the imitation is made. *Phônê*, however, means primarily the voice and only metaphorically sound in general. That voice is not meant as a strict parallel to color and figure is also clear by its place in the sentence. Some are said to make imitations with or by means of colors and figures (*chrômasi kai schêmasi*), while others imitate through the voice (*dia tês phônês*). The difference is highlighted by Aristotle's apparently parenthetical remark about how imitations with color and figure can be through either art or habit.[14] We are therefore tempted to say that voice is to be compared with art and habit rather than with color and figure. But voice would then be a way of imitating and not a medium of imitation. Vocal imitation would be of the same order as artful imitation or habitual imitation. This makes sense so long as the sentence stands by itself, but the sequel seems to demand a distinction between visual imitation and imitation in sound. However, *phônê* as voice is not sound; it is not a being in its own right. To speak of a voice means to

11

have assumed something that speaks through voice, that has a voice. That we do not speak in voice but through voice is perhaps the most fundamental sign of our natures as mimetic. Color and figure might be understood as the simples out of which painted images are constructed, but voice is not simple; it is already mimetic.[15] A voice is only a voice when it has something to say, even if only an expression of pleasure or pain. Only when taken metaphorically as all of sound does *phônê* compare to color and figure.[16] As a first thing, therefore, it is only metaphorically first, and so, although Aristotle hints that it is the "primordial" stuff of poetic imitation, he must further resolve it into its elements to reveal the "in which" of poetic imitation. We must get to the first things behind the first thing.

That in which all the arts mentioned[17] are imitated (their medium) is rhythm (*rhuthmos*), speech (*logos*) and the putting together of notes in a pleasing way that seems to mean both harmony and melody (*harmonia*)— the three taken either alone or mixed together, either all or in part. Unlike the first things of painting (figure and color), these are already all dispositions, arrangements, or modifications of sound. The stuff of poetry is already compounded. This seems to be the consequence of building poems out of words. Images are made out of elements that are themselves already images.[18]

This apparently applies not only to that in which the poetic imitation is made but also to that which is imitated. Empedocles will be cast from the ranks of the poets despite the metrical form of his work. If form is not decisive, is the issue content? In representing the transformations of earth, air, fire, and water under the influence of love and strife, Empedocles is attempting to imitate the first things directly. But it is characteristic of poetry always to take as its beginning point second things. Is this also why the *Poetics* concentrates on tragedy and not comedy? In his list of poetic imitations Aristotle let comedy stand alone without any connection either to making or to art. There is a sense in which what comedy imitates is less made than what tragedy imitates. This would be in accord with Aristotle's later remark (1451b11–32) to the effect that tragedy uses old stories whereas comedy relies much more on natural types. Comedy in this sense is prior to tragedy. The situations in tragedy seem strange and artificial; we have to work our way through the play to see why the events defining Oedipus should be in any way paradigmatic for human life or what Philoctetes incurable wound has to do with us, but the first lines of Aristophanes' *Clouds* are sufficient for any parent of teenagers to recognize what is happening between Strepsiades and Pheidippides. And yet still, Aristotle concentrates on tragedy and not comedy. He concentrates on what seems derivative because the truth of the human condition is that, however familiar situations appear to us, the first things are of necessity derivative or second. All action is imitation.

Aristotle's examples of the ways in which *rhuthmos, logos,* and *harmonia* stand alone and mix together are instructive. Instrumental music is a combination of rhythm and harmony. The art of dancers is supposed to be an example of rhythm standing alone. By making "dancers" parallel "pipes," Aristotle suggests that the dancers are to be understood as instruments, but, by commenting on how they imitate even passions and actions by the rhythms of their figurings (*schêmatizomenôn*), he calls us back to the obvious fact that these figures are not audible. There is no dance without sight. Rhythm may be able to stand apart from the other two aspects of sound, but this example scarcely shows it standing alone. *Logos* alone and *logos* mixed with rhythm (metrical *logos*) are both said to have no name. Aristotle ends the first chapter with a discussion of the various kinds of poetry in which all three are mixed together.

What possibilities have been left out? Aristotle does not discuss what *harmonia* by itself would be—presumably because to be more than a sound, notes must move; that is, they must have rhythm. Thus Aristotle does not mention the combination of *logos* and *harmonia* because when music moves it has rhythm. So, with the exception of *logos* alone, the fundamental feature of imitation in sound seems to be rhythm or time.

Why would *logos* be an exception? Aristotle "explains" by means of a long digression.

For we would not be able to give any name in common to the mimes of Sophron and Xenarchus and the speeches [*logous*] of Socrates, not even if someone should make the imitation through trimeters or elegaics or any other such things except that men, putting together the making with the meter name them elegaic poets [makers] and epic poets, not addressing them as poets with regard to the imitation, but with regard to the meter they have in common. For even if they bring out/publish something in meter about medicine or natural science, they [men in general] are accustomed to call it this. But nothing is common to Homer and Empedocles except the meter. Hence it is just to call the one poet, but to call the other, rather than poet, one who gives an account of nature. And similarly, if someone should make an imitation by mixing together all the meters, as Chaeremon made *Centaur*, a mixed rhapsody from all meters, it would be necessary also to address him as poet. (1447b9–23)

The mimes of Sophron and Xenarchus seem to have been character sketches in prose. The speeches of Socrates, whether we take them to be Platonic dialogues or Socrates' actual speeches, were also in prose. Aristotle suggests that, just as we have no common name for these two simply because they are in prose, we should have no common name for other *logoi* simply because they are in meter. Homer is as different from Empedocles as Socrates is from Sophron, but the presence of meter in the former case obscures the difference, whereas the lack of common name in the latter case is evidence that the two are not identified. This last is especially puzzling since Aristotle uses a word that might easily have been applied to both—mime (*mimos*). He might have said that *mimos* is a generic term that, like *poiêsis*, came to be restricted to a species within the genus. Thus, Socratic *logoi* and Sophronic mimes would both be mimes in the generic sense. In not making remarks of this sort Aristotle suggests that there is a radical difference between the two, a difference that is analogous to the difference between the poems of Homer and the metric writings of Empedocles. There is then a difference within imitations in sound in addition to the difference between sounded and visual imitations, and it is so important that it threatens the unity of the genus *mimêsis*. What is it that makes it possible to call Socratic speeches, Homeric epic, and Chaeremon's mixed rhapsody, as well as dithyrambs, nomes (*nomos* could also mean law), tragedy, and comedy, all poetry but excludes mimes and metric treatises?

Aristotle's intent becomes clearer at the end of the digression:

> Concerning these things, then, let them be defined in this way. For there are some which use all the things mentioned—I mean [*legô*], for example, rhythm, song and meter—such as the making [*poiêsis*] of dithyrambics and of nomes [*nomôn*], and both tragedy and comedy. But they differ because some [use] all at the same time and others [use them] severally [*kata meros*]. These then I say [*legô*] to be the differences among the arts in that in which they make the imitation. (1447b23–29)

This is a reworking of the first account. Rhythm has remained constant, but *logos* has become meter, and *harmonia* has become song.[19] Aristotle calls attention to what has happened by introducing the new list with *legô*—I mean or I say. He has incorporated speech or *logos* into the other two parts. Harmony or melody plus speech is song; speech plus rhythm is meter—there can be no meter without words.[20] Aristotle has thus first introduced the possibility that *logos* can stand alone as the "in which" of poetic imitation only to take it back at the end of chapter one. Furthermore, harmony was never said to be alone, and rhythm was only problematically alone in the art of dance. Well after their introduction, we discover that none of the original first things can stand by themselves. Why does the argument proceed in this way? As spoken, *logos* is necessarily sounded, and thus rhythmical if not metrical. Even talking to ourselves is rhythmical. For *logos* to exist apart from rhythm, then, it would have to bear its other sense—something like "meaning" or *ratio*. In this sense it would, like a painting, exist all at once and so not unfold in time. The key to the first chapter of the *Poetics* is that the distinguishing feature of poetic *mimêsis* is rhythm or time.[21]

On its face, this makes sense. Although it is true that we do not always take in a painting all at once but move from part to part, the painting itself does not force us to begin with any part and thus treat one as necessarily prior to another. This is of course not the case in poetry. A poem about a Grecian urn could describe it in some detail, but only by moving through the description piece by piece—thus literally bringing pieces of the urn into existence before others to display them. Poetry of necessity represents difference as temporal difference. It is the paradigm for *poiêsis*—making, from which it borrows its name. Poetry must present the parts of things as independent of one another even when it means to demonstrate their necessary connection.[22] It treats the parts of an analysis as though they were the parts out of which something is generated. Of necessity poetry presents *eidê* as though they were parts. But this is true of any *logos*. What distinguishes Homer and Socrates from Empedocles and Sophron is that, being aware of this limitation of speech, they use it.

Aristotle's own mode of argument in the *Poetics* imitates the problem of the *Poetics* and must do so. He began with rhythm, harmony, and speech as separate to combine them so as to show that they cannot exist separately. It is the nature of poetic imitation to present temporally what can only be understood as a whole, as though it could be put together part by part. In poetry, the longing for autonomy may get worked through as killing one's father and intercourse with one's mother—being the cause of oneself coming to mean literal self-generation. One therefore might retranslate the penultimate sentence of chapter one.

> But they [the arts mentioned] differ in that on the one hand they use all, but on the other hand they proceed by parts. (1447b27–28)

The general movement of chapter one of the *Poetics* is from poetry to imitation to a subset of imitation that is set off from the visible as its medium and seems to have to do with sound. Yet Aristotle allowed this subset to include dance so as to make clear that the underlying feature of this imitation was in fact not sound but time. At the same time it turned out that the "in which" specified by Aristotle as being threefold (rhythm, harmony, and speech) was problematic. The three cannot be understood as parts of poetry separable from one another, and so they cannot be first things in the sense of constituent elements existing independently of one another. Thus, Aristotle's account, which at first seems to be concerned with how to put poetry together—a genetic account, proves to be an analysis of poetry—an eidetic account. Now, this putting together obviously extends over time. What is peculiar to poetic imitation, then, is that it appears to be a putting together of elements in time but in fact is not. Why then does it conceal its eidetic character?

We have noticed repeatedly that Aristotle reproduces this movement in his own writing. The degree of this self-reflexiveness is not at first obvious. The *Poetics* sometimes seems poorly written; there is little introduction, atypically no account of the goal of the inquiry, few methodological remarks, and no account of the views of his predecessors. The book also seems full of digressions and incomplete. Think only of the famous "lost" second book on comedy that some take to be promised at 1449b21. The *Poetics*, then, which is about literature, seems least able of all Aristotle's books to fit his description of tragedy, and since tragedy is paradigmatic for poetry generally, of all poetry as an organic whole made up of beginning, middle, and end (chapter seven). Nevertheless, the book is replete with signs that Aristotle means it to be taken as an example of what he is talking about.[23] As a general rule, the *Poetics* tends to do some version of what it is talking about just after having talked about it. In the chapter one Aristotle begins by treating rhythm, harmony, and speech as separable and ends by forcing us to realize their inseparability. This way of proceeding is the way of poetry and at the same time his way in the *Poetics*. If we recall the connection between *mimêsis* and thinking, this coincidence should not surprise us. If time is the "in which" of poetry, perhaps it is that in which thought necessarily takes place as well. If doing or acting takes the form of poetic imitation, and thinking takes the form of poetic imitation, then poetry would be the meeting point of doing and thinking. It would be a way of understanding them as one. If human beings are the rational animals, then the two parts of human nature can be understood as one in terms of poetic imitation. Or, poetic imitation—imitation in time—will be the key to what it means that the actions of human beings are rational. This, in turn, will have something to do with our way of making independent and separate beings out of the things we attempt to understand. And, in time, Aristotle connects this with metaphor as the fundamental characteristic of human thought (chapter twenty-two). But it is clear at least that the account of the medium of poetic imitation in chapter one has paved the way for the discussion of the object of poetic imitation in chapter two. If the medium of poetry is time, it should come as no surprise that the object of poetry is what in some sense always unfolds in time—action.

3

What and How
(1448a1–b3)

[2]   If it is inappropriate to call Homer an epic poet, form cannot be what gives poetry its character. Are poets, then, to be distinguished by the content of their poetry? Unlike the other arts, poetry has no peculiar content but ranges over all of what is. And yet Empedocles, whose concern was the whole, was a *phusiologos* and not properly a poet. If neither the what nor the how define poetry, perhaps it is distinguished by the togetherness of the two—*hetera* and *heterôs* understood as one.[24] This is the key to understanding what Aristotle means when he says that "those imitating imitate those acting" (1448a1). Acting—the proper object of poetic imitation—is not a thing at all; it is a way.

   Chapter two begins with its own ambiguities.

> Since those imitating imitate those acting, it is necessary for them to be either good/earnest [*spoudaios*] or base/paltry [*phaulos*] (characters almost always follow such things alone, for all differ with respect to characters by vice [*kakia*] and by virtue), either better than what relates to us or worse or such [as relates to us], just like painters. (1448a1–5)

By this time it is no surprise that it should be so perfectly unclear whether Aristotle's "them" refers to those who are imitating or to those who are being imitated.[25] Both must be thought of as better or worse since imitation is not only of action but is itself a species of action. Whatever it teaches us about action generally must also apply to itself. In a discussion presumably about the things imitated in poetry, Aristotle goes out of his way to confuse imitators and imitated. But why? And why the shift in emphasis from actions as objects of imitation to character as that according to which they differ? Is it that we can get at what men are like inside only by depicting what goes on outside even though what goes on outside has meaning only because of what we presume to have gone on inside?

Those acting—in whichever sense—are first said to have to be either good (*spoudaios*) or base (*phaulos*), but that proves to mean either better or worse. Aristotle's concern is the relative goodness of men as made manifest in their actions, but how is this measured? Some will be better than what relates to us (*kath'êmas*), some worse, and some such as relates to us. We are the standard. Now, "we" may be the audience, or it may be the imitators, but in either case those detached from the action use themselves as measures of the action from which they are detached. This is not hard to understand if it is those imitated who are understood to be good or bad. We measure Antigone against ourselves, and whether we find her good or bad, we know that she is not like us. But what if it is those who are imitating who are to be understood as good or bad? Insofar as the question of the goodness or badness of something arises by way of comparison to "us," there is always an implied spectator to the evaluation. That characters differ solely by virtue and vice seems to mean that we differentiate on the basis of what is worthy of imitation and what is not—what we would like to be versus what we would like to avoid. This, in turn, is only possible insofar as we represent the alternatives to ourselves. Poetry does this explicitly; we learn of the wrath of Achilles by observing the actions of Achilles. But all evaluation—of ourselves as well as of others—necessarily takes a poetic form. If this is so, then the point of Aristotle's ambiguity is that it does not matter whether he is referring to those imitating or to those imitated since the action of those imitating—the representation of the good and the bad— is that without which men cannot be good or bad. Hence the action of those imitating is in its way the action of those being imitated. The ultimate object of poetic imitation is the way of poetic imitation itself.

Without something akin to poetry there would be no good or bad in the world. In that sense *kath'êmas* is the pivot on which the moral world turns. Were we identified only with what we do, we would have no distance from our actions and so no way of posing alternatives for ourselves. Action stripped of intention is indistinguishable from motion. Alternatives cannot simply be identified with ourselves because, as options for us, they must be sufficiently apart from us to be understood as better or worse according to us. The good man does not do good deeds mechanically; he must be aware of the alternatives and intend one of them. Now, truly imitating his action in poetry would require imitating this awareness and intention; it would require imitating imitation.

There must be a distinction between "us" and what we represent to ourselves even when it is thought to be "such" as we are. Depending on what is imitated the imitation will vary.

And it is clear that each of the aforesaid imitations will have these differences and will be different [*hetera*] by imitating different things [*hetera*] in this way [or: by imitating this way differently, or: by imitating differently in this way]. (1448a7–9)

The triple claim here is that the imitation of different things amounts to imitating differently which is the same as imitating imitation differently. Painting, dance, flute, kithara, speeches, poetry without music, dithyrambs, and nomes—all the previously mentioned forms of imitation save comedy and tragedy—admit of the three varieties of objects.

With respect to this difference tragedy also stands apart from comedy; for the one tends [or: wishes] to imitate worse [men] and the other better than those now [existing]. (1448a16–18)

Drama appears to exclude the middle possibility: the imitation of men such as we are. And comedy and tragedy tend or wish to imitate the better and the worse but perhaps do not succeed in doing so. In drama everything is acted. There is no possibility of explaining in a detached way what was going on in someone's mind because every explanation is itself a part of the action. If the imitation of men "such as we" meant the imitation of the essential characteristic of all men—our imitative nature, it would be an object excluded from drama in which the detached "we" of imitation could never appear. For that reason—let us call it the ultimate invisibility of intention in the action of which it is the intention— drama could only tend or wish to imitate the actions of better and worse men. But because of this fact it would come closest to representing our true condition in the world; it would in a way imitate us "such as we are" by virtue of its peculiar failure to imitate those better and worse.

There can be no direct revelation of the invisible in tragedy and comedy. Homer can tell us that the man who appears to be Mentor is really Athena, but drama could only show us Mentor.[26] Drama, therefore, most truly represents the way our world resists the direct representation of the invisible. Comedy and tragedy are distinct forms of poetic imitation because of the way they imitate action without making its intention visible, a way identical to their objects of imitation—better and worse men but not men such as they are. For men such as they are could be imitated only by assuming a perspective beyond men such as they are. Taking a painter's view, Homer must make it look easy to determine a man's

motives and so know whether he is good or bad or like us. The what of
poetic imitation is thus in part determined by its how.[27]

[3] An action is not only a movement; it must also have some meaning, a *logos*. Accordingly imitating action involves imitating both of its
elements. How action is imitated, the question to which Aristotle turns
in chapter three so as to complete his account of the various ways in
which imitations differ, will determine which aspect of action is highlighted. The how of imitation affects what is imitated so that there is a
sense in which narration and drama cannot be imitations of the same
thing.

> Further, how someone might imitate each of these [*toutôn*] is a third difference
> of these [*toutôn*]. (1448a19–20)

The first "of these" must refer to the objects of imitation discussed
in the previous chapter; they can be imitated in various ways. The second would seem to refer to poetic imitation, the three *differentiae* of which
have been the subject matter of chapters one through three. The ambiguity introduced by the double use of the word *toutôn* becomes clearer
in an alternative translation of the sentence: "how someone might imitate each of these is a third difference of them." In other words, either
how one might imitate the objects of imitation is a third way of differentiating the objects of imitation, or how one might imitate poetic imitation is a third way of differentiating poetic imitation. This reading helps
make sense of the notoriously difficult text that follows.

> For even imitating the same things and in the same things, it is possible to
> imitate when reporting/narrating—either becoming something else as Homer
> does [*poiei*] or as the same and not changing—or [to imitate] all those imitating
> as acting [*prattontas*] and being in action [*energountas*].[28] (1448a20–24)

Narration represents or imitates action by providing its inner *logos*; drama
is restricted to presenting action as external. Because drama cannot represent action from the inside, it cannot in any direct way do justice to
the imitative nature of all action. It therefore imitates "all those imitating" as though they were merely acting or as though their actions were
energeiai—activities altogether complete in themselves.

While narration and drama are the fundamental alternatives, Aristotle's
insertion of a third between these two seems to question their purity.
Pure narration is all speech. It is about action, but we can appreciate
this action only by ignoring the real action before our eyes—a man speaking.

The sign of the gulf between the two is that the time of the narration moves on a different plane from the time of the action. In a few hours a narrator can tell the story of a whole war, moving forward and back through time as it seems convenient. Pure drama, on the other hand, is all action; imitative time is identical in duration and sequence to the time of the action imitated. By indicating what Homer does (*poiei*) (i.e., coming to be something else), Aristotle points to one epic poet who both reproduces dialogue and, perhaps more importantly, who uses the voice of another to narrate long parts of his poem.[29] Homer's introduction of drama into narration is an indication that a mixture of the two forms is possible. In fact it is more than possible; it is necessary. Just as narration is action rendered in speech, drama is speech displayed as action. The action of *Oedipus* begins long before the play begins and so must be made available to us by way of the narration of characters in the play.

That Homer becomes something rather than someone other is a curious way of putting this point, as is Aristotle's use of the verb *poiein* for what Homer does or makes or poetizes. Homer cannot be said to become someone else when his poem lapses into dialogue, for the characters may be many but there is only one actor. Homer's action, what he does (*poiei*) by becoming different characters, is really the same as what Sophocles does in writing tragedy. But the action of Homer persists in the poem, while that of Sophocles disappears into the actors in his play. Thus making the act of acting visible, Homer's doing or action—his *poiêsis*— shines through his poem—his *poiêsis*. He is not present with us as a narrator would be present in his act of narration (i.e., in person). Nor is he present solely in the actions of persons in his play—his characters. He has neutralized himself—become, not someone, but a neuter something (*ti*).

This might be put somewhat differently. When a man narrates without lapsing into quotation he is speaking about doing. His action in speaking is constant, but it is different from the actions about which he is speaking. His action is, so to speak, in the same world as that of his audience, and so he acknowledges them directly. In a dramatic performance, however, different characters speak. Their actions in the play are in a world discontinuous with our own. They mimic action; theirs is a doing that is not really doing. Because drama requires the illusion that what is acted on the stage is real action, that acting is acting (if you can fake honesty, you can fake anything), it does not acknowledge its audience. To do so would be to acknowledge its own essential dishonesty. As imitation, poetry demands the suspension of our own sense of reality. We must enter into the world represented. But if we really enter into this world it ceases to be a representation and becomes reality. Poetry thus requires our simultaneous belief and disbelief in the world it represents. Aristotle uses Homer to point to the mixture of narration and drama which is the essence of all poetic imitation.

Sophocles is the same as Homer with respect to what is imitated (i.e., good or earnest men); he is the same as Aristophanes with respect to the how of imitating men in action (i.e., drama). This would seem a clear statement of the difference between the how and the what of poetic imitation were it not that Aristotle has just used Homer as his example of a mixture of narration and drama and later emphasizes Homer's dramatic skill and credits Homer's imitation of the base in the *Margites* as central to the development of comedy. And, of course, a moment's reflection reminds us of Thersites in the *Iliad* and the guard in *Antigone*—neither Homer nor Sophocles makes only the good the objects of his poetry. The high cannot be imitated apart from some representation of the low, for to see men acting requires that we see their choices, and for that we must see what they have rejected. Similarly, although the *Clouds* is funny and *Oedipus* is not, is Aristophanes' reflection on what moves Pheidippides to beat his father so far removed from Sophocles' reflection on the crime of father killing?[30] Sophocles is like Homer but not simply because both imitate the *spoudaioi*, and like Aristophanes but not simply because both imitate in the same way. In each case the way of imitation is more intimately bound with what is imitated.

Why then the pretense of a strict distinction between form and content? It would be foolish to let the underlying similarities cause us to lose sight of the obvious differences among epic, tragedy, and comedy. Aristotle begins with these surface differences, but the fact that he gives his own account of the relationship among epic, tragedy, and comedy in chapters four and five is enough to show that he is not satisfied with the simpler version of chapter three. There is a difference between what is first to us and what is first by nature. The digression at the end of chapter three about the Dorians' claim to have originated tragedy and comedy holds the key to Aristotle's intention.

Whence some even say they are called dramas [*dramata*] because they imitate those acting [*drôntas*]. Hence the Dorians also lay claim [*antipoiountai*] to tragedy and comedy—for the local Megarians [lay claim to] comedy as having originated with their democracy. And those in Sicily [lay claim to it], for Epimarchus, the poet, lived there, by far antedating Chionides and Magnes. And some of those in Peloponnesius [lay claim to] tragedy—making [*poioumenoi*] names the sign. For they say that they call their outlying districts *kômai*, but [they say] the Athenians call them *dêmoi*, as if comedians [*kômôdoi*] were so called not from reveling [*kômazein*], but by wandering from *kômê* to *kômê*, being dishonored in the towns. And they say they name doing [*poiein*] *dran*, but that the Athenians name it *prattein*. Concerning the differences of imitation then, both of how many and of what, let these things have been said. (1448a28–b3)

The Dorians' claim depends on the connection between their verb "to act" and the word for acting on stage. Although he says that they lay claim to both comedy and tragedy, Aristotle gives arguments only for drama generally and for comedy. He says of the local Megarians that comedy is naturally at home in democracy and that in Sicily they trace their claim to the dates of Epimarchus's life. It is not clear whether these historical arguments are Aristotle's or the Dorians'. However persuasive, they are nevertheless inconclusive. Megara is not the only democracy, and Epimarchus need not have been the first comic poet. However, if they could trace the names universally given in Greek to comedy, tragedy, and drama to idiosyncracies of their own language, then their case would seem much stronger. However, their attempt to do this is problematic. Comedy derives as easily from "to revel" in Attic as it does from "village" in Dorian, and there seems no reason to prefer the etymology of place to that of activity. The emphasis on *dran* is also difficult, for if "to do" and "to do on stage" are not distinguished, if to act means to act, it is hard to see how a notion of drama could develop. The Dorian etymology of drama therefore turns on itself.

What then is wrong with the Dorian account? Aristotle says they lay claim—*antipoiountai*—to tragedy and comedy. Since we are in the middle of a digression involving a forced etymology, what about this word? It means "to lay claim to," "to exert oneself over," or even "to have something done in return to one." But literally, which is to say not really, it would mean something like antipoetize. What might be antipoetic about the Dorian claim? And why, if he means us to take this hint, does Aristotle then speak of the Dorians making (*poioumenoi*) names the sign of their claim. Their claim is antipoetic but is the use of names on which the claim rests poetic? Does Aristotle mean that the Dorian claim reveals something about tragedy and comedy despite the fact that it is not true? This book about Greek tragedy seems to have learned something from the use of names in Greek tragedy. As names Antigone and Oedipus seem at first to be particular and accidental, but antibirth is the essence of the tragedy of Antigone as the tension between swell-foot and know-where is of the tragedy of Oedipus. Only in poetry or by accident is an anti-hero named Loman. The Dorians make the mistake of using a poetic argument in the real world. If their goal had been to clarify the nature of drama, they would have succeeded; as it was to give an account of its historical origin, they failed.

Chapter three is about the how of poetry. Having said that Sophocles and Aristophanes are alike in their imitation of men doing (*drôntes*), Aristotle appears to become distracted and move to a discussion of the connection between *dran* and drama. In the course of this etymological digression he reveals the antipoetic character of the Dorian claims to consist in their mistaking poetry for reality. They literally trace drama to *dran*— acting to acting—and thus obscure the distinction between the two. And yet their willful etymology was poetic insofar as it did reveal the essential connection between drama and reality. In a poetic account what appears at first to be idiosyncratic is shown to reveal something essential. But isn't this what Aristotle himself has done in chapter three? An apparently irrelevant and inessential digression reveals to us the poetic mode as the appearance of irrelevance and accident. This is the how of poetic *mimêsis*. Its forced separation from the what was a fiction necessary to reveal the intimacy of their relation.

4

Dramatic Imitation
(1448b4–49b20)

[4] Thus far, the argument of the *Poetics* seems to have something like the following structure. Aristotle first splits *mimêsis* into spatial and temporal; he then divides imitation in time into music and poetry (chapter one). He divides poetry into narrative and drama (chapter three) and drama into comedy (chapter five) and tragedy (chapter six). The whole book has been moving toward the isolation of tragedy as Aristotle's principal object of inquiry. However, this systematic division is complicated by several problems. Although *mimêsis* is clearly the beginning point for Aristotle, we are not told what it is until chapter four, and there it proves rather indefinite. Does *mimêsis* mean the act of imitating or the thing imitated? And are the two natural causes of the art of poetry to be understood as our natural tendency to imitate and our delight in imitations, or is *mimêsis* in all its ambiguity to be taken as one cause and harmony and rhythm the other (1448b20–21)? Aristotle had earlier claimed (1447a20–21) that poetic imitation is in *logos*, harmony, and rhythm, but if harmony and rhythm are with *mimêsis* the co-causes of *poiêtikê*, are we to understand that *mimêsis* has replaced *logos* as one those things in which *mimêsis* takes place? What could that mean? Is *mimêsis* that in terms of which poetry must be understood, or is it itself what is to be understood; and does this difficulty have anything to do with the ambiguity within *mimêsis* itself (i.e., *mimêsis* as activity and *mimêsis* as product)?

We need to begin again from the beginning of chapter four.

Some two causes, and these natural, are likely to have generated the art of poetry as a whole.[31] For imitating is natural to human beings from childhood—and in this they differ from the rest of the animals in that they are [literally: it is] the most imitative and do [*poieitai*] their first learning through

145,8 9/7

25

imitation—as it is [natural] for all to take pleasure in imitations. And what happens concerning works [or deeds—*erga*] is a sign of this; for we are pleased in beholding especially precise images of things which themselves we might see painfully, for example, by the visible forms both of the most dishonored of beasts and of corpses. And the cause of this is that not only is learning most pleasant for philosophers, but also for the rest of men, although they only seldom share in it. On account of this, they are pleased in seeing images because, by beholding, it happens that they learn and think through [*sullogizesthai*] what each thing is, for example that this [*man*] is that, since if by chance he has not seen an imitation [*mimêma*] before, it will not produce [*poiêsei*] pleasure except on account of its workmanship or color or on account of some other such cause. Since to imitate is natural for us, as well as harmony and rhythm (for it is manifest that meters are parts of rhythms), from the beginning those especially having these things by nature, advancing little by little, generated poetry [*poiêsis*] from their improvisations. (1448b4–24)

The issue is the double cause of the art of poetry, which seems at first to be identical to a doubleness within *mimêsis*. Children imitate from the very beginning. They learn to speak that way. Imitation here does not mean performance or representation as much as a natural tendency to have the content of one's own doing reproduce what others have done. Such action is fully absorbing; it does not require an awareness that one is imitating. Children are frequently serious about their play. On the other hand, to delight in representation as representation, also natural to us, involves being aware of the playful character of what is being represented. These two versions of *mimêsis*, akin but not identical, repeat a pattern present from the outset of the *Poetics*. *Poiêsis* means both doing or acting and poetry. Poetry in turn is connected to *mimêsis*, which encompasses both mimicry and representation. Delight in representation also proves to have two senses: one is common to most men, the other is philosophical. In whatever we are dividing we come upon an active component and a reflective component, and even when we think we have fastened on the reflective part, as in the cases of poetry and *mimêsis*, each proves to have its own active and reflective component. We end up reproducing in a new form what we thought to have gotten rid of.

But what if the two natural causes of the art of poetry are not the two aspects of *mimêsis* but *mimêsis* as a whole, on the one hand, and harmony and rhythm on the other? This ambiguity about the two causes reinforces what we have already seen, for the active sense of *mimêsis* is to its reflective sense as harmony and rhythm are to *mimêsis* as a whole.[32] It begins to look as though the true doubleness of the cause of the art of poetry has to do with this simultaneous connecting and splitting of action and reflection everywhere present in the account. By replacing *logos*, harmony, and rhythm (the elements of *mimêsis* in chapter one) with *mimêsis*, harmony, and rhythm here, Aristotle suggests that *mimêsis* and *logos* are interchangeable. On the one hand, *mimêsis* must now be understood as in some way an element of itself. On the other hand, *logos* must be understood as fundamentally mimetic. The latter makes sense if representation means first separating something from other things so as to give it a certain wholeness. Painting a portrait requires concentrating on the face to be painted—an act of thought before putting brush to canvas. This act of thought is precisely what is presupposed by all speech. To say "this is that" one must first think this as independent from that. Putting together may be the soul of both imitation and *logos*; however, it first requires thinking apart. *Logos*, no less than *mimêsis*, means framing objects in the world—setting them apart from what surrounds them so as to make them objects for contemplation. Thus, while *logos* is in one sense an element of poetic *mimêsis* (i.e., the stuff out of which poems are made), in another sense *mimêsis* is the stuff out of which *logos* is made. But this is only to say once again that for poetry the first things are second things.

If the art of poetry, or doing, or action is necessarily mimetic, and if being mimetic is the distinguishing feature of human beings, and if that is so because thinking requires putting things together that are not obviously already together (*sullogizesthai*), and if this putting together requires representing in the sense that the act of saying "for example" highlights and makes a whole out of what was previously only part of a continuum, then Aristotle's book on the art of poetry is about the distinguishing feature of human beings. The delight we take in imitations by nature is a delight in putting together. Sometimes this means delighting in the accuracy of representations, but Aristotle makes clear that similitude is not always the source of our pleasure since we can delight in an image even though we have never seen that of which it is supposed to be the image. To be sure *mimêsis* means imitation, and an accurate imitation calls attention to itself as an imitation. Realism in art is necessary to reveal the unreality of art. By seeing that a work of art is a copy of something else, we come to be aware of what a strange thing a copy is; otherwise, a work of art looks like anything else. Yet, it is not the exactitude of the copy that pleases us as much as our own activity of seeing things as copies. Although more obvious in looking at a painting, this activity is the core of all thinking, and so of the characteristically human. *Mimêsis* is above all our ability to stand back from the world to see its pieces as separate from one another so as to put them together again.

Aristotle connects this pleasure of being a spectator, of beholding or contemplating (*theôrountes*), with learning in the ordinary sense and in the extraordinary sense of philosophizing. Philosophy is explicitly present here alone in the *Poetics*, and it is introduced as the exemplary case of the distinguishing human feature. Philosophy is the perfection of the *mimêsis* that is central to poetry. Of the forms of poetry, drama most of all points to the separation of the spectator that is the core of *mimêsis*. Aristotle's choice of examples—corpses and the least honored of the beasts—foreshadows the importance of tragedy for him. The pleasure of thought is so powerful in human beings that it can transform the most fearful thing, death, into something pleasant. Yet corpses are terrible because of what they represent, and it is hard to know what would make animals least honored (*atimotatoi*) unless they stand in some relationship of representation to other things. Asses are perhaps contemptible as war steeds; as pack animals they have an undeniable utility. *Mimêsis* is what makes looking at dead bodies more than eating one's kill; only as beings who can represent ourselves to ourselves can we be aware of our own deaths. *Nekroi* are not meat or carrion but corpses, human beings once alive and now dead. They are horrible not because they are physically ugly, but because they make us aware of our own deaths. But *nekroi* can also mean the dead in Hades. The poetic imitation of the dead, by lifting us out of ourselves and making us spectators, transforms dead bodies into shades in Hades. In so doing it relieves us of our fear and makes it possible for us to pity others. This, the pleasure of tragic drama, makes most manifest the detachment of the spectator that is the defining feature of all *mimêsis*.

The special status of tragedy begins to emerge more clearly in Aristotle's own account of the histories of tragedy and comedy. The sequence of events in this history seems to be the following. While *mimêsis*, rhythm, and harmony are natural to men, some have them to a greater degree than others. The speech of these men is first spontaneous and extemporaneous in the spirit of mimicry. Noticing how well their speech is received, they do it again. The first speech is like pure mimicry—an imitation of action. The second is one step closer to *mimêsis* understood as representation; it is already an imitation of an imitation. In either case the *mimêsis* highlights the actual, as song highlights speaking or dance highlights walking. Now, this mimicry, as an action itself, must have a motive originating in the character of the one acting. Of character there are two fundamental sorts—the more reverent, dignified, or august (*semnoteroi*) and the meaner, cheaper, or more trivial (*eutelesteroi*).[33] The former imitate beautiful or noble actions and the actions of those who are beautiful or noble.[34] These imitations are hymns and encomia— the first praise gods, the second praise men. Does Aristotle mean that although men may do noble deeds, only the gods are noble? The latter, the meaner sort of men, imitate the actions of the base (*phauloi*)—not base actions, making invectives and lampooning (*iambizein*). The one leads eventually to tragedy, the other leads to comedy.[35]

The distinctness of the art of comic poetry from the art of tragic poetry seems assured from this account of their origins. Still, it is partly overcome in the person of Homer. Tragedy and comedy may originate in a disposition to revere and a disposition to hold in contempt, respectively, but Homer is the poet of the lampooning *Margites* as well as of the heroic *Iliad* and *Odyssey*.[36] Obviously, then, the two impulses—revering and belittling—cannot be incompatible. Drama seems to be the principle that brings the two together. But what does it mean that as the most dramatic poet, Homer can be both comic and tragic? The easiest answer is that because the dramatic poet does not speak in his own voice, drama requires that the poet recognize his own activity; he must be able to separate *drama* from *dran*. Comedy is no more simple invective than tragedy is simple praise. As a mimic who is no longer (except accidentally) an actor on the stage, the dramatic poet is essentially invisible. He has therefore made the distinction between the real and the imaginary much more pronounced. By muting the role of his own action—his imitating, he has muted the role of his own character. Chapter four moves from mimicry to representation. However, by beginning with the question of the motive for mimicry, Aristotle has forced us to keep in mind that as an action itself, representation also requires a motive. We still do not altogether understand Homer.

This issue emerges in yet another way when Aristotle cites the various contributions of Aeschylus and Sophocles to the development of tragedy (1449a15–19). Aeschylus reduced the role of the chorus by increasing the number of actors to two, thereby making the *logos* the star of the performance. In fact, by bringing two actors on the stage, Aeschylus created actors. He made it possible for performers to talk to each other and so to ignore the audience. This innovation makes it possible for drama, the action on stage, to present itself as an absolute reality, thus pushing the tension between the two levels of action—*dran* and *drama*—to its most extreme stage.

This history of tragedy is thus of some interest. Poetry begins as natural imitation that is not so different from real life. A man starts performing, but he is still talking to us about things familiar to us. He therefore uses the meter closest to everyday speech—iambic—for his lampooning (*iambizein*). Then, however, to affirm the difference between itself and the world, between *drama* and *dran*—acting and action, poetry becomes stylized. Its meter changes to heroic hexameter. Finally, to affirm the

precision of its imitation of the real, it is driven back to something like
iambic meter, but now in a form, drama, that allows it to assert its absolute reality—it is an accurate representation—and its absolute unreality—it is only a play—simultaneously. This is what Aristotle seems to
mean when he refers to the need to judge tragedy in two ways—itself
according to itself and with regard to its audience (1449a7–9). For itself it must be real—an action; to the audience it must be unreal—acting. This double standard to which all drama, as mimetic, must adhere,
works differently in comedy and tragedy. Because a play is obviously
play (i.e., discontinuous with our real lives), it is harder to take seriously than not. But insofar as what goes on in a play is mimetic, what
we find it easier to laugh at is an imitation of our real lives. In comedy
these two levels agree; it is a playful representation of the playful. In
tragedy the levels are at odds; as the playful representation of the serious, tragedy requires the suspension of one's own concern for one's own
world and its actions in a way not necessary in comedy.

[5] Aristotle had earlier claimed that Sophocles and Aristophanes were
alike insofar as both imitate men doing but differed in the worthiness of
the objects of their imitation (1448a25–28). Now we begin to see more
clearly what he means.

> Comedy, as we said, is an imitation of the base, not however with respect
> to all evil, but with respect to the laughable part of the shameful/ugly. For
> the laughable is an error [*harmartêma*] shameful, but painless and not destructive,
> such as for instance the laughable mask [*prosôpon*] is something shameful
> and distorted, but without pain. (1449a32–37)

Comedy may imitate the base but only those we do not fear. It thus encourages
a sense of superiority on the part of its spectators. From our perspective
of divine detachment we are inclined to wonder at "what fools these mortals
be." We can do that because they do not threaten us by pulling us into
the action of their world. Comedy therefore emphasizes the playful character
of plays. Our acts are serious; those in the play are not. Because there
is no tension between the playful mode of comedy and its playful content, its spectators are encouraged to feel a double sense of superiority
and so detachment. It comes as no surprise, then, that its history should
be less known than the history of tragedy, for, "comedy, on account of
not being serious [*spoudazesthai*], was from the beginning forgotten"
(1449a38–b1). To be an actor—a player—is not to be serious; it is to
substitute acting for action. To be a comic actor is even less serious since
it is not even to imitate things that are serious. Queerly enough, the double
playfulness of comedy allows us to take its actors seriously. Because

the nonseriousness of being a player fits the nonseriousness of the play, it is easy to confuse the two. We are inclined to think "What a fool he is!" and not "What a extraordinary actor he must be to look such a fool." That is why comic choruses were so long left to volunteers—amateurs (1449b1–2). Comedy is seen as more natural, as needing less artifice.[37] It slurs the difference between the actor acting and the action of acting and therefore between the two forms of *mimêsis*—mimicry and representation.

We know little of the history of comedy, but we do know who introduced plot. This change was crucial. Stand-up comics are not qualitatively distinct from their audiences; they talk to the people around them even if in an artificial way. Plot, however, announces that we are in the presence of an alternative reality. Plot is more than an imitation of action; it is a putting together of actions into a coherent whole. Comedy ceases to be invective at the moment when the poet invents the person he is making fun of.

> The making [*poiein*] of plots came on the one hand originally from Sicily, but of those in Athens, Krates first began discarding the form [*idea*] of the lampoon to make speeches [*logoi*] and plots [*muthoi*] of the general [*katholou*]. (1449b5–9)

Comedy cannot avoid the doubleness of drama.

If comedy and tragedy are alike in form, we have seen tragedy and epic to be alike in content (1448a25–27). Epic follows tragedy, although clearly not temporally, as an imitation in metric speeches of the good, or worthy, or serious (*spoudaioi*). The two differ in form. Epic is narrated; tragedy is dramatic. The meter of epic is hexameter, tragedy is iambic. They differ too in length. The time of an epic is not bounded as it is in a tragedy to about one day. The final two differences are traceable to the first. The drama of tragedy, its presentation of an alternative reality, requires the meter of speech, and it requires that fictional time and real time be more or less the same.

Aristotle singles out tragedy because of its emphasis on the simultaneous separation and identity of *drama* and *dran*, acting and action. He can do this and still entitle his book *Concerning the Art of Poetry* because the principles of tragedy are the principles of all poetry. With regard to epic, Aristotle makes this relation explicit.

> For some parts are the same and some are peculiar to tragedy. Hence, whoever knows about good [*spoudaios*] and base [*phaulos*] tragedies knows also about epics [*epôn*]. For what epic-making [*epopoiia*] has exists in tragedy, but what is in it is not all in epic-making. (1449b16–20)

The principles of tragedy are the principles of comedy and epic as well; they are the principles of all poetic imitation. All poetry, as *mimêsis*, must affirm itself as apart from the world even as it imitates the world. Tragedy, which shares its form—its how—with comedy and its matter—its what—with epic, makes this doubleness of imitation most manifest and so is in a way most mimetic. At the same time, tragedies are not only about the *spoudaios*; they are measured in accordance with the *spoudaios* and the *phaulos* (1449b17–18). In addition to applying to actions imitated in comedy and tragedy, the worthy and the base apply to the actions of tragedy and comedy themselves. Seeking to be apart from the world is the characteristic action of tragedy within the world. If tragedy is exemplary for all poetry, and poetry is exemplary for human action as such, then the doubleness within tragedy will be the character of human action as such. The part of the *Poetics* about poetry proved to be about tragedy. The part about tragedy (chapters six through eighteen) will prove to be about action.

Part II

Praxis

Methinks I see these things with parted eye,
When everything seems double.

—Shakespeare
A Midsummer Night's Dream IV:i

5

Tragedy
(1449b21–31)

[6] In the previous two chapters Aristotle gave an account of the genesis of tragedy out of rudimentary imitation. At first it looks as though chapter six continues that argument.

> Concerning imitation in hexameters, then, and concerning comedy, we will speak later; but let us speak concerning tragedy, taking up the definition of its being coming to be from the things having been said. (1449b21–24)

Aristotle's account of the coming to be of tragedy was apparently at the same time a coming to be of an account of tragedy. As contemplating the *genesis*, the coming to be, of tragedy, we are spectators to a drama. But our detached contemplation, also an action, has been the *genesis* of the definition of the *ousia*, the being, of tragedy. This will be the central issue in the long account of tragedy, which constitutes the bulk of the *Poetics* (chapters six through eighteen). Tragedy, which looks like a series of elaborately connected events—a fated coming to be, is in fact a coming to be of an interpretation of those events. The rule of necessity (i.e., fate) looks rather arbitrary on the level of plot. Only on the level of understanding the meaning of the events of the plot does this arbitrariness disappear.

Aristotle defines tragedy in what is probably the most famous passage of the *Poetics*.

> Tragedy, then, is an imitation [*mimêsis*] of action which is good/serious [*spoudaios*] and complete/perfect, having magnitude/greatness, by speech pleasing separately by each of the species [*eidê*] in the parts/in turn [*en tois moriois*], acting and not through narration/report, accomplishing through

35

pity and fear the purification/purgation [*katharsis*] of such passions [*pathêmata*].
(1449b24–28)

Many things are dark in this much commented on definition. As the translation
indicates, its key terms are unusually equivocal. In addition, what exactly are these species or *eidê* of, and what does it mean that each pleases
separately in the parts or in turn? Aristotle hastens to clarify these issues in the sequel.

I mean [*legô*] by pleasing speech [*logos*] that having rhythm, harmony and
song, and by separately in the species [*eidê*] sometimes through meters alone
accomplishing its task and again at other times through song. (1449b28–
31)

The species seem to be the species of pleasing speech (i.e., speech accompanied and unaccompanied by music); "in the parts" seems to mean
that the choral odes are sung and the episodes not.[38] Still this is a convoluted way of saying something rather simple. Could the awkwardness
in Aristotle's text be an invitation to reconsider its meaning? Could we
be meant to see that tragic imitation characteristically shows *eidê*—species or forms—to us as parts, so that, for example, Oedipus's swollen
foot is literally the cause of his solving the riddle of the sphinx—he knows
about needing a staff, and at the same time it is symbolically the cause
of his solving the riddle—only the man who does not fit the definition
of man can see what it means to be a man?[39] Tragedy presents the eidetic genetically; the intellectual elements into which an action must divide
if we are to come to understand it—its *eidê*—are presented as elements
of its coming to be—its *genesis*. Plot may prove the most important part
of tragedy only after it thickens.

    With the exception of the part concerning pity, fear, and catharsis,
Aristotle seems to have prepared the ground for his definition of tragedy.[40] *Mimêsis* was treated in chapters one and four, the *spoudaios* action in chapter two, and the difference between narration and drama in
chapter three. Still, all this applies as well either to comedy or to epic;
what is altogether distinctive to tragedy is its purpose—the catharsis of
"such passions" by means of pity and fear.[41] It is therefore peculiar that
we are left to figure out for ourselves the meaning of catharsis—a word
that has a religious significance of purifying as well as a medical significance of purging. Furthermore, why are pity and fear singled out as
that through which catharsis is effected, and even accepting their importance, what does it mean that the catharsis effected is of "such passions"? What are the relevant passions other than pity and fear, and why
are they comparable to pity and fear?

For more than a century the scholarly debate has focused on whether catharsis means purification or purgation.[42] The *Poetics* seems to give us little help; catharsis is mentioned only one other time in an apparently unrelated context. At 1455b15 Aristotle refers to the ruse practiced by Iphegeneia in Euripides' *Iphigeneia among the Taurians* (1156–434). Pretending that the statue of Artemis has been polluted by the attempt to offer a matricide as sacrifice, on her authority as priestess, Iphegeneia tells the Taurians to remain inside while she purifies the statue in the sea. Meanwhile, she escapes with her brother, Orestes. In this context, catharsis must mean purification; what could it mean for Iphigeneia to purge the statue? The word, then, is at least ambiguous in the *Poetics*; it does not simply mean purgation.

In fact it is not even clear that catharsis has this medical meaning in the passage most frequently used to support the view that the purpose of tragedy is a purging of emotions by pity and fear. Aristotle discusses the cathartic effect of music in Book VIII of the *Politics*.

> For the passion which occurs strongly concerning some souls exists in all, but it differs by less and by more—such as pity and fear, and further, inspiration [*enthousiasmos*], for some are also capable of being possessed by this motion. But from the sacred songs—when they use songs stirring the soul to frenzy— we see them being restored as though obtaining a cure and a catharsis. It is necessary that those pitying and those afraid undergo this same thing, as well as the rest who generally suffer/undergo [*tous pathêtikous*], according to the extent to which it belongs to each of such men. And [it is necessary] for some catharsis to come to be for all and [for all] to feel relief/lightening with pleasure. And similarly cathartic songs produce harmless joy among human beings. (1342a5–16)

This has been frequently understood to mean that tragic catharsis is like a homeopathic cure in which we undergo a version of the disease to be purged of the disease. Accordingly, the passion in question would be a disease the removal of which would bring pleasure. On the face of it, however, this is not a particularly persuasive account of what happens to us in the theater. We certainly do not feel sick with a passion when the house lights dim and pleased to be relieved of it when they come up, as though our satisfaction from seeing *Othello* consisted in being purged of jealousy. Do actively jealous people enjoy *Othello* more than those who have the green-eyed monster under control? Aren't they less likely to be open to reflection about jealousy and so less moved by its drama? The pleasure we experience seems rather to arise from the experience of passion than from its annihilation. The passage from *Politics* VIII seems to indicate that the passions for which music provides a catharsis, although present to different degrees, are nevertheless present in all souls. It certainly does not suggest that they are ever simply purged. If sacred songs produce a cure and a catharsis, one might as easily conclude that there is a difference between the two as that a catharsis is a cure.

But perhaps this is not entirely fair. Perhaps tragedy is meant to serve as a vaccination. In inducing a semblance of the disease it would purge its reality before the fact. We would then go to *Othello* to prevent ourselves from becoming sick with jealousy rather than to cure us of an already contracted case. Yet this would hardly account for the pleasure of the experience. This pleasure seems in some way connected to the paradigmatic character of the passion that is aroused by a particular tragedy. Othello is not just a jealous man; he is somehow the jealous man. Like "shapes of dishonored beasts and corpses" (1448b12), passions rendered in their perfection can be experienced with pleasure even when their impure versions are painful. Even if one result of tragedy is that we are purged of certain dangerous passions, this purgation is accomplished by a representation of a purified version of the passions in question. When Aristotle says that tragedy is an imitation that through pity and fear accomplishes the catharsis of such passions or undergoings, catharsis means purification, but it is the passions, not the spectators, that are purified. Still, we need to know what exactly this purification consists in and why it is effected by pity and fear.

If tragedy accomplishes a purification, it does so as an imitation—as *mimêsis*. Aristotle's claim would seem to be that tragedy is a representation that through pity and fear purifies passions such as pity and fear (i.e., presumably there are other passions in some way like them). We have seen that the claim leads to troubling questions. Why is the purification accomplished by pity and fear? And whose pity and whose fear? Why, too, are the passions to be purified said to be "such as these" (i.e., like pity and fear, but not only pity and fear)? What is paradigmatic about these two? In the *Rhetoric* Aristotle defines pity and fear in a way particularly instructive for the *Poetics*.

Let pity be a pain from some apparent evil, either destructive or painful, happening undeservedly which someone himself might expect to suffer or [might expect] any of those belonging to him [to suffer], and this when it appears near. (1385b12–16)

Let fear, then, be a pain or disturbance from imagination [*phantasia*] of an imminent evil, either destructive or painful. For not all evils are feared, for example whether one is to become unjust or stupid, but whichever make possible great pains or destructions, and these if they are not far off but appear nearby so as to be imminent. (1382a21–25)

Comedy was concerned only with certain evils (*kakiai*), those that were ridiculous because they belonged to that part of the shameful or ugly that was neither painful nor destructive (1449a32–35). Pity and fear seem then to be the tragic analogue to the laughable or ridiculous. Thus, while the response to comedy was single, the response to tragedy is double. If the evil appearing before us is destructive or painful, we are forced to acknowledge the distinction between our perspective as spectators—*ta theatra*—and the perspective of the character undergoing what is destructive or painful—*autho kath'auto* (1449a8–9). As spectators we pity; as participants we fear. But this is simply the consequence of the double character of all imitation exemplified by tragedy—the mixture of the utterly real and the utterly unreal, of *dran* and *drama*.

Imitations announce to us their simultaneous reality and falsity. They can only affect us insofar as they are real; we must therefore enter into the perspective of the character. On the other hand they can only affect us as images if we are aware of their unreality; this distance allows us to separate ourselves from the plight of the character. If a ferocious beast leaps at a character in a movie, we in the theater cannot properly appreciate the film unless we are at some level afraid. On the other hand, were we simply afraid, we would leave our seats and run for the exits. We can savor our fear only insofar as our experience is simultaneously real and unreal. Although it is usefully understood as the split between the perspective of the character in the drama and that of the audience, this initial dualism is not stable. Pity is not so easily separable from fear, for if we did not fear on some level we could not pity the plight of one in danger. To be worried about the danger facing a character means to in some sense feel it as danger. While tragedy emphasizes the disparity between *drama* and *dran*, it, no less than any other form of imitation, must also depend on their togetherness.

All *mimêsis* involves purification. To say "this is that" requires a simplification of what "this" is. All poetry, therefore, involves purification—catharsis. In part, Aristotle begins the *Poetics* by describing *poiêtikê* as an account of how to put plots together so as to make the *poiêsis*, the thing made, beautiful (1447a10). For something to stand apart from the ordinary things of our experience so as to be able to be a representation of them, for us to be able to say that "this" is "that," it is necessary for artificial boundaries to be placed around the thing so as to make it discontinuous with reality. To be something else, it must itself come to sight as a whole. But nothing in the real world possesses this sort of splendid isolation. Successful imitation depends on this essential unreality of the *mimêsis*, and successful imitation is beautiful imitation.[43] It is not an accident that the question "But is it real?", when answered negatively, is sufficient to destroy our sense of the goodness of something but leaves our sense of its beauty in tact. A beautiful illusion remains beautiful even after we have become aware of its illusory nature.[44] Poetry, as *mimêsis*, is necessarily connected to beauty in this sense. Even when not beautiful in any obvious way, in representing, it is an idealization of that which it represents. It distills reality so as to be a purer version of the real. Even a poem meant only as a "slice of life," by being sliced from the continuum of life, becomes paradigmatic—an idealization of the ordinary. Life does not come in slices.

The beautiful, *to kalon*, is the measure of poetry because of its connection to the unreality of poetry. Poetry is an imitation of the real that is known not to be real. What then does this have to do with the representation of passions? As spectators or readers we can be moved to feel righteous indignation in an almost pure form. When Penelope's suitors treat Telemachus with contempt in the beginning of the *Odyssey*, we long for Odysseus to return and punish them. We feel such passions in reality—if we did not there would be no foundation for eliciting them from us in poetry—and yet we do not feel them so purely. Righteous indignation moves us to defend our honor, but when our lives are really at stake, it is accompanied by a diluting admixture of fear. Our passions are mixed together in such a way that we can never be said precisely to fear, or to be angry, or to pity. In reality we tend to look more like the sensible Ismene than the passionate Antigone.[45] If poetry effects a catharsis of the spectators' passions, then it does so by way of a different kind of catharsis of the passions it depicts. In depicting them, it idealizes them. The wrath of Achilles is a paradigm for human wrath, but it is not a wrath ever felt by human beings in reality. This very purity, however, means that the passions of poetry go unchecked. Because they are pure, their internal contradictions ultimately show themselves. Macbeth is the courageous man, but unchecked courage leads him to attack the very conditions for human freedom without which courage is impossible.[46] Ajax is the fully loyal man whose loyalty leads him to attempt the slaughter of the whole army to which he is loyal.[47]

Poetic characters are idealized types even when, as is usually the case, they are more complex than representations of single passions. Is *Hamlet* about revenge, love of one's father, love of one's mother, fear of death, ambition? Any of these singly, and indeed all taken together, are too simple. And yet *Hamlet* is the putting together of a finite number of actions. As much as it seduces us to think that there is a Hamlet with a full human soul behind these actions (so that the unwary will start to wonder what Hamlet's childhood experiences were like), the character is only the collection of deeds in the play. While this collection is ex-

traordinarily rich and compels us to think through the competing elements of Hamlet's soul, still Hamlet is not a human being always with
an undetermined future ahead of him. To describe a character by selecting a finite number of his actions is to burden those actions with a weight
they could not bear in reality. To make them significant to such a degree is to remove from them the accidental features present in all the
actions of real life. Only because they are given a finite magnitude can
they have this greatness (1449b25), and yet in reality no action is clearly
bounded in this way. When does a real act of murder begin or end? This
very selection that makes *mimêsis* possible and significant at the same
time ensures the unreality of the imitation. The world is significant but
incompletely so; the world of poetry is fully significant but unreal.

All poetry, as imitation, involves purification, but what does it mean
that the cause of this purification in tragedy is pity and fear? The object
of pity and fear is the same—they both involve being pained by an approaching evil that is either destructive or painful. They differ with regard to whom the evil is approaching—myself or another.[48] By eliciting
both pity and fear, tragedy highlights the tension between these two
perspectives; on the one hand, we enter into the character's perspective,
and on the other hand, we are detached. We are simultaneously practical (concerned with action) and theoretical (concerned with looking or
contemplating), and must be so because we are theorizing about practical matters. Our fear is the sign that we have suspended ordinary reality. Our pity is the sign that we have reaffirmed our ordinary reality but
not altogether. To pity *Oedipus* we must accept his purified and simpli-
fied experience as real experience. Pity and fear belong together as the
co-causes of tragic catharsis because tragedy always deals with approaching
evils, and these two passions represent our double response to approaching
evils. The ordinary ambiguity of our situation in the face of an imitation is highlighted in this way when the object of imitation is evil.

However, what is most peculiar to tragedy is neither the purification
that is constitutive of all poetry nor the fact that this purification shows
itself in a double way through pity and through fear. The most puzzling
part of Aristotle's definition is what is purified—"such passions." Why
does the purification that shows itself through pity and fear have to be
of passions like pity and fear? As a pair, pity and fear pointed to the
simultaneously real and unreal character of all *mimêsis*. Does "such passions" mean passions of this sort, passions that make us at once spectators and actors, theoretical and practical, rational and animal? All poetry is subject to the beautiful—*to kalon*; it purifies what it represents.
Taken together, pity and fear point to the discrepancy between the real
and the beautiful. We really pity those for whom we can fear only be-

cause we have bracketed reality. Passions "such as these," then, would be passions pointing to this discrepancy. Tragedy would be that form of poetry that has as its subject matter the discrepancy between the real and the beautiful understood as the idealized. That is, all poetry, as cathartic, purifies or beautifies what it is about. While specific issues vary, tragedies are always concerned with this process of purification or beautification. All poetry is beautiful; the subject matter of tragedy is the beautiful.

But tragedy is still poetry and, as such, cathartic in its representations. From the outset of the *Poetics* Aristotle has indicated that the principle governing the putting together of parts is the beautiful (1447a10). Tragedy is, therefore, the beautiful representation of the beautiful. Tragedy imitates human life in such a way as to display the dangers of the characteristic element of human life. By representing our lives to ourselves, we purify our lives; we make them simpler than they really are. Oedipus understands a king to be a father to his people. Sophocles shows us what happens when Oedipus fails to realize that this metaphor is a suppressed simile. Oedipus really thinks of himself as the father of his people and so fails to remember that he is also their "brother," that he is as much one of them as he is superior to them. Oedipus's fate is tragic. He is forced to face the consequences of his own purification of reality. But his story is a purified version of what happens to the man who takes his own purification of reality, his role as father-king, too seriously. Tragedy is, therefore, no more real than any other form of poetry. In exposing the dangers of idealizing, it is a pure critique of purity that, in idealizing the contradictions in human life, exaggerates their effect. It makes us feel that we are all Oedipus when Oedipus could only exist within a poem. Tragedy thus beautifully depicts for us the consequences of the disparity between the beautiful and the real. It accomplishes through pity and fear the purification of such passions and, in doing so, takes as its object its own manner.

Tragedy can be taken as paradigmatic for poetry generally because it makes poetry as real as it can be. The subject matter of tragedy is poetry. This preoccupation of poetry with itself would not be of so much interest were it not identical with a preoccupation with our natures as imitative. Since our natures as imitative underlie our natures as rational, tragedy is like a pure critique of pure reason.

6

The Parts of Tragedy

(1449b31–50b20)

After defining tragedy Aristotle moves to an enumeration of its parts and their order.

> Since they make [*poiountai*] the imitation by acting [*prattontes*], first the adornment/order [*kosmos*] of sight/spectacle/visage [*opsis*] would be a part of tragedy of necessity. (1449b31–33)

On the most obvious level this means that because tragedy imitates action, and action must be visible, the actors will have to be dressed in clothing of some sort, and they will have to be in a specific place.[49] This is to say only that what it is possible to see and the laws governing what it is possible to see are a part of tragedy. Aristotle subsequently seems to undermine the importance of *opsis*.

> But *opsis*, while it leads the soul, is the most artless [part] and least proper to the art of poetry. For the power of tragedy is possible without a contest and performers, and further, concerning the production of spectacles [*opseis*] the art of the costume-maker is more sovereign than that of the poets. (1450b16–20)

Here *opsis* seems scarcely a necessary part of tragedy. Yet this need mean only that, although tragedy requires a scene, it does not have to be seen. A tragic poet must begin with *opsis*, for it places limits on what can and cannot be done. Characters not on stage cannot speak, but characters must be brought on stage in a manner consistent with the previous action. A playwright must envision the action in his play so that things like entrances and exits are done correctly.[50] Drama involves putting an

43

action into speech as though it were to be seen. However, there is no need for it to be seen. That tragedy is written as though to be seen means that the action must be particularized, but once that has been understood the play need not actually be performed. It can simply be read.[51] *Opsis* thus rules tragedy by placing limits on its content while at the same time not being a proper part of tragedy. It is in a strange way the most important and least important of the parts of tragedy.

However, this seems to fly in the face of the obvious argument of chapter six as a whole—plot, the putting together of incidents (*pragmata*) so as to imitate an action (*praxis*) is the most important part of tragedy, especially compared with character.

> And the greatest of these is the putting together of incidents. For tragedy is an imitation, not of human beings, but of actions and of life. Happiness and unhappiness exist in action, and an action is the end not a quality. But men are of a certain quality according to their characters and happy or the opposite according to their actions. Therefore, they do not act in order to imitate characters, but they embrace characters because of actions. So that the events and the plot are the end of tragedy, and the end is the greatest of all. (1450a15–23)

> Plot, then, is a first principle and like a soul of tragedy, and characters are second. (1450a38–39)

Plot is important for obvious reasons. As drama, tragedy is an imitation of action; it is not a description of men's inner being but a display of what men are by what they do. This is not simply a limitation of a poetic genre, as though narrative poetry would surpass tragedy by being able to do what tragedy cannot—namely, show us the insides of men. Aristotle means rather that the limiting conditions of tragedy are the same as those of human life generally. Tragedy is an imitation of life because we only know our own souls through the actions they perform. We are knowable only by what we do. All of the other parts of tragedy are thus instrumental to plot; they serve the imitation of action.

Nevertheless, it is clear from Aristotle's enumeration of the parts of tragedy that there is something special about *opsis*. There are three lists of these parts in chapter six, as illustrated in Table 1. Aristotle makes certain changes from list to list. Plot, first in the order of importance, is last in the order of *genesis*. It is the last thing that poets learn to construct effectively (1450a35–38). Character is second in order of importance, but, at least on one reading of the first list, second to last in order of *genesis*.[52] The relative orders of thought and *lexis* are also inverted. There seem, then, to be two orders of significance with regard to the parts of tragedy, and according to one of them *opsis* comes first.

Table 1: The Parts of Tragedy Enumerated in Chapter Six

1449b30–50a4	1450a8–10	1450a38–b20
1. *opsis*/spectacle	1. *muthos*/plot	1. plot
2. *melopoiia*/songmaking	2. *êthos*/character	2. character
3. *lexis*/diction/dialogue	3. *lexis*	3. *dianoia*/thought
4. character (or thought)	4. thought	4. *lexis*
5. thought (or character)	5. *opsis*	5. songmaking
6. plot	6. songmaking	6. *opsis*

The importance of *opsis* is confirmed when Aristotle, recalling the argument of chapters one through three, says of the six parts that two are that in which imitation takes place, three are that which is imitated, and one is how the imitation takes place (1450a10–11). The two in which the imitation takes place are clearly *lexis* and songmaking (1449b33). Since the object of imitation for tragedy is action (1449b24), the three parts serving as objects of imitation would seem to be plot (the putting together of an action out of incidents) and the two causes of action— character and thought. This leaves *opsis* as the part that deals with the how of imitation. *Opsis* governs the manner of tragic imitation because of the way in which reality limits tragedy. Tragedy effects a catharsis— a purification, but there are nevertheless limits on how pure the object of tragic imitation can become. The *kalon* is the standard for poetry generally and for tragedy particularly, but the idealized passions of poetry must nevertheless remain rooted in reality. The anger of Achilles has to be recognizable anger—it must be related to love, envy, shame, and so forth as is ordinary anger—if it is to be idealized anger.[53] *Opsis* has this structure. That the tragic poet must constantly envision the action of his tragedy means that this action must conform to the conditions of what is possible in our day-to-day world.[54]

Opsis is the how of tragic imitation insofar as it points to the fundamental conditions governing human life. But we have already seen that Aristotle invites us to collapse the distinction between the how and the what of tragic imitation (1447a16–18). Here this would mean *opsis* is somehow the what of tragic imitation as well as the how, but in what way? Aristotle first introduced *opsis* in the phrase *ho tês opseôs kosmos* (1449b33)—the cosmos/adornment of sight/spectacle. As the overarching order of visible things, *opsis* might easily be understood as the ultimate object of imitation. In a complicated way this is confirmed by the notoriously difficult sentence at 1450a13: *kai gar opsis echei pan kai êthos kai muthon kai lexin kai melos kai dianoian hôsautôs.* In the context one would expect this to be a repetition of the claim that "all [tragedy] has *opsis*, character, plot, *lexis*, song, and thought," but, because *opsis* is in the nominative case this reading requires an emendation.[55] Furthermore, the sentence immediately preceding this says that "not a few of them [poets?] have, so to speak, used these forms (*eidê*)." It is puzzling that Aristotle should so suddenly refer to the parts of tragedy as *eidê*, but it is yet more puzzling that he should sandwich a claim that "not a few use these *eidê*" between two statements of the necessity for all tragedies to have these six parts. Some of this mystery is dispelled if we translate the sentence cited above as it stands: "For also *opsis* has everything— character, plot, *lexis*, song, and thought similarly." Given our suspicions about the centrality of *opsis*, this reading seems not so strange.[56] *Opsis* in this sense is not simply the concern with masks, costumes, and scenery but with what makes it necessary to have masks, costumes, and scenery. In this sense, *opsis* includes all of the other parts of tragedy. Every tragedy has all six of the parts because they are all derivative from the nature of tragedy as an imitation of action. All tragedies, for example, as imitations of human actions force us to posit a motive behind the action. Otherwise the actions would be only motions; human actions presuppose a character behind the action, a character that will determine thought (*dianoia*) and show itself in speech (*lexis*). This does not mean that every tragedy will be about the relation between invisible character and visible action; some, however, will be. Sophocles' *Ajax*, for example, is largely concerned with what it means that the motives for human action are necessarily invisible.[57] Thus, all six of the parts mentioned are necessarily present as parts in every tragedy; however, "not a few" poets use these parts as *eidê* (1450a12). They feature them to make them problems to be examined by means of tragedy. This is possible because all of the parts of tragedy are present in *opsis* understood as the conditions governing our everyday lives.

Looked at from one point of view, *opsis* is trivial and scarcely a part of tragedy. As the accidental part of tragedy, it is what directors most play with. It is Malvolio in Edwardian dress or Angelo in jackboots. Looked at from another point of view, *opsis* is the crucial part of tragedy. As the "cosmos of sight" it places limits on what can be shown; it is what is showable in principle and so reveals to us the limits of our world. Tragedy in some way shows us what cannot be shown. Aristotle has understood that to show us why we cannot know what is in Ajax's mind when he attempts to slaughter the herds belonging to the Greek army, Sophocles must show us what is really in his mind. The plot of the *Ajax* is contrived in such a way as to make visible to us the limits of our vision. It is in this sense that *opsis* is the ultimate object of tragic imitation.

7

The Unity of Action

(1450b21–52a11)

[7] Roughly speaking, the *Poetics* thus far has been structured in the following way. It begins with an account of *mimêsis*, which divides into an account of spacial *mimêsis* and temporal *mimêsis*. Temporal *mimêsis* then divides into an account of music and an account of poetry. The account of poetry divides into an account of narrative and dramatic poetry, and the account of dramatic poetry divides into accounts of comedy and tragedy. The account of tragedy divides into accounts of plot and of the other parts. The explicit treatment of plot begun in chapter seven continues, although with several interruptions, through chapter eighteen. Chapters seven, eight, and nine are concerned with the unity of plot. Accordingly, chapter seven is concerned with plot as having parts (i.e., as many), chapter eight with what makes a plot truly one, and chapter nine with the relation of the parts of plot to the whole.

Chapter seven begins with a statement of the importance of the unity of plot.

> These things having been determined, after them, let us say what sort the putting together [*sustasis*] of the incidents [*pragmata*] ought to be since this is the first and greatest [thing] of tragedy. We have posited tragedy to be an imitation of a complete/perfect and whole action having some magnitude/ greatness. For there is also a whole which has no magnitude. (1450b20– 26)

The question, then, is what turns a series of incidents (*pragmata*) into an action (*praxis*) that is complete and whole. *Sustasis*, or putting together, was the fundamental feature of *mimêsis* as Aristotle described it in chapter four. But if imitation is required to make a whole out of oth-

49

erwise disunited incidents, one must wonder whether actions, properly understood, exist other than in poetry.

   To understand the nature of this *sustasis* we must first see what Aristotle means by a whole.

> What has beginning [*archê*], middle [*meson*] and end [*teleutê*] is a whole. A beginning is what itself is not of necessity after another [*allo*], but after which another [*heteron*] by nature is or comes to be. But an end [is] the opposite, what itself on the one hand is by nature after another [*allo*]— either of necessity or for the most part—but after which there [is] no other [*allo*]. And a middle [*meson*] [is] that which [is] both itself after another [*allo*] and after which there [is] another [*heteron*]. Plots well put together, then, ought neither to begin from wherever they chance nor end from wherever they chance, but use the aforesaid forms [*ideai*]. (1450b26–34)

As usual, what seems simple is not. The language here contains a number of peculiarities.[58] Beginnings are said not to be after another (the word is *allo*) while another (the word is *heteron*) is said to come after them. An *allo* by nature precedes an end (why this should be "of necessity or for the most part" is unclear), and no *allo* follows it. An *allo* precedes a middle, but a *heteron* follows it. Generally then, while that after which something comes to be is an *allo*, that which comes to be after it is a *heteron*. Now, the difference between these two words is slight and not always consistently maintained. However, when there is a difference, *allo* means other simply, and *heteron* is an other which is one of a pair; it is an other intimately related to another.[59] In the present context this seems to mean that when something comes after another, it is related to that other as an *allo*—as utterly other. But when something is the origin of another it is related to that other as a *heteron*—as an intimately connected other. Relative to its beginning, then, every middle is an *allo*, while relative to its end it is a *heteron*. Under the guise of perfect symmetry Aristotle has thus introduced two different perspectives. From the perspective of the end, one's action looks independent and unconnected to what caused it; from the perspective of the beginning (i.e., looking forward), one's action looks like a cause, and what follows it looks caused. For this reason parents tend to look on their children as products and so lament their mistakes in childrearing as though children were altogether formed by that rearing. Children, on the other hand, tend to think of themselves as free agents. And yet, as though to emphasize the peculiarity of this double perspective, the parents who lament the mistakes they have made in rearing their children do not ordinarily blame their parents for these mistakes, although perfect consistency would require them to do so. Now, apart from tragedy, our perspective is always that of the middle—there are no absolute beginnings or ends. Accordingly, we always view the incidents or events (*pragmata*) of our lives "with parted eye." Every event is simultaneously *allo* and *heteron*. Putting events (*pragmata*) together into an action (*praxis*)—a whole— was the crucial characteristic of tragic imitation. This wholeness proves to be the difference between the actions of tragedy and the actions of life. Such wholes are "put together" because only by hypothesis can we get hold of a beginning, and only arbitrarily can we posit an end from which to survey our lives.

And yet, since only a whole that has magnitude is potentially beautiful (*kalon*), it is clear that the actions of our daily lives cannot be beautiful.

> And further, since the beautiful, both animal and every matter [*pragma*] which is put together from certain things, ought not only to have these things ordered but also [ought to have] a magnitude which does not exist by chance— for the beautiful exists in magnitude and order, whence neither could a very small animal be something beautiful (for the contemplation [*theôria*] is mixed up by coming to be in an almost imperceptible time) nor could a very great [animal] (for the contemplation comes to be not at the same time, and the oneness and wholeness is gone from the contemplation with respect to those contemplating) such as if there should be an animal of a thousand stades, so that, just as in the case of bodies and of animals it is necessary to have a magnitude and for this to be easily seen at one time [*eusunopton*]—so also [is it necessary] in the case of plots to have a length and for this to be easily remembered [*eumnêmoneuton*]. (1450b34–51a6)

To be beautiful a whole must have magnitude because the order of its parts must be visible or sensible.[60] If the whole is too little, no parts, and therefore no order among them, will be discernible. If it is too big, no whole, and therefore no principle governing the order of the parts, will be discernible. The optimal magnitude, therefore, would contain the greatest number of parts discernible together, since, the more parts, the greater the display of order. This does not mean order in any narrowly conceived sense; it means rather that the parts are such that each has to be what it is and where it is in order that the whole be what it is.

It is surely no accident that Aristotle reveals his teaching on the whole to us in a sentence that is so long and convoluted. The sentence is an example of what it describes. It may seem to contain digressions and irrelevancies—very orderly wholes frequently do, but in the end the pieces all fall into place. It is not hard, therefore, to see how something can at first seem ugly but on more careful inspection prove extremely beautiful. This is one of the principles of Aristotle's own writing and of his peculiarly understated sense of humor.

Having established this general principle of beauty, Aristotle turns to the question of the optimal magnitude of tragedy. A beautiful plot will contain as many incidents as possible while preserving its beginning, middle, and end. This is what Aristotle means by saying that plot is the heart of tragedy and consists in the putting together of *pragmata* to form a single *praxis*. He uses the image of a beautiful animal to make this point, but there is a crucial difference between a beautiful animal and a beautiful plot. The beautiful animal must be *eusunopton*—easily seen at one time; the beautiful plot must be *eumnêmoneuton*—easily remembered at one time. With respect to tragedy, magnitude—*megethos*—is not understood spacially but temporally. Accordingly, Aristotle uses a new word—*mekos*, length—to indicate that what is at stake is a sequence of events over time and not their simultaneity. The image of a beautiful animal, borrowed from Plato's *Phaedrus* (246c), is deceiving. It makes simultaneity of perception seem to be the goal of beautiful plots, as though the parts of a tragedy were like the parts of a painting. But the putting together of tragedy is more like the putting together of Aristotle's own account here. Its wholeness has to do with the necessity of its sequence.

How, then, are we to understand the limit *eumnêmoneuton* places on the length of tragedy? Aristotle goes out of his way to indicate that this limit has to be something internal to the art of tragedy itself and not imposed externally. The lengths of tragedies would be limited if tragic contests included one hundred plays, and for the same reason individual tragedies are limited in length; to judge one against the other would mean remembering them all, but our memories have limits. Judging one hundred tragedies at a time would require shortening each but not because of any limit intrinsic to tragedy. Aristotle also rejects perception (*aisthesis*) as an intrinsic limitation on the length of tragedy. As the discussion of *opsis* made clear, tragedy is an imitation of action, not necessarily a presentation of that imitation. There are certain limits on the performance time of a tragedy—people tire, and the daylight lasts only so long.[61] But once again, this is not intrinsic to the action of the tragedy.

Tragedy is limited intrinsically not by what we can perceive at once but by what we can hold together in our memories so as to think at once. This holding together is not spacial but logical; Aristotle must therefore articulate the principles that govern the logical connection of the incidents of the larger action:

But the limit according to the nature of the matter [*pragma*] itself is this: the greater is the more beautiful with respect to magnitude as long as it remains altogether manifest. So to speak delimiting it simply, in howevermuch magnitude of things coming to be in succession according to the likely [*to*

eikos] or the necessary [*to anagkaion*], a change occurs either to good fortune
from ill fortune or to ill fortune from good fortune is a sufficient limit of
magnitude. (1451a11–15)

By now, much of this is familiar. What is not, and is crucial, is the double
standard used to evaluate the relations of one incident to another within
the action of the plot—the likely and the necessary. What does it mean
that either can connect the pieces of the whole? Aristotle's language here—
good fortune (*eutuchia*) and ill fortune (*dustuchia*)—is an indication of
the extent to which chance (*tuchê*) must figure in the action of the plot.
At the same time, from the perspective of the spectator outside the plot,
the action of a good play looks as though it had to happen the way it
did; it seems subject to necessity. Once again, then, we have chanced
upon the double perspective of tragedy—that of spectators and that of
characters within the play. The likely governs the action from within
since from the perspective of the character, the relationship between action
and what follows from it is causal but not fated. To do *X* may make *Y*
likely—that is after all why one does it, but it does not make it necessary. However, from the perspective of the spectator, *Y* must seem somehow
inevitable and so not contingent on what the character decides.

   This double standard of the connectedness of action is connected to
several previous issues. In chapter six Aristotle spoke of character (*êthos*)
and thought (*dianoia*) as the codeterminants of action (1449b38–50a1).
These are the terms used to distinguish the two kinds of virtue in the
Nicomachean Ethics (1103a5–10). It is not difficult to see why. Moral
virtue is impossible without a certain indeterminacy of events in the world
(i.e., chance). For anything to be at stake, we must be able to change
the course of events. For our actions to be significant, we must able to
predict the outcome of our actions with some success but not perfectly.
The world must be intelligible but not perfectly so. But this is simply a
description of what it would mean for "the likely" to govern the connection between events. The perspective of the character within the play
is simply the perspective of moral virtue. On the other hand, if to know
is to know the cause, then, in attempting to put the incidents of a larger
action together, thought will aim at a principle beyond the likely. Thought
always tends toward the necessary as its measure of the wholeness of a
whole. In doing so it necessarily places itself outside the action it seeks
to comprehend; in its contemplation (*theôria*), it assumes the perspective of spectator (*theatês*). This will to make sense of things takes the
perspective of the end after which there is nothing else (*allo*) and before which there is necessarily something other (*allo*) but not intimately
other (*heteron*).

[8] The action of tragedy is governed by a double standard—the likely and the necessary. This doubleness points once again to a tension between the perspective of the character and that of the spectator. As we have seen, this is characteristic of all imitation. What is peculiar to Aristotle's claim here is that this double standard governs the action within tragedy. The spectator has been brought on the stage.[62] In combining these standards tragedy imitates human life, for the necessary and the likely are simply the standards we apply to our children and to ourselves, respectively. At the same time, in chapter eight Aristotle makes it clear that the poets who simply imitate everything that happens in a single life err. Tragedy may imitate life, but life is not like poetry.

The action of tragedy must be one, but those who think that they can make a plot one by making it about one person "are likely to err [*hamartanein*]" (1451a19–20). Later in a famous passage of the *Poetics* (1453a7–12), Aristotle singles out error (*hamartia*) to be the cause of our pity and fear in tragedy. Is it possible that bad poets err tragically by believing that life is like poetry? They attribute a oneness to human life that it does not have, and so they think they can imitate the deeds of a single man, and those deeds will form a unified plot.

Perhaps we can better understand their error by understanding why Aristotle thinks that Homer avoids it. Homer differs because he sees beautifully/nobly (*kalôs*) that real life is not one in the way a poetic life is.[63] Accordingly, the *Odyssey* is not like the *Herakleids* and *Theseids* of lesser poets.

> For, in making [*poiôn*] the *Odyssey*, he did not make [*epoiêsen*] everything which happens to him [Odysseus], such as being smitten at Parnassus and making out as if [*prospoiêsasthai*] he were crazy at the call to arms, of which it is neither necessary nor likely that because the one [*thateron*] comes to be the other [*thateron*] comes to be. But, concerning one action, as we say, he put the *Odyssey* together and the *Iliad* similarly. (1451a24–30)

The claim is that Homer does not include extraneous events in the "life" of Odysseus. That the young Odysseus visited his grandfather Autolukos and was wounded in the thigh by a wild boar has nothing to do with the action of the *Odyssey*. Odysseus also attempted to avoid going to Troy with the rest of the oath-bound suitors of Helen by feigning madness. He sowed his own fields with salt and was only discovered when Palamades placed Telemachus, Odysseus's baby son, in front of the plow. Odysseus had either to stop, and show his sanity, or to continue, and kill his son. This too has nothing to do with the plot of the *Odyssey*. The claim, then, is that Homer includes only such things as contribute to the wholeness of the plot by making it one action with beginning, middle, and end. In this way, each event within the plot can reasonably be thought to be the means to the next, and retrospectively, each can be understood to have been necessitated by what came before. With respect to what comes after each is an *archê*—a beginning, and with respect to what comes before each is a *teleutê*—an end. Homer sees that for a plot to be one action, each part must be inseparable from the whole. It must be what it is and where it is; were it to be changed in content or position, the whole would be fundamentally altered.

Homer sees "beautifully" compared with other poets, because to see beautifully means to make a whole in which every part is necessary. The other poets err because they think that human life can just be imitated. But, while the life of a single person is marked by a beginning, birth, and an end, death, ordinary life is haphazard and not necessary. However, the lesser poets do not imitate the haphazard thinking it to be haphazard. They attribute unity and meaning to their imitations. Is this, then, the characteristic tragic error—to seek to see life as though it were meaningful? It would then be ironic that to show that real life is not altogether meaningful, tragedy must create a world in which it seemed to be. In tragedy men are punished for attributing too much significance to things, but this punishment makes their actions significant.

Homer, however, sees the lack of wholeness of ordinary life "beautifully." His virtue is not so simple as making beautiful poems in which events are connected perfectly as they never are in reality. To see what this means we must return to Aristotle's examples. Lesser poets imitate all of the events of the lives of men like Herakles and Theseus. But are Herakles and Theseus real human beings? If they are fictional characters, then there is some reason to think that the various exploits attributed to them have some connection. This difficulty is compounded by the examples cited to illustrate Homer's superiority. Not only does the *Odyssey* not omit the incident at Parnassus (XIX:392–466), certain things about it are absolutely central both to the plot and to the meaning of the poem. The story is introduced as an explanation for how Odysseus acquires the scar that enables his old nurse, Eurykleia, to recognize him as she bathes him. In the course of telling the story of the scar, Homer introduces a seemingly unnecessary detail about how Autolukos names Odysseus from the verb *ôdussao*—to be angry.[64] The scar provides the necessary proof of Odysseus's identity to Eurykleia; this recognition proves important for the plot (she later aids him in his revenge). The digression concerning Odysseus's name also reveals who he is, but more deeply in terms of his anger. Homer, therefore, provides us with an event within the poem to give a hint of how to read Odysseus's nature so as to make

it possible for us to make sense of the rest of the poem—especially its
bloody conclusion.[65]

On the one hand, Aristotle's meaning is clear. The exclusion of extraneous events is necessary for the wholeness of the poem. This is a
powerful argument for reading a poem—especially a tragedy—from beginning
to end and for not doing an analysis where one studies something like
bird imagery in Sophocles' *Antigone*. Because tragedy is not a simultaneous whole—a *megethos*—but a length—a *mêkos*—it cannot be read
like a painting. Part of its order is its sequence. Each part is what it is
by virtue of coming after what it comes after and before what it comes
before. This is what beginning, middle, and end mean.[66] However, were
the argument of a tragedy to develop in this way, only the end could
point to the play's intention as a whole. Such a play would be completely
intelligible because each part would be necessary in its place, but the
characters in the play could have no idea where the action was really
going. Furthermore, as spectators we would be in the same position, but
because the action was not ours, we would have no inducement to an-
ticipate its completion as we watched. However, drama requires that spectators
be induced to attempt to complete the whole before it is complete; this
is what it means to feel that the plight of the characters is somehow our
own. By inserting incidents like the story of Odysseus's scar, a poet provides
us with an occasion within the play for reflection on the play as a whole.
The story of the scar thus stands to the world of the *Odyssey* as the *Odyssey*
itself stands to reality. As whole and detached from the larger wholes
that surround them, both seem discontinuous with that larger whole, and
so, disruptive. The one seems like an unnecessary digression, the other
like play. Yet, for this reason, both induce us prematurely to make whole
what is not yet whole. Of course this means inducing us to make the
error characteristic of the poets who wrote *Theseids* and *Herakleids*. In
tragedy we are induced to make this error so as to come to see why it is
an error.

In tragedy, as opposed to life, action is whole and so, in principle,
totally intelligible. The action of tragedy must end as it does. But this
is to deny any element of freedom within the action, or, what amounts
to the same thing, to deny any element of chance. At the same time,
tragedy demands that each event follow from others according to what
is likely (i.e., according to the probable effect of a given cause). But
this is to accept the perspective of the actor, and so, of freedom. Tragedy is the combination of these two perspectives. The character within
the play assumes the absolute nature of his beginning point (*archê*)—it
is an *allo* not a *heteron*. In one way or another the consequences of this
assumption are brought home. The tragic error consists in this assump-

tion of the completeness of one's own action; the spurious whole that results from such an assumption is what we mean by "the beautiful." Tragedy is thus a beautiful *exposé* of the beautiful. Insofar as tragedy demands the simultaneous presence of the two perspectives, it is an imitation of life. Insofar as it accomplishes this end by showing the tension between the likely and the necessary, freedom and intelligibility, action and thought, or actor and spectator in an idealized way, it is also an imitation of itself.

[9] Although Aristotle might seem to begin something new when he turns to the differences between history, poetry, and philosophy at the beginning of chapter nine, in fact he is continuing the discussion of the double standard to which the action of tragedy is subject. For the contingency of history is only a version of the likely, and the standard governing philosophy is the necessary. How poetry can combine the two is what is at issue.

> It is also apparent from what has been said that this is not the task [*ergon*] of the poet—to say things that have come to be [*ta genomena*], but [to say] what sort might come to be and [to say] what things are possible [*ta dunata*] according to the likely or the necessary. For the historian and the poet do not differ by speaking either in meters or without meters since even should the [writings] of Herodotus be put in meters, they would no less be a history with meter than without meters. But they differ in this; the one says things that have come to be while the other says what sort could come to be. Whence also poetry [*poiêsis*] is more philosophic and more serious [*spoudaioteron*] than history. For poetry says rather the universal things [*ta katholou*] while history says the particular things [*ta kath' ekaston*]. (1451a36–b7)

The poet doesn't say *ta genomena*—the things that have come to be. He rather says what might or could come to be (i.e., the possible things [*ta dunata*] according to the likely and the necessary). Aristotle then cites a particular example, Herodotus. In doing so he uses *eiê*—the third person singular optative of the verb to be—to wonder what might happen if Herodotus's history were written in meter. So, just before distinguishing history and poetry by saying the one is concerned with what actually happened and with the particular, while the other is concerned with what could happen and with the general, Aristotle introduces a particular historical example to reflect on what might or could have been. In the context, his example is poetic as opposed to historical even though it involves a real person, Herodotus. This should make us suspicious of the absoluteness of the distinction Aristotle is in the midst of formulating between poetry and history.

Aristotle not only calls poetry more philosophic than history, he also says it is more serious—*spoudaioteron*. Now, the distinguishing feature of poetry over and against history is that it is concerned with the general (*katholou*) rather than the particular (*kath'ekaston*). *Katholou* literally means "with respect to the whole," and *kath'ekaston* means "with respect to the particular." If the superior seriousness of poetry depends on its distinctive feature, it would be more serious because concerned with the *katholou*—that which is general, universal, or "with respect to the whole." Tragedy is an imitation of an action that is *spoudaios*—worthy or serious—and *teleia*—complete or perfect (1449b24–25). Complete action has a beginning, middle, and end and so is a whole—*holon* (1450b23–27). Tragedy is therefore concerned with the serious and with what is *katholou*—"with respect to a whole." We saw that this wholeness tragedy imitates, while the cause of the beauty of tragedy, is at the same time the cause of its unreality. There is something counterfactual about tragedy; it presents action as it "might be" but never as it is.

If tragedy is an imitation of the general, then the life of which it is an imitation cannot be the life of a particular human being.

> The general [*to katholou*], what sort of things one happens to say or do to what sort of man according to the likely or the necessary, is what poetry [*poiêsis*] aims at in setting down names/words [*onomata*] while the particular [*kath'ekaston*] is what Alcibiades does or suffers. (1451b8–11)

History treats actions as in some way self-subsisting and independent— what happened to happen. They may but need not affect what comes after them. Poetry, on the other hand, imitates actions that are whole. But "that which by being present or by not being present makes nothing clear is no part of the whole" (1451a31–35). A part necessarily makes a difference to the whole of which it is a part. An action that is part of a genuine whole is essential to that whole and could not be replaced without fundamentally altering the whole. In being about wholes (*katholou*), poetry is concerned with relations that, because necessary, are generalizable. Tragedy, therefore, finally has to do with what sort of thing certain sorts of men do in certain sorts of circumstances. The sign of this, says Aristotle, is names. Poets do not begin with a name and build a character around it. The names are tacked on later to fit the character. The character of a character precedes his name, the sign of his absolute individuality. Indeed, a name that at first seems simply to be a sign of the individual frequently reveals the class character of that individual. It is no accident that Antigone means antibirth and Oedipus is a pun on swell-foot, knows-a-foot, or know-where.[67] General significance shines through these individual names.

All of this is supposed to differentiate poetry, and especially tragedy, from history, which is concerned with the particular. However, Aristotle's example of a particular—what Alcibiades did or suffered—is not decisive for this differentiation. Does he mean to call to mind the Alcibiades of Thucydides' history or of Platonic dialogues? Neither simply supports his claim. In Plato's dialogues, Alcibiades is the beloved of Socrates and seems to be a paradigm for the necessary particularity of any actual love. It is arguable that Thucydides' Alcibiades, both in his virtues and in his vices, gradually comes to stand for Athens and finally for a certain kind of political order. Aristotle's own example of a particular, Alicbiades, thus calls attention to what has thus far been suppressed in the argument—the extent to which the particular can be used to stand for the general. This is, of course, the peculiar power of poetry.

If history is not as concerned with the particular and contingent as at first seems the case, neither is poetry as detached from the particular. Aristotle makes it seem as though comedy never uses historical characters but consists of fictional plots whose characters are named as a sort of afterthought, the names frequently conforming to their characters (1451b11–15). Indeed, in a general way this agrees with the history of comedy put forward in chapter four. Initially comics ridiculed particular public figures; with the addition of a plot, the situation becomes comical in itself. This is the difference between comedy and lampoon. Still, what are we to think of the plays of Aristophanes? Are the *Clouds*, the *Frogs*, and the *Knights* thinkable without Socrates, Aeschylus, Euripides, and Kleon—all historical figures? It is surely not possible that the works of the greatest Greek comic poet do not qualify as comedies. Aristotle has clearly overstated the case, but there is a case. Comedy is connected to the plausible. Because its plot is constructed with a view of likelihoods (1451b13) and not so much with a view to the necessary, the perspective of the spectators is closer to that of the characters.

Unlike comedy, tragedy must use "historical" names to add to the likelihood of its plots. Things that have happened clearly must be possible (1451b17–19). However, these two—things that have happened and things that are possible—are precisely what Aristotle wanted to separate in order to distinguish between history and poetry. Here he seems to admit that when we do not know the general, there is some sense in which the particular can serve as a substitute to establish what is possible. Still, tragedy cannot finally rely on these particulars.

Nevertheless even in tragedies, in some one or two of the names are of those known while the rest have been made up [*pepoiêmena*], and in some none [are of those known] such as in the *Antheus* of Agathon.[68] For in this one, both the incidents and the names alike have been made up [*pepoiêtai*], and it is no less enjoyed. So that one ought not seek to cling completely to the plots that have been handed down which tragedies are about. For to seek this would also be laughable, since even things known are known to few, but nevertheless they please all. (1451b19–26)

Although Aristotle gives an example of a play with no historical content, it is instructive that this is the only play that we know about of this sort.[69] Still, Aristotle means to say that because such a play is thinkable, and because even when the names and situations are "known" they are not known to all, tragedy cannot in principle be dependent on such knowledge. Now, it is interesting that Aristotle should say that even things known are known only to a few. Of what things can he be speaking? Surely the Greeks who filled the theaters knew about Troy and about Oedipus.[70] In the *Rhetoric* (1416b26–27), for example, Aristotle indicates that to praise Achilles one need not tell the audience what he did since everybody knows that. Of course, everyone will not everywhere and always know the things that everyone now knows. Aristotle's remark must, then, have to do with the universality of the appeal of tragedy. A passage that began by distinguishing comedy from tragedy by their use of historical individuals ends with the claim that such a use is not essential to tragedy. Tragedy is thus not so different from comedy. To bring this point home, Aristotle says that it would be laughable—*geloion*—to think only the old stories are proper subjects for tragedy because to do so would be to mistake particulars for the universal. It would be to locate the appropriateness of the stories in their familiarity—a contingency—rather than in what probably caused their familiarity—their universal significance. It would be to mistake a spurious whole for a whole. But this was the formula for a "tragic error." Contrary to our initial impression, the comic and the tragic have the same root.

Still, as we have seen, almost all tragedies and many comedies do make use of known individuals. Aristotle seems to distinguish the poetic from the historical only to undermine his own distinction. Histories turn out to be "poetic"—Alcibiades is an image of a kind of democracy, and poems, both comic and tragic, turn out to be historical. But Aristotle's argument does not undermine itself. He first says that poets imitate not what does happen but what could happen. But since what does happen could happen, poets can imitate what happens if they do not understand themselves to be doing so historically. As poets, they get at the general within the particular.

There must be particular incidents within the plot that point to its wholeness. This is only to say that human beings always understand actions in progress in light of where they are heading (i.e., as incomplete wholes). Some animals seem always locked in the present; their conscious activity consists in choosing what seems best for them at the moment. Their action can, therefore, be described as purposive without their ultimate purposes being objects of consciousness for them. Dogs chase sticks without ever thinking to themselves that these actions in which they are engaged constitute "chasing sticks." Were human beings like that, they might do geometric proofs by moving from step to step simply because it was logically possible to do so. But such proofs would never end, and such provers would not really be human. A geometer has "to see with parted eye"— one eye directed toward what justifies moving from step to step and the other toward the ultimate goal of the proof. One eye is on the likely, the other is on the necessary. The likely is therefore not possible by itself; because it involves the anticipation of a yet to be completed whole, it is yoked to the necessary.

If there must be events within the plot through which the necessary shines (the likely cannot supersede the necessary), there must also be a way of preventing the plot from becoming altogether predictable (the necessary must not supersede the likely). This is the last of the issues to which Aristotle turns in chapter nine. He begins with what looks like a digression about the worst of simple plots and actions—those that are episodic.[71] He does not tell us what simple plots are until the following chapter, and this brief mention of episodic plots seems only to point back to the beginning of chapter eight. If, by episodic, Aristotle means not corresponding to the likely or the necessary, then this digression seems to be an example of what it is about. Such plots are put together by bad (*phauloi*) poets because they are bad poets (1451b35–36) or by the good "on account of the performers." "For," according to Aristotle,

> by making [*poiountes*] contests and stretching the plot beyond its capacity, they are compelled to distort the sequence. (1451b37–52a1)

Is it the good poets who distort the sequence? What would it mean that they make contests and stretch the plot "on account of the performers?" Does Aristotle mean that they write plays with certain performers in mind? It seems more likely that he means to say that it is the performers who make contests and stretch the plot beyond its capacity or power. In other words, the subtle connections of the sequence of events in a play may not be understood by those who perform it. What a "good poet" understands as a connection may be perceived as a digression. If that is true of tragedy, perhaps it is also true of the apparent digression Aristotle has made concerning episodic plots.

That something like this is in fact the case is clear from the sequel— the end of chapter nine.

But since the imitation is not only of a complete action but of fearful and pitiable [things], and these come to be both especially and more when, contrary to expectation/opinion [*para tên doxan*], these come to be on account of one another. For this will be more wondrous than if they came to be of themselves or by chance, since even among chance things those seem most wondrous which appear to come to be as if for a purpose, for example, as the statue of Mitys at Argos killed the one who was the cause of the death of Mitys which fell while he contemplated it. For it is likely [*eoike*] that such things do not come to be at random [*eikêi*] so that such plots are of necessity more beautiful. (1452a1–11)

There is a curious reversal in Aristotle's argument here just before his introduction of reversal and recognition as the most important features of tragic plot in chapter ten. And it is pity and fear that force Aristotle's reversal. The distinctive feature of tragic drama, that it arouses pity and fear, requires that the plot unravel in such a way as to produce *to thaumaston* (the wondrous or surprising)—the cause of philosophy (*Metaphysics* 982b12–17). Up until this point the criteria of the wholeness of the action of tragedy have been the likely and the necessary. The two are problematically related but nevertheless inseparable. Here what happens must be a surprise, and so, presumably not likely. The sequence of Aristotle's argument is as follows. He first argues plausibly that plot must be plausible. Then he surprises us by reversing himself to show plot is more powerful still when something unlikely can be shown to be likely. And finally this is understood as a necessary consequence of the previous argument of which it seems at first to be the denial (1452a10–11). This reversal of Aristotle's argument comes just before the discussion of reversal in Aristotle's argument.

Both of these reversals turn on a curious way of unifying the likely and the necessary and so the action of which they are the standards. Aristotle's example points the way. Mitys's killer is killed by Mitys's statue. Now, it is likely enough that a man should die from a falling rock. And it is likely enough that someone close to Mitys should attack Mitys's killer. However, on the surface, it is extremely unlikely, and so surprising that the rock that is Mitys's image should cause the death of Mitys's killer. How is it that the combination of two likelihoods results in something so surprising? We wonder at the death of Mitys's killer not because it is unlikely but because it is too likely. That is, we are accustomed to have chance play a role in our lives. The death of Mitys's killer is so unlikely only because it is so appropriate. It is one of those things that happen only in books—that is in artificial situations where the meaningful is made to happen. For that reason, when such things do happen in real life, we are moved to say that they could not have come to be randomly. It is not accidents that are unlikely. Most people are not killed by falling rocks, but there is nothing astonishing in such a death. Accidents do happen. It is the meaningful—the intelligible—that really counters our expectations and so is *para tên doxan*, against opinion—paradoxical.

The unlikely is so unlikely in its meaningfulness that once it happens it seems to be by design. What couldn't have happened unless it were "meant to be" becomes no longer only likely but necessary. The likely and the necessary are thus unified in tragedy when tragic reversal reveals the sequence of likelihoods leading to a conclusion which is unlikely because it is so full of meaning. As the double standard that governs tragic action is also characteristic of human action generally, this unification will be more than a technical question of literary form. With that in mind we turn to Aristotle's account of reversal and recognition.

8

The Structure of Action

(1452a12–56a32)

[10] The *Poetics* is about the dual meaning of *poiein*; the verb "to do" can mean to act or to make poetry. Human doing has an unself-conscious part and a self-conscious part; this is what it means that we are rational animals. However, when we turn to the self-conscious part in the form of poetry, we discover a new version of the old dualism. Imitation, the heart of poetry, proves to have a self-conscious part and an unself-conscious part. Now, what is true of poetry in general is especially true of tragedy. Tragedy is the most perfect manifestation of poetry because more than any other form it embodies this doubleness. The heart of tragedy, plot, is governed by two principles—the likely and the necessary—that point back to the distinction on which all drama is based, between the perspectives of actor and spectator. The demand of the spectator—of the part of us that is engaged in *theôria*—is for total intelligibility. The demand of the actor—of the part of us that does—is for openness, contingency, and freedom. Neither of the two ever exists pure. But this is only to say that their necessary combination in poetry is characteristic of their necessary combination in human action.

Tragedy characteristically displays this double demand by showing how intelligibility and freedom are at odds. The principal character in a tragedy ordinarily takes for granted the absoluteness of his beginning point, assuming something to be altogether fixed and known, an *allo* and not a *heteron*. Oedipus, for example, assumes that he knows who he is— that his parents are Polybus and Merope. In one way or another the consequences of his mistaken assumption are brought home to the character. Ironically, in assuming his own situation to be completely determined, the character treats himself as though he were a character in a

65

play whose actions were part of a whole. Because his assumption is an action in a play, he pays for it. This assumption of wholeness is the connection between tragedy and the beautiful. Tragedy is not only a beautiful whole of ordered parts, it is also about the beautiful. It is about the consequences of the assumption that one's life is a whole of ordered parts.

If plot is the heart of tragedy, what Aristotle calls reversal (*peripeteia*) and recognition (*anagnôrisis*) are the heart of plot. They make plots complex rather than simple (1452a15–16) and so reveal the doubleness of tragedy, poetry, *mimêsis*, and ultimately human action. Reversal and recognition are the thread running through the section of the *Poetics* beginning with chapter ten, where Aristotle distinguishes the plots they characterize from simple plots.

> Of plots, some are simple while others are complex, for the actions, also, of which the plots are imitations, are such from the start. And I say action to be simple that comes to be as continuous and one, as was defined, and of which the change comes to be without reversal or recognition; but [I say action to be] complex from which the change is with a recognition or a reversal or both. And these ought to come to be from the myth's composition [putting together] itself, so that, from what went before, these things happen either coming to be from necessity or in accordance with the likely. For that things come to be on account of others is quite different from coming to be after them. (1452a12–21)

Just as simple plot was previously introduced with only a hint of what it was (1451b33–34), here it is presented negatively in contrast to reversal and recognition, terms not defined until chapter eleven. Aristotle does not mean that a simple plot contains one story and complex plots more than one. This possibility is excluded by what he says later (1453a12–13)—that the beautiful plot must be single rather than double. Because the most beautiful plots involve reversal (1452a10–11), such plots must be single. Simple plots, then, cannot be the same as single plots. A double plot is two stories parading as one. A single plot is apparently one story but is not necessarily simple. A simple plot, on the other hand, seems to be an imitation of an action where one incident follows on another but containing no incident in the sequence that points to the necessity to look back over the whole to see that it conceals a deeper sequence of equal likelihood or necessity. Such a plot would point to the doubleness of action only insofar as we in the audience reflect on our relationship to the action as it unfolds on the stage. However, this relationship itself is not made a part of the plot.

A complex plot has to weave reflection on the action into the incidents that make up its action. For this reason the most beautiful tragedy is not simple but complex (1452b30–32). Because a complex plot is built on the discrepancy between what seems to be and what is, its movement will turn on a question of knowledge, of penetrating through seeming to what is. For a connection of incidents to seem woven together into a whole, it must be plausible or likely. When a plot reveals the real story underlying this plausible appearance and makes this revelation a turning point in the action (i.e., the cause of the change from good fortune to ill or ill fortune to good), then it is lack of knowledge that is constitutive of this change of fortune. In a simple plot one's expectations are never reversed. A strong nation goes to war with a weaker nation and defeats it. This simple plot might contain many incidents, and they might be unified into a genuine whole. But only the reversal of our expectations by the defeat of the stronger by the weaker could force us to wonder about the seeming strength of the stronger.

[11] Reversal is defined in chapter eleven of the *Poetics*.

> And reversal is the change of the things acted/done to the opposite, as was said, and this, just as we say, according to the likely or necessary. (1452a22–24)

Aristotle's example is from *Oedipus the King*. A messenger has just come from Corinth with the "good news" that the king, Polybus, whom Oedipus believes to be his father, has died. Oedipus expresses some doubts about returning as the oracle had also concerned his future intercourse with his mother, and Merope, Polybus's wife, is still alive. This messenger, never given a name or even a pronoun by Aristotle,

> coming so as to cheer Oedipus and to release him from his fear regarding his mother, making clear who [he] was, [he] did [*epoiêsen*] the opposite. (1452a25–26)

To whom does the "he" refer, Oedipus or the messenger? Because disclosing Oedipus's identity proves to require disclosing the messenger's identity, the ambiguity seems to make no difference. In either case the good news proves bad. Intending to free Oedipus from the fear of parricide and incest, the messenger reveals that it was he who had brought the baby Oedipus to Polybus and Merope. The result is "a change to the opposite."

Now, it is clear that reversal must involve some violation of expectation; it must be *para tên doxan*. But whose? Since, as Aristotle makes clear, the reversal need not coincide with any recognition within the play (1452a14–17), the expectations cannot be those of characters in the play.

The *Oedipus* would not be dramatically affected were the messenger to leave before he discovered that his good news backfired. At the same time, since the turn of events involves not so much a change as a reinterpretation of what has already occurred, some recognition seems necessary. Therefore, reversal must be our recognition as an audience that what we thought to be is not what we thought it to be. Reversal occurs at that moment when it becomes clear that all of what has gone before meant something other than what we thought it to mean. A plot containing a reversal is not double because the action remains the same, but it is complex because the action has been revealed to be something other than what it first seemed to be. Until Cassandra speaks to the chorus of Argive elders *(Agamemnon* 1035–330) we do not know of Clytemnestra's adultery with Aegisthus, and we do not know that she plans to kill Agamemnon. In light of what she says, the whole action of the play must be rethought, beginning with the purpose of the signal fires warning her of the end of the war *(Agamemnon* 21–39).

The account of recognition begins with a reference to its etymology.

> And recognition [*anagnôrisis*], just as the name signifies, is a change from ignorance [*agnoia*] to knowledge [*gnôsis*], either to friendship or to enmity of those having been defined with regard to good fortune or ill fortune. (1152a29–32)

Recognition, as *an-agnôrisis*, is a privation of ignorance.[72] But might we not understand its etymology as *ana-gnôrisis*—knowing back or re-cognizing? As the same syllables give us two different etymologies, it is not so obvious what "the name signifies." Now, when the kind of ambiguity exemplified in Aristotle's language here arises within a play, the conditions are present for recognition.

In Sophocles' *Trachiniae* (1157–178) Herakles first interprets Zeus's promise that he will not die at the hands of anything living to mean that he will not die but later understands it to mean he will be killed by the poison from the blood of the dead centaur Nessus. Nothing has changed here but his understanding of the meaning of the events leading up to this recognition. Still, for such a change to become an incident (*pragma*) in a play it has to have consequences; it must lead to a change that makes a difference to the action as a whole. Recognition can turn on lifeless things—for example a ring or a lock of hair, but it is only because these things are signs that they are important. Thus, while recognition may be of things (*tinôn*), it must ultimately be of people (*tinôn*)—whether oneself or others. For it is only in one's relationships to other people that the world is significant and so subject to interpretation, reinterpretation, and recognition. For Electra to recognize a lock of hair or a footprint

(*Libation Bearers* 164–211) would mean nothing unless they were signs of Orestes, her brother. Since recognition always involves a change, it must then be a recognition that one thought to be *philos*—dear, a friend, or kin—was really *echthros*—enemy or foe—or vice versa. In either case, a prior confusion is discovered in a way that alters the action of the play. Recognition is thus the awareness of a character within the play that parallels the audience's awareness of a reversal.

Recognition is most beautiful when it coincides with reversal—when the discoveries within and outside the play come to be simultaneously, or when the act of understanding and the action itself are somehow one.[73] Aristotle describes the recognition that "especially belongs to plot and especially to action" as the "one having been said" (1452a36–38). Now, presumably this means the most beautiful kind mentioned at 1452a32–33, the kind where recognition and reversal coincide. At the same time, certain recognitions occur when a character comes to understand the significance of things that he has previously said. Oedipus does this all the time. He promises to pursue the murderer of Laius as though Laius were his father (264–66). And he begins *Oedipus the King* by addressing those assembled around him as *tekna Kadmou*—children of Kadmus. Oedipus treats them as though they were his children (1, 58); he does not realize that he too is a child of Kadmus, that those under his care as king may be like children, but they are also his brothers and sisters, his fellow citizens. For Oedipus, really recognizing who he is would involve discovering the significance of "what has been said." Of course, the beauty of Aristotle's claim that the best recognition is "the one having been said" is that, when we recognize what it means, it becomes an example of itself.

A plot in which events simply followed one another predictably, in which the likely turned out to be the necessary, in which, to cite the previous example, a strong nation attacked a weaker enemy and won, would contain *pathos*—suffering or experience—but not reversal or recognition. Reversal makes an audience reflect on the necessity of action that at first seems unlikely, for example in the *Trachiniae*, that Deianira's attempt to make Herakles love her should end by killing him. Recognition introduces inference into the play so that reflection on the likelihood and necessity of the action becomes a part of the action and so has further consequences within the play itself.

Aristotle concludes chapter eleven by calling these three—*pathos*, reversal, and recognition—parts of plot. While they are parts, they are not parts that stand along side each other. Every plot has *pathos*, a sequence of plausible actions. Simple plots contain only *pathos*. Complex plots contain an incident in which something that at first seems unlikely proves to be necessary; this is reversal. Plots are more complex still when such a reversal of the likely is experienced within the play; this is recognition. The turning point in *Oedipus the King* is Oedipus's discovery of who he is.[74] This kind of action—in which coming to knowledge is decisive—is, not surprisingly, especially revealing of the rational animal.

[12] Having introduced reversal and recognition, Aristotle moves without explanation to a short chapter on the parts of tragedy. Our only preparation for this disruption comes from the description of *pathos*, reversal, and recognition as "parts of plot" (1452b9) in chapter eleven. But these parts are clearly different from the sequential parts of chapter twelve.

> We stated [*eipomen*] before the parts of tragedy which ought to be used as *eidê* [forms or species], but these [*tade*] are [the parts] with respect to quantity into which, having been separated, it is divided: prologue, episode, exode, choral part—and this into parode and stasimon, these being common to all, and, peculiar to some, are [choral parts] from the stage and *kommoi*. A prologue is a whole part of tragedy before the parode of the chorus. An episode is a whole part of tragedy between whole choral songs. An exode is a whole part of tragedy after which there is no choral song. Of the choral part, a parode is the first whole speech [*lexis*] of the chorus, a stasimon is a choral song without anapests or trochees, and a *kommos* is a lamentation common to the chorus and those on stage. We stated [*eipamen*] before the parts of tragedy which ought to be used as *eidê*, but these [*tauta*] are [the parts] with respect to quantity into which, having been separated, it is divided. (1452b14–27)

So out of place does chapter twelve seem that many editors (beginning with Heinsius in the seventeenth century) have suggested moving it, and many others (e.g., Butcher and Else) do not accept it as genuine. The chapter is certainly queer; at first glance, its list of parts—prologue, episode, exode, parodos, stasimon, and *kommos*—seems connected to nothing else in the *Poetics*. Upon reflection, however, one recognizes that each part is defined in terms of its relationship to the chorus. The prologue is what comes before, the exode after and episodes what come between choral odes. The parode is the first chorus and stasimons are the others. A *kommos* differs from a chorus by the participation of the actors, but is still defined as a variation of a choral ode.

Now the chorus has a funny function in tragedy. It is a character insofar as what it says grows out of the plot—to understand the famous chorus in *Antigone* (331–83) about man as the being most *deinos* of all (simultaneously most canny and uncanny), one must understand what they make this claim in response to. At the same time the chorus reflects on the action of the plot and so talks directly to the audience. Thus, while chapter twelve seems at first unconnected to what surrounds it on both sides (the discussion of reversal and recognition), in fact, the role of the chorus is unusual in allowing it to participate on the levels of both reversal and recognition. The chorus is, in a way, the defining feature of tragedy. Nietzsche notwithstanding, the chorus is the spectator within the drama.[75] At the same time it is an actor. It is, therefore, especially meet that Aristotle should discuss the chorus in a "digression." Chapter twelve of the *Poetics* functions like a stasimon. There is something poetic in the almost exact duplication of its first sentence by its last sentence (the two differ only in using different forms of the aorist "we stated" and different words for "these"). Because it seems only marginally connected to what surrounds it, a choral ode looks like a reflection on what comes before and after. It is both still within the dramatic time of the play and at the same time atemporal. This "choral ode"—chapter twelve— has as its content the double perspective of the chorus as a paradigm for the structure of tragedy. The apparent break in continuity with the surrounding discussion of recognition and reversal is what connects chapter twelve to that discussion, for the chorus makes manifest the double perspective of tragedy of which recognition and reversal are the deepest expression.

[13] In the first sentence of chapter thirteen Aristotle goes out of his way to assert the connection between what he is about to say and what came before. He goes so far as to use a word, *ephexês* (1452b30), to mean something like "thereupon," which he had used at 1452a1 to mean the "succession" of events in a tragedy. It is typical of Aristotle to describe something in his account just before using it on the level of his account. This will prove to be especially true of his discussion of error—*hamartia*.

If plot means a change of fortune, and the best change involves the coincidence of reversal and recognition, in which direction ought the change to occur? It would be *miaron*—polluted or disgusting—were a man who is *epieikês* (decent, meet, equitable) to move from good to bad fortune (1452b34–36). In *Nicomachean Ethics* V (1137a31–138a4), Aristotle gives an account of *epieikeia* as a virtue more just than justice because correcting the necessary imprecision of law as general. The equitable man (*eipeikês*) characteristically demands less than his share because he recognizes that justice does not prevail in the world. *Epieikeia* is therefore morality that is at the same time critical of moral idealism.[76] To show a man with such moderate expectations moving from good to ill fortune would be shocking. On the other hand, to show the wicked moving from lack of fortune to good fortune would arouse neither pity nor fear but righteous indignation.[77] This would be the least tragic of all (1452b37) since it would produce neither pity and fear nor something Aristotle introduces here for the first time, *philanthrôpia*—literally, love of or kinship with human beings. Pity and fear are absent because the wicked who fare well do not suffer; *philanthrôpia* is missing because there is no sense of solidarity with such men. Plots of this sort would arouse a deep sense of injustice. Tragedy is apparently not meant to cause utter despair of goodness in the world. Finally, it is not especially tragic to show the fortunes of the villainous change from good to bad. Such a plot might encourage *philanthrôpia* (insofar as justice prevails), but it would result neither in pity (the villain gets what he deserves) nor in fear (the one who suffers is not like us). Tragedy, then, does not simply support morality and subverts moral naiveté. Accordingly, Aristotle is silent about the plot in which the good man's fortune alters from ill to good. That tragedy is no simple morality play is signaled by a change in Aristotle's language. The "good" man, previously *spoudaios* or earnest (1448a2), has become the *epieikês*, the man aware of the impossibility of perfect justice.

What remains then is what lies in between the equitable and the bad man.

> Such a one is he neither distinguished by virtue and justice nor changing to ill fortune on account of vice and wickedness, but [one who changes] on account of some error and is one of those being in great repute [with a great opinion] and of good fortune such as Oedipus, Thyestes and renowned men of such families. (1453a7–12)

The subjects of tragedy are those who are thought to be great. Are they also those who have great opinions? Their error (*hamartia*) seems to have to do with being too little aware of the fuzziness of moral principles— they are too little *epieikeis*. In one way such men are not virtuous; in another they are too virtuous. This is borne out by Aristotle's list of examples: Alkmeon and Orestes killed their mothers but to avenge their fathers; Oedipus sought to become master of his own fate, but to avoid the necessity to kill his father and have intercourse with his mother; Meleager was killed by his mother after accidentally killing his uncles; Thyestes, brother of Atreus, seduced Atreus's wife, and, to punish him, Atreus fed him his children; Telephon was punished for accidentally killing his uncles. Although these are cases that scarcely admit of straightforward solutions, the characters involved are ordinarily sure of themselves and filled with moral indignation. Each commits some "great error" (1453a16) connected to some "great opinion" (1453a10), which is the reason for his "great repute" (1453a10).

In the midst of this discussion of great errors in tragedy, Aristotle remarks that

> those accusing Euripides of the same thing err [*hamartanousin*] [or, those accusing Euripides err with respect to the same thing] because he does this in his tragedies, and most of them end in ill fortune. (1453a24–26)

The critics of unhappy endings commit the same error (*hamartia*) committed by men of big opinions. In demanding happy endings, they demand that justice prevail in the world; they demand that the world make sense. Aristotle goes so far in defense of Euripides as to say he is not only right but

> even if he does not manage the rest well, yet he appears of all the poets the most tragic. (1453a29–30)

It is not that Euripides is the best tragic poet—elsewhere he is compared unfavorably with Sophocles (for example, at 1456a27)—but that he is the most tragic of poets. Those who criticize him err, not recognizing in themselves the tragic demand that justice fully prevail. Euripides is the most tragic of poets because his plays most conform to the rule that tragedies end unhappily. In being the most rigorous in his practice, the least *epieikês*, he behaves most like the character in a tragedy. The thrust of this remark is to call attention to the fact that tragic poets are subject to the same necessities of action as the characters about whom they write.[78] Chapter thirteen concludes with a remark locating the weakness of the spectators as the cause of the making of inferior plots. Poets flatter their audiences with plots that are *kat'euchên*—according to prayer. This is connected to the error of tragic characters who make the mistake of living their lives *kat'euchên*. Tragedy necessarily violates prayer understood as what we would most wish for.

[14] According to chapter thirteen, the change in plot must move from good to ill fortune. This is the source of our pity and fear. In chapter fourteen Aristotle considers how it is that pity and fear are produced. The easiest way, through spectacle (*opsis*), is rejected as inferior, but why has it suddenly been reintroduced? Although it is common to feel pity at the sight of terrible suffering, by itself sight cannot tell us whether the suffering is just or unjust. For that we need a story—a sequence of events in which the suffering is placed in a context and each moment is linked causally to previous events.[79] Because *opsis* can so easily engage our passions without justification—any picture of a mutilated child arouses

pity—it is a great danger to the proper task of tragedy. A good actor can make a play seem better than it is; a bad actor can make it seem worse. When an actor interprets a role, he frequently must resolve certain ambiguities that the role as written leaves unresolved. We may prefer Laurence Olivier's Hamlet to Richard Burton's, but neither is Hamlet. At its best, acting may call attention to the necessity of the sequence of events of the plot, but even here it mutes the ability of the events themselves to call attention to the necessity of their sequence. And this is not simply a matter of conscious interpretation. Whether in her own person or behind a mask, once Antigone walks out on stage she must be either tall or short, beautiful or ugly, speak with a high or low voice. When we go to the films of our favorite actors, it is frequently the person we want to see, a personality who reappears in various stories and so transcends the details of any particular story. We say we are going out to a Clint Eastwood movie. It is a bit like spending an evening with a good friend. However entertaining, such an evening contains nothing of the necessity of the pity and fear generated solely from the putting together of actions. Aristotle has once again warned us about drama. While it is written as though to be seen, its deepest effect is independent of performance,

> for the plot should be put together so that even without seeing, the one listening to the actions which occur will shudder and pity from what happens. (1453b3–6)

Chapter thirteen makes clear that a tragic plot must move a character of less than perfect virtue from good to ill fortune. Curiously Aristotle seems to reverse himself in chapter fourteen. As actions may be done with or without knowledge, there are four possibilities for the action in tragedy. A character may intend to do something knowing what he is doing, but because of some accident not do it—this is not really drama. A character may intend to do something knowing what he is doing and do it— this is the case of Medea. A character may do something without intending to have done it and then discover what he has done—this is the case of Oedipus. Finally, a character may intend to do something, discover that he did not really know what he was doing and not do it—this is the case of Iphigeneia. Aristotle calls the last the best (1454a4). But how can it be best for Iphigeneia not to kill her brother, that is, for the play to have a happy ending, when tragedy requires a change from good to ill fortune?

    Aristotle's language here is revealing. What the ancients did (*poiein*) as well as what Euripides did (*poiein*) in the *Medea* was to make the doing (*prattein*) come to be with knowledge. Sophocles makes Oedipus do (*prattein*) terrible things in ignorance and then discover it. The "best" form is characterized as intending to do (*poiein*) and then, discovering, not to do (*poiein*) it. Now, up to this point Aristotle had been using *poiein* to refer to the activity of the poet and *prattein* to apply to the activity of the character. Leaving that distinction intact, what he calls best here would not be an action within the play but rather the action of the poet.

Let us try to see what this means by putting some of these issues together. Reversal is an event in a play that leads the spectator to reflect on the events of the play. Recognition introduces this sort of reflection into the play as a piece of the action. By introducing the *epieikês* Aristotle pointed to a virtue of action, the highest kind, which is possible only as a reflection on the imperfection of virtue. But why is this highest action of man not the subject of the highest form of poetic imitation? Poetry could never present the highest virtue if the highest, like *epieikeia*, necessarily takes the form of a reflection on the imperfection of the "best." No action could ever reveal the virtue that always takes the form of a reflection on action. Insofar as a poet wished to "present" the best he would have to present an action that causes reflection (i.e., reversal) rather than presenting the reflection itself (recognition). And insofar as human action approaches its best, the actor would have to present to himself an action that causes reflection. The activity of the *epieikês* is something like literary criticism; it consists in seeing where others have gone wrong.

Still, Aristotle certainly says that the best plot, and so the best tragedy, combines reversal and recognition—it makes reflection an action. Tragedy thus distinguishes itself from other forms of poetry by making the poetic character of human action thematic. However, to present in action a successful reflection on action (*epieikeia*) would not arouse wonder and so not lead to reflection; it would be too pat and so essentially invisible. The goal of tragedy is the stimulation of pity and fear because reflection is stimulated only by failure—"All happy families are alike; each unhappy family is unhappy in its own way." There is no wonder without some appearance of discrepancy. Therefore, the options for combining reversal and recognition seem to be these. The poet can show the failure of genuine *epieikeia*, which does not seem possible since *epieikeia* consists in the ability to foresee the ways in which one cannot expect virtue to be manifest in the world. For it to fail to see where things fall short of perfection would be for it to fail to be *epieikeia*. Or, he can show the failure of spurious reflection. This occurs when a character who thinks he understands his situation comes to recognize that he was wrong; reversal becomes recognition. However, as an action in a play, an action with dramatic consequences, for such a recognition to lead to wonder, it too will have to be spurious. Recognition will always in some sense be false recognition. It will therefore always be subject to a higher order reversal in which it is possible for the audience to recognize something remaining opaque to the character. This is how it stimulates wonder. Oedipus thinks that he knows who he is, but when he takes the pin of Jocasta's brooch, stabs himself in his eyesockets (*arthra*), and pleads to be set out on Mount Kithairon, he is simply reproducing what had been done to him as a baby when his joints (*arthra*) were pinned and he was abandoned on Mount Kithairon.[80] If he really knew "who he was" Oedipus would not once again be attempting to take his fate into his own hands. Blinding himself was not humble. Oedipus still has not learned that he too is one of the *tekna* of Kadmus. However, had he learned who he was, we would have been unable to learn who he was. The *epieikês* can express his knowledge, even to himself, only by articulating what would happen to him were he not to know. Oedipus could have expressed wisdom only by writing his own tragedy. Self-knowledge outside of tragedy, therefore, requires the creation of something like poetry. Human action is self-aware only insofar as it is poetic.[81]

This is all particularly important in light of the way in which the form of the *Poetics* has mirrored its content throughout. Does Aristotle mean to give his book the form of tragedy? Certainly the argument of the *Poetics* is, like the argument of tragedy, very radical. The highest action, as reflection on action, is necessarily invisible. *Epieikeia* appears only as the correction of an error. But the action of the *Poetics* is precisely its reflection on action, disguised by Aristotle as a reflection on poetry. Perhaps the tragic error of the *Poetics* will prove to be this conflation of poetry and action, indicating that the willful identification of *poiein* and *prattein* in chapter three was too pat—too *kalon*. That all doing is a species of production suggests that all doing has a beginning, middle, and end, and that is not so obvious. Understanding the *Poetics* will require that, once having come to see how poetry and action are the same, we recollect how they are different. But such a reflection can be made visible, only as a correction of the error of the identification. Like a spurious recognition, it will necessarily appear as something other than it is. Aristotle's warning against our susceptibility to the visible at the beginning of chapter fourteen was another way of telling us that it is not possible for us to "see" what the poet is showing us. This is why a book on thinking shows itself as a book on poetry. This displacement is surely poetic. Insofar as tragedy is paradigmatic for poetry, it should be no surprise that the *Poetics* has proved peculiarly "tragic."

[15] At first glance chapter fifteen looks like another interruption of the argument. The discussion of plot begun in chapter seven has led by

stages to reversal and recognition. In chapter sixteen Aristotle will return to this pair, and plot will once again become central until chapter nineteen. Furthermore, even in chapter fifteen the discussion of character quickly gives way to a discussion of plot. Why, then, is something as important as character given such a perfunctory treatment?

Aristotle lists four things "at which one should aim concerning characters" (1454a16):

one and first that they [characters] be good [*chrêsta*]. (1464a16–17)

Chrêstos, used here for the first time in the *Poetics*, means good but with emphasis on utility. It, therefore, suggests the question "useful for what?" Goodness of character is introduced as relative to something other than character. It depends first of all on the class or kind (*genos*) into which the character fits. Aristotle suggests a good man is not the same as a good woman or a good slave, for "of these the one is perhaps worse and the other altogether base" (1454a21–22). Goodness, then, means goodness relative to the standards that constitute a class. A good slave is servile, a good man is not. Of course, only in fiction is a role ever this univocal. In real life slaves are also women and men, as well as mothers and fathers, daughters and sons, former citizens, and so on. Even in tragedy such "good characters" are forever acting out of character in a way not "appropriate" to their class. Deianira's surprise at the unexpectedly freeborn behavior of the nurse in the *Trachiniae* (49–63) is what defines the character of her nurse just as Antigone is defined by her refusal to follow Ismene's advice to behave like a woman (*Antigone* 49–77), and Electra's peasant husband is defined by his unexpectedly noble refusal to consummate a marriage that Aegisthus has forced upon Electra (Euripides' *Electra* 246–70). Aristotle makes clear that for character to be present some intention (*proairesis*) must be made manifest by a speech or action. However, the intention, which comes before the action (*pro-hairesis*), only shows itself in the choice (*hairesis*) finally made.[82] When the choice easily conforms to our expectations—when slaves act slavishly—the intention behind the choice, and so the character in question, is invisible. Aristotle's "good" characters do not seem to be the characters of tragedies unless when he says that they must first be good, he means that they must conform to a class so that they can be seen to deviate from it.

At first glance, Aristotle's second stipulation, that they be suitable or appropriate, seems only a repetition of the first. Women characters must not be *andreiê* (manly or courageous), nor are they to be *deinê* (clever, terrible, simultaneously canny and uncanny). The appropriate does differ from the good, however. Taken together, the first two criteria mean that a character must not only accurately represent a class of human beings, but must also represent the excellence of that class. If a bad slave were to behave in a disobedient way we would learn nothing much about what it means to be a slave. If, out of his desire to serve, a slave is forced to disobey, we learn something more interesting.

Unless Aristotle rejects Antigone as an appropriate subject for tragedy, it is clear that these first two criteria cannot stand by themselves. Antigone is the woman who is not only courageous and manly but whose burial of Polyneices' corpse gives rise to the famous stasimon on human beings as the most *deinos* of creatures (*Antigone* 332–83). One might, then, expect the final two criteria to effect some revision of the first two. With respect to the third, it is difficult to tell. Aristotle simply says that characters must be similar or like (*homoion*); he does not bother to tell us what or whom they are to be like but tells us only that to be like is not the same as to be good or appropriate. The final criterion of character is somewhat more complicated. A character must be even or consistent (*homalon*); it must be like itself. And when inconsistent, it must be consistently inconsistent. Characters are not supposed to surprise us gratuitously by their actions. If they are forever acting out of character, then they cannot properly be said to have any character. On the whole, then, characters must be predictable. Yet, were they wholly predictable, the plot would have no surprises—no reversals. It seems clear then that characters must be uneven or inconsistent in some sense. However, these inconsistencies ought to make sense. Once they have shown themselves, after our surprise, we ought to be able to say "I should have seen that coming. I should have known that this was that."

Aristotle presents four criteria for evaluating character in tragedy. Curiously enough, all these criteria measure character not in terms of itself but in terms of plot. Aristotle seems to call attention to this at 1454a33–36.

> It is also necessary similarly [*homoiôs*] in characters just as in the putting together of incidents always to seek either the necessary or the likely so that for such a one to say or do such things is either necessary or likely, and for this to come to be after that is either necessary or likely.

At 1454a24 he had left us dangling with regard to the meaning of *homoion*.[83] What were characters to be like? Us? Real people? Here he uses the adverb *homoiôs* to say that characters have to be put together like plots. Does *homoion* then mean that, like plot, characters must conform to the double standard of the likely and the necessary? This seems to be the meaning of Aristotle's final qualification of his final criterion. The actions of consistent characters seem to issue from them out of necessity. Perfectly consistent characters would be perfectly predictable. Inconsistency in characters is therefore a necessary condition of all drama. Characters must seem free to act in a way other than is perfectly predictable. At the same time, were their actions to be utterly inconsistent, there would be nothing to hold them together as characters. That they are consistently inconsistent seems to mean that although their actions are not predictable, they are retrospectively intelligible. But this is simply the togetherness of the necessary and the likely.

Aristotle's account of character has shown it to be governed by the same double standard that governs plot. Whatever else this means, it serves to introduce a digression on plot.

It is apparent, then, that even the resolutions [*luseis*] of plots should occur from the plot itself, and not, as in the *Medea*, from a contrivance [*mêchanê*], or the things concerning the sailing away in the *Iliad*. But contrivance ought to be used concerning things outside the drama, either whatever comes to be before and is not possible for a human being to know, or whatever [comes to be] later which requires foretelling and narration. For we assign it to the gods to see everything. And nothing absurd [*alogon*] [should] be in the incidents, but if there is, [it should be] outside of the tragedy, such as in Sophocles' *Oedipus*. (1454a37–b8)

A contrivance or machine (*mêchanê*) was a cranelike device used to lift gods into a scene from above. It is therefore a rather nice image for what Aristotle has in mind. Medea, in Euripides' play by that name, until the end of the play shows no supernatural powers. At the moment when she needs them, she suddenly shows prophetic powers and the ability to transport herself magically to Athens. In Aristotle's second example, Athena tells Odysseus to stop the flight of the Greeks in *Iliad* Book II. In both of these plots there is an external and unexpected cause of a crucial event that might have been linked by the likely or the necessary to something that came before.

Still, there is an important difference between the two. If the example from the *Iliad* were dramatized, it would look just as though Odysseus had acted in character. Athena's visit in *Iliad* Book II provides an occasion for a conversation that externalizes Odysseus's character so as to make it visible. It is fine for such devices or gods to be brought into a plot to make visible what would otherwise have remained hidden. Aristotle therefore connects this account of plot with the fact that the gods see everything. Accordingly, when knowledge of something invisible is crucial to the plot sequence, poets must introduce something like the gods. But the crucial invisible element of plot is character. For this reason Aristotle has introduced this digression about gods and their relationship to plot into his discussion of character. It is not a digression at all because the intervention of the gods, when well used, is a sign of the introduction of something that would otherwise remain *alogon*—absurd or unspoken. The gods are necessary to speak the unspeakable, and that is paradigmatically character. Sophocles' Ajax begins with a mystery: Why has Ajax slaughtered the Greek herd animals? His intention is invisible; the Greeks cannot know that he thought he was slaughtering the army in revenge for not having been awarded Achilles' armor. To them it looks like madness—something the reason for which is utterly invisible. But, without knowledge of Ajax's intention, the plot cannot proceed. They would not know whether to pity Ajax or punish him, whether he was friend or enemy. Athena must therefore be introduced to do what the rest of the play is designed to show us is impossible. Because the gods see everything, even the invisible, she is able to look inside Ajax to know his intent and tell Odysseus what she knows.

This digression on the role of the gods and devices in tragedy leads directly to an interestingly ambiguous suggestion:

> Since tragedy is an imitation of those who are better, we ought to imitate good image-makers.[84] For, while also rendering likenesses with regard to individual form, they also paint so as to make more beautiful. So also, while imitating the irascible and easy-going and those having the rest of such things concerning characters, the poet [should] make such men be equitable [*epieikeis*]. . . . (1454b8–13)

If we are to imitate the painters, we are not to take those they paint as models. Insofar as tragic characters become *epieikeis*, they do so by recognizing their errors. Presumably we are to imitate their recognition without their errors. But we cannot do that other than by expressing their errors to ourselves. Such expressions are imitations of the poet, not of his characters. Aristotle therefore cautions us.

> These things should be observed, and in addition to these, the things concerning perceptions following from necessity with regard to the art of poetry. For there is often erring with respect to these. But enough has been said concerning them in the speeches which have been given out [*en tois ekdedomenois logois*]. (1454b15–18)

While perceivable things follow of necessity in tragedy, in reality they do not do so. We must therefore remember that it is for us to imitate the poet, not his characters. Not to do so is to err (*hamartanein*), and it is a frequent error. The final twist of chapter fifteen is Aristotle's joke about his published speeches. These explanations are *ek-dedomenoi*—they have been given out. Aristotle refers us to external writings to explain what he means since it is appropriate for devices and godlike intervention to be restricted to what is "outside of the drama" (1454b3).

Character is perhaps the true object of imitation in tragedy, but it is invisible except through plot. The discussion of character in chapter fifteen was derailed and turned into a discussion of plot as an image of the dependence of character on plot, of the inside on the outside. At the same time, the "digression" on character was necessary for the discussion of recognition that continues in chapter sixteen. Like character, recognition is invisible. How, then, is it to become the crucial event in a plot?

[16] Chapter sixteen is a ranking of the forms of recognition in ascending order based on the priority of what emerges through the plot rather than by signs (i.e., by the visible). Aristotle lists five forms. The first and lowest, recognitions by signs, he divides in two. Signs may be either congenital like Orestes' hair, or they may be acquired. If the latter, they may be on the body of the person recognized, like the scar of Odysseus, or they may be things possessed, like necklaces or the cloth embroidered by Electra and shown to her by the returning Orestes to prove he is her brother (*Libation Bearers* 231–32). All recognitions by signs are better when they arise out of the plot itself (e.g., as Odysseus's scar was inadvertently seen by the nurse who was bathing him in *Odyssey* XIX), and worse when they do not (e.g., when Odysseus has to show the same scar to prove his identity to Eumaeus and Philoetius in Book XXI). Somewhat better than recognition by signs is the sort willed by the poet when a poet has a character declare his identity. Third, it is possible that recognition will occur because some sense perception of a character in the play arouses a memory. Odysseus, hearing a song describing the Trojan War, cries; as a result, he is recognized (*Odyssey* VIII). Second best are those recognitions that result from reasoning or inference of one of the characters in the play. Aristotle mentions in passing that sometimes such recognitions result from bad inferences (1455a14–16). Finally, chapter sixteen closes with an assertion that the best recognitions arise out of the events of the plot themselves. Here he cites Sophocles' *Oedipus* and Euripides' *Iphigeneia among the Taurians* as examples, although the *Iphigeneia* had seemed to be an example of the second sort.

A number of things are revealing about this list. Aristotle seems to prefer signs that are not used as tokens of trust. Such signs do not involve any plan or act of will on the part of the character recognized. Odysseus has a scar by which he is recognized in the first instance, but he uses this scar to show who he is in the second instance. On the same grounds, Aristotle objects to Orestes' attempt to prove who he is by showing

what he knows (*Iphigeneia among the Taurians* 805–26). In both cases
the recognition is a direct revelation; it does not emerge out of the action. When poets make the recognition in this way, it is as though they
transform *anagnôrizô* from a transitive to an intransitive verb with a passive
sense. What previously demanded a direct object—to recognize something—comes to mean "to make oneself recognized." In fact, Aristotle
uses the verb intransitively three times in this and in the subsequent chapter—
much to the puzzlement of editors and translators.[85] Ironically, the effect of this transformation is to make what motivates the recognition—
intention or *proairesis*—altogether invisible, with the result that the
recognition looks not necessary but somewhat arbitrary and indistinguishable
from chance. What we experience is someone's claim. Only when recognition appears to emerge out of the events of the plot can invisible
intentions be truly revealed. Otherwise we are always in the position of
the audience at Euripides' *Bacchae* when, in the first line, a character
declares himself to be Dionysus, son of Zeus. In reality, we would, like
Pentheus, have a right to be a little skeptical.[86]

Aristotle's account of the recognition scene of the *Iphigeneia among
the Taurians* seems unfair to Euripides. Iphigeneia, now the priestess of
Artemis in the land of the Taurians, offers Orestes, known to her only
as an Argive, escape from being offered as a human sacrifice to Artemis.
She will release him if he promises to carry a letter from her to her kin
in Argos. Orestes convinces her that Pylades, his friend and fellow captive, should go in his stead. Iphigeneia then tells Pylades to commit the
contents of the letter to memory so that, if it should be lost at sea, he
can still deliver it. The letter reveals her identity to Orestes and Pylades,
who then reveal their identities to her. Under the circumstances, then,
the recognition is not simply "willed by the poet." It is perfectly natural
that a man whose sister's identity has just been discovered should say
"But I am your brother."[87] What could be more appropriate under the
circumstances than attempting to prove his identity? That a woman, captive
in a strange land, should reveal her identity to those she takes for fellow countrymen in order to send a message home, and that hearing her
identity her brother should say who he is, is surely no less a recognition
"out of the events" than the suggestion Aristotle cites by Polyidos that
the captured Orestes should say how appropriate it is that he whose sister was sacrificed should also be sacrificed. As an imitation of human
action, tragedy must allow for characters to be aware of their own situations. While it may be true that recognitions must be rooted in the action
of the plot and not simply effected through speech, it is also true that a
large part of human action is speech. One cannot build a plot around a
case of mistaken identity without considering that human beings ordi-

narily introduce themselves to each other. On the other hand, an introduction by itself is simply an act of will. After marrying Procne, Tereus
rapes her sister Philomela and cuts out her tongue to prevent his deed
from being discovered. Philomela weaves an image of the event into a
tapestry. However clever this accusation, its indirectness does not en-
sure its truth. It is still a claim, and as an artificial sign—a picture—we
must still be wary of it. Only embedding it in a situation would reveal
it to be more than an assertion of will.

The importance of this awareness of situation emerges in the discussion of recognitions effected through *sullogismos*—inference or thinking together. Finding a lock of hair on Agamemnon's tomb, Electra has
to think through its significance. Since it is like her hair, it must belong
to a member of her family. It is not hers, and Clytemnestra would not
have left it. Therefore, it must belong to Orestes (Aristotle conveniently
omits to mention that she does not believe her own inference). Now, while
not all of Aristotle's examples are from extant plays, it is nevertheless
possible to draw some general conclusions. In each case, *sullogismos* seems
to occur when a character steps back from his own life to reason about
his situation as though he were a spectator of it. In each case cited, however,
the reasoning is suspect. Electra can draw the conclusion she draws only
by assuming that for her to be like Orestes is for her to be Orestes. This
becomes clearer in her interpretation of the second sign, the footprint,
which she concludes to be Orestes' because it is identical to her own.
Do brothers and sisters always share the same hair color and texture,
not to mention shoe size?[88] Similarly, although we know nothing of the
Phineidai other than what Aristotle tells us, we know enough to wonder
about the reasoning.

> For seeing the place, they inferred their lot, that in this place it was allotted
> them to die, for here also were they cast out. (1455a10–12)

Why on earth should one die where one was exposed as a child? It may
be poetic justice, but poetic justice is ordinarily reserved for characters
in poems. These characters all make the mistake of behaving as though
they were viewing a tragedy. This moves them to think events together,
but they do it badly. Their *sullogismoi* are really contrary to reason; they
are *paralogismoi*. To the extent that we accept such reasoning,

> there is also a [recognition] put together from misreasoning [*paralogismos*]
> of the audience. (1455a12–13)

The introduction of paralogism serves as a transition to the final and
best form of recognition. Aristotle's examples are Sophocles' *Oedipus*

the King and Euripides' *Iphigeneia among the Taurians*. Both involve willed revelations with unexpected consequences. Iphigeneia does reveal herself to her brother through a letter but not in the way she had intended; she believes Orestes to be in Argos (although she also has indicated that she believes him to be dead), but he is standing in front of her. The messenger from Corinth tells Oedipus "who he is" but, instead of releasing him from the fate foretold by the oracle, the messenger confirms it. In the best tragedies, then, a willed recognition becomes an event serving an end other than the one intended. Put somewhat differently, if recognition were possible simply through signs, it would be effortless and involve no willing. Because signs all involve some interpretation, however, such recognition is impossible. Since a sign must signify to someone, recognition through signs must always involve some "thinking together" or *sullogismos* on the part of a character in the play. On the other hand, recognition purely through an act of will means nothing apart from the situation in which the revelation occurs. Orestes seems to make a habit of dramatically revealing his identity to his sisters only to be asked for proof.[89] Recognition is accomplished neither by pure showing nor by pure saying but always involves *sullogismos* of the two. But how is this act of inference to be presented in a play? It cannot simply be shown, for then it would be a sign subject to a variety of interpretations. If it is to be said, it must be uttered by a character in the play. But pure inference would remove a character from the action, as though he were a spectator outside the play. Sherlock Holmes can unravel the knot of a mystery only because he is, as a private investigator, not really a part of the action but an audience to it. Holmes's action is thinking. Accordingly, the reader of a genuine mystery novel does not so much sympathize with a character as want an answer to a question.[90] Wherever this is not the case, recognition in a drama will necessarily involve the presentation of an inference that is itself part action. Now, while such inferences can be correct, the only way to make clear that they are a part of the action is for there to be a flaw in them that is traceable to something in the action. When Oedipus, despite the fact that the evidence is inconclusive, concludes that he has killed his father, we can understand his willfulness in light of the tendency toward anger that he has manifested throughout the play (both to us and to Kreon and Teiresias). Where inference is correct, no such connection between it and the action can become manifest. In all tragedies it is impossible to separate recognition through willing from recognition through showing because all human action involves inference. Human beings are rational animals. In the best tragedies, thinking is shown to be a part of action, but with the consequence that thinking about one thing leads to the discovery of another. For recognition to be "from the action," it must display the character of all recognition as a combination of thought and action, but, to do that, it must be a false recognition. Something like paralogism—a displacement of thought—is what tragedy does at its best.

[17] Aristotle's account of recognition forces us to think through what it means for the spectator to be brought into the play as part of the action. In chapter seventeen, this understanding of action is applied to the poet's own action—the composition of tragedy.

> Plots should be put together and worked out with speech [*lexis*] while being put as much as possible before one's eyes. For in this way the one seeing most distinctly, just as though he were among things being done [*prattomenois*] themselves, would discover what is appropriate and [he would] least fail to notice contradictions. A sign [*sêmeion*] of this is what censured Karkinos. For Amphiaros was returning from the temple, which, had the spectator not seen, he would have failed to notice, but on stage, it flopped because the spectators were annoyed by it. (1455a23–29)

Aristotle thus returns to the question of sight or spectacle—*opsis*—in its relationship to the possible. To see underlying contradictions, one has to visualize the plot (this need not mean removing the contradictions exposed). If the dialogue indicates that Orestes has a plan to get inside his mother's house by claiming to be someone who is bringing home the ashes of the dead and cremated Orestes and includes a speech in which Orestes indicates that to support his story he will approach the house carrying a funeral urn, visualizing the scene reveals a difficulty. If Orestes just thought of the idea, where did the urn come from? If he carried the urn and had the idea all along, why, after traveling all this way, has he just bothered to mention what it was for? Wouldn't his companions have been curious?[91] The words do not reveal this difficulty by themselves; they must be seen in their situation for it to emerge. When the chorus of the *Oedipus at Colonus* enter for the first time they are looking for Oedipus who, they have been told, has violated a sacred place. As they speak, they say that they must neither speak nor look when they pass the place, but they are speaking as they tell us this, and what they tell us is that they are looking. Furthermore they are walking over ground that we have previously been told is not to be stepped on. Oedipus has forced them to these sacrileges by hiding in the grove.[92] Seeing all of this requires that one not only listen to what they say, but also imagine what their actions have to be as they say it. It requires that the plot be "worked out with speech while being put as much a possible before one's eyes."

Having just criticized recognitions by way of signs, Aristotle now gives us a sign of the importance of visualizing the plot. His sign, the Karkinos example, seems to point to the necessity to block the action on stage so that a character never has to emerge from a place or a direction that is at odds with where the previous action of the play has already placed him. Here, it is interesting to note, the sign in question is an example. Do examples perform the same function in a treatise as visualizing does in a drama? That is, are they a means for testing the possibility of an argument?

Visualizing the plot as a whole is not enough; one must also envision how each actor will portray his character.

> To whatever extent possible [he should] work out [the plots] with gestures, for apart from the nature itself, those who are amidst the passions are most persuasive, he most driven by a storm drives by a storm, and he who is angry most truly enrages. Whence, the art of poetry belongs either to one of good nature or a madman, for of these, the former are easily molded [*euplastoi*] and the latter out of their minds [*ekstatikoi*]. (1455a29–34)

A good poet does not tell his audience that his character is angry; he shows that anger by making his character do and say things that an angry man does and says. The poet must, therefore, know what the outward manifestations of anger are—its *schemata*. But to know that they are genuinely signs of anger, the poet must distance himself from his anger to observe it. To match up internal passion and external signs he must be simultaneously actor and spectator. He must practice the first sort of imitation—mimicry—to practice the second—representation. Accordingly, poets must either have natures that are good in the sense of plastic, or they must be mad in the sense of out of their minds. Poets cannot be what they are, for they can watch themselves in the midst of their passions. Apart from everything else, this teaches us something of considerable interest about the relationship between poets and their poetry. One who is either outside of himself or of such a plastic nature that he can take on any nature could never display outward manifestations of his nature. A poet could never appear in a drama as a poet. Aristotle first suggests that one must have experience (*pathos*) of what one writes— *mimêsis* must be mimicry—only to show how problematic that is—*mimêsis* must be representation. The one requires the immediacy of experience, the other the detachment of thought. That the two must be put together is implied by that to which Aristotle next turns.

The remainder of chapter seventeen consists of plot summaries of Euripides' *Iphigeneia among the Taurians* and the *Odyssey*. Aristotle introduces them as illustrations of a third principle of poetic composition.

One himself making/poetizing [*poiounta*] should set forth in general the speeches [*logous*] and men having been made up [*pepoiêmenous*], and then add episodes and stretch them out. And in this way I mean [*legô*] the general would be contemplated [*theôreisthai*], for example in the *Iphigeneia*.[93] (1455a34–b3)

It is clear that *logous* cannot mean the precise words uttered by a character, for which Aristotle would have used *lexis*. The poet must imagine in general terms what is said and done without yet bothering about precise details either of language or of situation. To know that those assigned to guard the unburied corpse of Polyneices will have to tell Creon that it has been buried despite them, is to know what must be said—speeches—generally. It is not necessarily to know the peculiar manner in which it will be said in Sophocles' *Antigone*. A report about a buried corpse doesn't have to contain a doctrine about the soul however appropriate a place it is for such a doctrine.[94] In general then, the poet is to begin with a plot summary. He contemplates this general account and then adds the details of action and speech necessary to turn a plot summary into a play. What is done in general becomes a specific series of episodes; what is said becomes a specific series of speeches.

This all seems a simple, if a little too formulaic, account of how poets compose. However, Aristotle's plot summary of the *Iphigeneia* omits a lot that is relevant to the action. He doesn't tell us that Orestes is on the run because he killed his mother, Clytemnestra. He doesn't tell us that Apollo sent Orestes to the land of the Taurians to be purified. We don't know that Orestes is mad or that his madness is the result of the Furies. These omissions obscure the most interesting tensions and difficulties expressed by the play. For example, we need to be reminded that, while Orestes killed his mother for killing his father, his mother killed his father for "killing" Iphigeneia. This might well have an effect on her sisterly affection for him. The maiden is thus not just a sister, and the man to be sacrificed is not just her brother. Aristotle has given a plot summary but not of the *Iphigeneia*.

Similarly, the specific language of a play is never so incidental as it first seems, as even Aristotle's brief summary indicates. Orestes is captured on account of his madness (*mania*) and saved through a purification (*katharsis*) (1455b14–15). The language here corresponds to the language of Euripides' play (*Iphigeneia among the Taurians* 83, 1191) Now, Aristotle had called the poets *manikos* earlier in the chapter (1455a33), and the goal of tragedy was said in chapter six to be *katharsis* (1449b28). Without the specific language in which Aristotle discusses the *Iphigeneia*, there would be no reason to connect his summary of it with his account of tragedy. Once we notice this language, however, we wonder whether it is not Aristotle's interpretation of the play that Orestes is meant to be the poet in his role as standing apart from his own passions. Orestes is the spectator "purified" by the action of the play. This confirms Aristotle's earlier suggestion in chapter fourteen that the *Iphigeneia among the Taurians* is an attempt to present the action characteristic of the best man—the *epieikês*—by bringing the spectator on the stage. All of this would be invisible were we to pay no attention to the specific language of Aristotle's account.

Can we doubt that the same is true of tragedy? To understand Sophocles' *Philoctetes* one must understand the connection between the two things that are unique about Philoctetes—his famous unerring bow and his self-renewing wound. However accidental it is that *bios* means both life and bow in Greek, Sophocles exploits the coincidence. The deeper meanings of ordinary events are frequently brought to light in Greek tragedy by extraordinary language. In tragedy, unlike life, how things are said is the clue to what they are. One might begin thinking about the *Philoctetes* by wondering what it means that Philoctetes moans metrically.[95] A poet may begin with a general notion of speeches and deeds, and only later stretch it out with episodes, but it is in the stretching out that a poem becomes what it is. Aristotle is right that Euripides must have begun with a sister's discovery of her longed-for brother, but the episodes of *Iphigeneia* do not merely stretch this plot out by adding the details that must be present in any real event. They and the language in which they are expressed constitute an interpretation of the meaning of the plot they have stretched out.

Aristotle's summary of the *Odyssey* is still barer than his summary of the *Iphigeneia*. As it does not mention the Trojan War or Odysseus's refusal of Calypso, we know neither what moved Odysseus to leave home, nor that the whole of the *Odyssey* is an account of his decision to forego immortality in favor of going home. Aristotle does not name Odysseus, calling him merely someone, but, curiously, and in apparent violation of his own principle of generality, he goes out of his way to say that Odysseus's troubles stem from Poseidon. By mentioning a specific god, Aristotle shows how difficult it is to purge his summary of all particulars, for the general emerges only by way of the particular.[96] In the plot summaries Aristotle twice uses the verb *anagnôrizô* in a sense only found in the *Poetics*, and only three times in the *Poetics*.[97] Although ordinarily it means "to recognize," Aristotle uses it here to mean "to make oneself recognized." Earlier (1454b32) he had done the same thing in a discussion of the form of recognition willed by the poet. The *Odyssey* and the *Iphigeneia among the Taurians* both involve recognitions in which characters "make themselves known" and then must prove who they are. This distinction between saying and showing, central to the nature of drama, is invisible in a plot summary where there can be no distinction between what emerges from the action and what is willed by the poet. Without the addition of episodes and speeches, anger, for example, always shows itself as "he was angry"—a bloodless synthesis of "I am angry" and the signs by which anger shows itself. The doubleness of human action—its nature as a combination of external and internal, sign and will—is suppressed in a plot summary, and with it the most important feature of tragedy.

Chapter seventeen as a whole is meant to point to this doubleness. Its account of how tragedy is generated by the poet splits in two. Aristotle first says the poet has to feel the *pathos* of those whom he imitates. He must experience anger to know the signs of anger. On the other hand, the poet must begin from a universal plot. But the account of the poet as immersed in *pathos* made it impossible to understand his contemplation of his own *pathos*. The poet has to be angry to write authentically about anger, but, talk of angry young men notwithstanding, writing poetry is a rather contemplative occupation. At the very least, the anger of the poet cannot be the same as the anger of his poetic creation. When Homer spoke of Achilles' anger at Agamemnon, was he angry in the same way?[98] If the detachment and universality of contemplation threaten the particularity of *pathos* in the first part of chapter seventeen, the general or universal plot summary of the second part does not escape some admixture of particularity. Aristotle began chapter seventeen with an account of the importance of envisioning—*opsis*. It was his way of indicating that, in tragedy, talk (*lexis*) is not the same as a rational account (*logos*) but an act of speech, unintelligible apart from specific circumstances. Talk is something that takes place. Aristotle couldn't get rid of Poseidon. In its form, chapter seventeen tries to give an account of the activity of the poet that splits *pathos* off from universality—*lexis* from *logos*. Its failure to do so indicates their necessary togetherness, demonstrating that *pathei mathos*—learning through suffering—applies not only within tragedies.

The *Poetics* begins with the following sentence:

> Concerning both the art of poetry itself and the forms [*eidê*] of it, what particular power each has, and how one should put plots together if the poetry is to hold beautifully, and further from how many and from what

sort of parts it is, and similarly also concerning whatever else belongs to
the same inquiry, let us speak, beginning according to nature first from
the first things. (1447a8–13)

We have seen that there are two thrusts to this beginning. On the one
hand, the *Poetics* is a "how to" book; Aristotle claims that he will tell
us how to put various forms of plot together and out of what parts. On
the other hand, it is an analysis of the various forms of the art of poetry—presumably by seeing how the parts of each form fit together differently. It is, therefore, both analytic or eidetic and synthetic or genetic.
    Now, the difficulty with this double intention of the *Poetics* is that
Aristotle does not seem to maintain a clear distinction between part (*meros*
or *morion*) and form (*eidos*). Consider, for example, the beginning of
the definition of tragedy in chapter six.

> Tragedy, then, is an imitation of action which is good/serious and complete/
> perfect, having magnitude/greatness, by speech pleasing separately by each
> of the species [*eidê*] in the parts/in turn [*en tois moriois*]. . . . (1449b24–
> 26)

Here part and *eidos* seem quite distinct. However, the two seem to be
conflated at the beginning of chapter twelve.

> We stated before the parts of tragedy which are the *eidê* one ought to use
> . . . . (1452b14–15)

In the context, Aristotle calls the six parts of tragedy (plot, character,
thought, *lexis*, song, and *opsis*), which he is distinguishing from the
"quantitative parts" of chapter twelve, *eidê*. The *Poetics* throughout slurs
the difference between making and analyzing even though Aristotle himself
begins with it. This tension between part and *eidos* is reflected in the
double meaning of *mimêsis*, in the tension between the perspectives of
actor and spectator, in the double standard of the action in tragedy as
both likely and necessary, and in the double role of the chorus. In chapter seventeen it emerged as the tension between the necessity for the
poet to experience what he was describing—*pathos*—and the necessity
to leave details behind and begin with a summary of the plot in its universal significance—*logos*. Presented as though they were moments in
the construction of plot, these two in fact prove to be moments into which
it is necessary to analyze tragedy if we are to understand it. It remains
to be seen how this is connected to chapter eighteen, the final chapter
of the second part of the *Poetics*.

[18]   Chapter eighteen divides into four parts. The first (1455b24–32) is concerned with *desis* (complication, involvement, binding, raveling) and *lusis* (denouement, resolution, loosening, unraveling). In the second part Aristotle indicates the four *eidê* of tragedy (1455b32–56a10). Third is a digression on epic (1456a10–25), and the fourth is concerned with the proper role of the chorus (1456a25–32).

If plot alone differentiates one tragedy from another, what constitutes plot is *desis* or *plokê* (complicating, weaving, knotting) and *lusis* (re-solving, unraveling, loosening). *Desis* includes the action from the be-ginning or *archê* (which frequently includes events before the beginning of the play) up to the extreme point (*eschaton*) where the weaving to-gether of the events of the plot stops and things begin to unravel. The *lusis* is all the rest from the *archê* of the change until the end (*telos*) of the play. Now, there is no question that in some sense Aristotle means us to take this account linearly or temporally. There is a part of any tragedy in which things are put together and a part in which they are taken apart. At the same time, the key terms of the account all allow for an alter-ative interpretation. Suppose *archê* means not temporal beginning but first principle, *telos* not temporal end but purpose, *eschaton* not tempo-ral or spatial extreme but utmost, and, most importantly, *lusis* not de-nouement but resolution understood as something like ana-lysis. For this last there is evidence internal to the *Poetics* where Aristotle uses *lusis* to mean solution or resolution (1460b6, 1461b24) and *luein* to mean to solve or resolve (1460b22). *Lusis* appears, before having been defined, in chapter fifteen (1454a37) where Aristotle indicates that it ought to come out of the plot itself and not be generated "from the machine." Now, if *lusis* meant analysis or interpretation here, Aristotle would be saying that tragedy is better when it supplies its own analysis.

The meaning of this first part becomes clearer after we look at the second.

> There are four forms [*eidê*] of tragedy (for the parts also were said to be this many): the complex [*peplegmenê*—plaited or woven], of which the whole is reversal and recognition; the [tragedy] of passion [*pathêtikê*], such as both the *Ajaxes* and *Ixions*; that of character [*ethikê*], such as the *Women of Phthia* and *Peleus*; and the fourth. . . , such as the *Daughters of Phorcus*, *Prometheus* and whichever are in Hades. (1455b32–56a3)

This passage is notoriously difficult.[99] Aristotle announces that there are four *eidê* of tragedy, and that this is connected to the fact that there are four parts of tragedy. But, although there are various lists of the parts of tragedy in the *Poetics*, nowhere are they four in number. Furthermore, Aristotle never says why the number of *eidê* should equal the number of parts. Finally, there is a textual difficulty at 1456a2 where only the letters *oêd* remain of the name of the fourth *eidos* of tragedy, and even these seem corrupt.

Nevertheless, certain things can be said. At the beginning of chapter twenty-four Aristotle makes the following remark:

> And further, epic should have its *eidê* the same as tragedy; for it is either simple, complex, of character, or of passion. And, except for song and sight [*opsis*], the parts are the same. (1459b7–10)

This strongly suggests that the missing fourth *eidos* of chapter eighteen is simple tragedy. While it is difficult to match the parts of tragedy with these *eidê*, since tragedy is meant to be understood as performed but not necessarily actually performed, one might argue that song and spectacle or sight are not parts of the same order as the other four. Thus, tragedy would consist most fundamentally of plot, character, dialogue, and thought. As plot is primarily reversal and recognition, it would correspond to the *eidos* of tragedy called complex. That is, the tragedy in which plot dominates is complex. The tragedy in which character as a part dominates seems obviously to be the *eidos* of tragedy called *ethikê*, of character. The final two are more difficult. However, Aristotle indicated in chapter seventeen that to know what angry men would say it is necessary for the poet himself to have the *pathos* of anger. Perhaps, then, one can say that the tragedy in which what men say to each other dominates is a tragedy in which *pathos* dominates; its *eidos* would be *pathêtikê*. Finally, in the tragedy in which thought dominates, where there is no discrepancy between what characters think and what they say or do, the lack of ambiguity would make reversal and recognition impossible; such a tragedy would be simple. This is confirmed when Aristotle remarks that the fourth form includes all those tragedies taking place in Hades. When Odysseus visits Hades in *Odyssey* Book XI, he finds Ajax unwilling to speak to him. Ajax, in Hades, is constituted by his hatred of Odysseus. Unlike the visible world, Hades (*Aidês*), the invisible (*aidês*) world, allows for no distinction between surface and depth, seeming and being. To be a shade is like being a character in a book. Because one's story has been completed, and change is impossible, there can be no reversal or recognition in a plot taking place in Hades. Similarly, plots involving only gods could not be complex, for the characters involved would see everything and so know what was to happen to them. Recognition and reversal require that characters not know what they are doing. Because actions in simple tragedies are not subject to the double interpretation that has proved so central to tragedy thus far, they seem to border on not being tragedies at all. Aeschylus's *Prometheus Bound* is a simple tragedy, for if Prometheus, whose name means forethought, knows his fate, how can a plot concerning him be anything other than simple?[100] In general, then, while any tragedy might have all four parts, its *eidos* would depend on which part was dominant.

The tragic poet ought to attempt to include all of these *eidê*, but, if that is not possible, to include the best and the most important. The most important of the *eidê* is clearly plot.

> For having come to be good poets with respect to each part, they deem the one [poet] to surpass the particular good of each. But it is also just to say that tragedy is other or the same in nothing but plot, those being [the same] of which the complicating/weaving and the resolving/unravelling are the same. But many, weaving well, unravel badly. Yet both should be brought to agreement/to be struck at once. (1456a5–10)

Poets are often good at *desis* (this is what it means to be a poet—to make up stories or put together plots) but less frequently good at *lusis*. This is Aristotle's version of what Socrates says of the poets (*Apology* 22c)—that "they say many beautiful things but know nothing of what they say." Poets, ordinarily good at the part of *poiêtikê* that involves putting the parts of a poem together, are not as a rule so good at the other part—analysis of poems according to their *eidê*. It is one thing to make a shocking movie and another to understand precisely why it is shocking. Tragedy is a crucial exception to this general rule, for in tragedy part of the plot is its *lusis*, an analysis of its action. Tragedy is distinct in being simultaneously synthetic or genetic—*desis*—and analytic or eidetic—*lusis*. On one level, then, the movement from *desis* to *lusis* is linear—there is a point in the play where things begin to unwind. On another level *desis* and *lusis* are the same (1456a9). Once Oedipus utters his first words, *ô tekna kadmou*, the meaning of his incest has already been revealed; he is the father who does not know himself to be a brother. In various ways he places himself altogether above those whom he rules, however benevolently. As he is not altogether above them, he cannot be who he thinks he is. The plot of the *Oedipus the King* is the series of episodes through which Oedipus as "brother" is revealed. This, however, is also the meaning of the plot. So the parts of the play turn out to be the principles according to which the play can be understood. Tragedy is something like a metaphorical analysis of metaphor in which events function simultaneously as parts of a play and *eidê* of its analysis. Things that at first look accidental in retrospect become absolutely necessary. *Lusis*, in its deepest sense, is not a part of the plot but a second sailing—a rereading that makes visible what was implicit from the outset but could never have been seen without first having been missed.

In slurring the distinction between part and *eidos*, the *Poetics* borrows from tragedy. Everything in Aristotle's book is susceptible to a double reading because we are simultaneously being given a productive or genetic account—a *desis*—and an analytic or eidetic account—a *lusis*. This is connected to Aristotle's earlier remarks that in the most beautiful tragedies reversal and recognition coincide (1452a32–33), that the composition of the plot in the most beautiful tragedies is complex rather than simple (1452b31–32), and that the whole of complex tragedy is reversal and recognition (1455b33–34). Reversal is a change of which recognition is the awareness. When the two are put, not side by side, but together, the result is the whole of tragedy—a doing that is simultaneously a thinking.

This whole issue continues in the third part of chapter eighteen where Aristotle turns again to epic. It is the simultaneity of *desis* and *lusis* that distinguishes tragedy from epic. It would be extraordinarily difficult to sustain this doubleness consistently for the length of an epic poem, although epic certainly borrows freely from the mode of tragedy. The issue of this part of chapter eighteen is thus once again *meros*—part. To attempt to render the whole of an epic like the *Iliad* in a drama other than by parts (*kata meros*—1456a15–16) would mean that some of the parts, instead of taking on their proper size, would come out "contrary to the hypothesis" (1456a15). That is, since it would not be possible to do everything, the poet would have to substitute for the unfolding of events either summary of the action or themes. In an epic about the whole of the Peloponnesian War, one might have to say that "the Athenians and Spartans carried on war that year" or describe the difference between the pious Spartans and the imperial Athenians without showing it, thus substituting an external account of events for an unfolding of the events themselves in time. But ideas that are brought to bear externally in this way are more like a *deus ex machina* than a *lusis*. The audience learns by being told rather than by having the necessity revealed of what they are being told.

Chapter eighteen as a whole points to the inseparability of part and *eidos* in tragedy. The real *logos*, or account, of a plot is inseparable from the events of the plot. Perhaps the *Oedipus the King* contains only the account of how a man comes to know that his very attempt to avoid killing his father and marrying his mother has led to those actions, but the deeper significance of his parricide and incest is revealed only in the specific events of the play. The *lusis* of a tragedy is simultaneously its unraveling and its analysis because the deeper significance of the events of play is always parasitical upon the fact that it is possible for them to constitute a good story—a *desis*—independent of our knowing why this is the case. What makes tragedy special is that it presents a story, a simple plot, involving reflection on the double significance of events, and so reveals the simple plot to have been complex. At the same time, in providing within itself its own analysis of itself, tragedy necessarily presents that analysis as part of a drama. Tragedy thus splits into a section that presents a story and a section that reveals the meaning of the first section, but the second section is also a part of a story and so not simply detached analysis. In the *Oedipus* the first *desis* consists of everything from the birth of Oedipus to the arrival of the messenger in Thebes who tells him who he is. The first *lusis* consists of everything from the discovery of Oedipus's incest to his self-blinding. On the other hand, there is another *lusis* that consists in the revelation of Oedipus's nature as it manifests itself in his role as king or tyrant (*tyrannos*). Oedipus fails to see that, as one of the "children of Kadmus," he is as much the brother of his fellow citizens as he is their father. The first *lusis* proves to be another event in the drama through which Oedipus reveals his unchanging nature. He never understands that he cannot take full control of his life. The pair *desis/lusis* thus means two things. It is first a division of the whole plot into two parts and second the supervention of a *lusis* over a *desis* as an analysis of what has been put together. In tragedy, the first is an imperfect representation of the second.

This doubleness of tragedy is confirmed by the conclusion of chapter eighteen. By emphasizing that the chorus must be one of the actors in the drama so that songs and episodes cannot be lifted out of one play to be used in another, Aristotle once again makes clear that the observations of the chorus must be rooted in the sequence of events of which they are a part. Otherwise their reflections on the plot would not grow from the plot so as to be simultaneously *lusis* and *desis*.

The *Poetics* is an account of human action by way of an account of tragedy. How then does it fit with Aristotle's other accounts of human action? In three books, Aristotle gives us three definitions of human beings. We are political animals in the *Politics*, rational animals in the *Nicomachean Ethics*, and mimetic animals in the *Poetics*. How, then, are the three connected? If the concern of the *Nicomachean Ethics* is the good and of the *Politics* the just, the concern of the *Poetics* seems to be the beautiful. Aristotle provides three definitions of human beings from the perspectives of the beautiful, the just, and the good. How, then, are these three connected? The superficial answer seems to be that politics is concerned with action—*praxis*. The *Poetics* is concerned with tragedy, an imitation or *mimêsis* of action in speech—*logos*. The *Poetics* is therefore somehow concerned with what links human beings as active with human beings as the animals with *logos*.

Chapters six through eighteen of the *Poetics* have been concerned with the structures of tragedy and human action. The heart of tragedy is plot, and of plot, reversal and recognition. This places self-conscious doing at the core of tragedy. Tragedy is especially revealing of human action because it not only tells a story that is significant or meaningful, but also makes the fact that the story can be meaningful a part of the story it tells. It makes an action of thought to show us what it means that our actions are rational. *Pathei mathos*, the lesson of tragedy, is at the same time the structure both of human action and of human thought. Aristotle can define human beings as at once rational animals, political animals, and imitative animals because in the end the three are the same. In human action as in tragedy everything depends on the intention of the actor. But that intention cannot be shown directly—it must be revealed through action. When a poet tries to introduce intention directly it looks arbitrary and so is indistinguishable from chance. The true *deus ex machina* is therefore the human soul; it disappears as soon as one makes it visible. Ironically, the significance of our actions becomes visible only by reversing what we thought the significance to be. But this requires the initial assumption that one can see significance without reversal. You must assume that you can see someone's character to see his action. This is what allows you to have your impression of the action reversed as the tragic plot turns on itself so that you can "see" the character in question. We must assume Oedipus innocent in order to understand his true guilt. Blundering would seem to be the fundamental character of human action and thought.

Tragedy reveals what it means for human beings to be rational animals. It is not that we are part rational and part animal with each of the two parts fighting for dominance. The mixture is more intimate . In articulating the structure of this intimacy, Aristotle has displayed in various ways the dependence of human action on rationality of an imperfect sort. What remains is for him to inquire into the nature of this imperfect rationality. This is the concern of the remainder of the *Poetics*.

Part III

Logos

Truth is stranger than Fiction, but it is because Fiction is obliged to stick to possibilities; Truth isn't.

—Mark Twain
Pudd'nhead Wilson's New Calendar

9

Parts

(1456a33–57a30)

As the long analysis of the structure of tragedy has made clear, there is something essentially poetic about human action; all human action is imitation of action. Our natures as mimetic are, in turn, connected to our natures as rational; human action is self-aware action. What happens in every tragedy—the distinction between actor and spectator—is only an unusually revealing version of what happens regularly within each of us. Chapters six through eighteen of the *Poetics* teach us that we are always to some degree the spectators of our own actions, that these actions would not be human were this not the case and that they are profoundly affected by the fact that it is the case. The *Poetics* thus far might seem to have been concerned with the manner in which all *praxis* is "poetic" because of the way in which it mixes with *logos*, as though speech or thought could exist either in connection with action or apart from it. So far, the standpoint of the audience as spectator has been taken for granted to make possible an analysis of the composite of spectator and actor within tragedy that characterizes human action generally. Yet this detachment is an illusion—a beautiful simplification. The remainder of the *Poetics* is concerned with thought as an action in its own right. That is, if chapters six through eighteen put thought together with action, chapters nineteen through twenty-six will put action together with thought. It should cause no wonder, then, that this concluding section of the *Poetics* is particularly self-reflective. In inquiring into the character of thought as an action, Aristotle is also inquiring into the character of his own activity. Philosophy will prove to be the ultimate theme of the *Poetics*.

[19] In chapter nineteen, Aristotle turns to a discussion of the two re-

maining parts of tragedy—thought and speech (*lexis*). Plot has been treated at great length. Character was the subject of chapter fifteen and *opsis* the subject of chapter seventeen. Song will be omitted, but Aristotle had indicated as much when he said that whatever power song had was altogether apparent (1449b34).[101] Still, why are thought and *lexis* paired in this way? They were first introduced in chapter six.

> I say that *lexis* itself is the putting together of meters, but what power songmaking has is altogether apparent. But since imitation is of action, and it is acted by those acting to whom necessarily certain qualities belong according to both character and thought, for through these we say actions to be a certain quality (by nature there are two causes of actions—thought and character) and according to these all things happen or fail to happen, and since plot is imitation of action, for I mean plot to be this—the putting together of events, and characters are certain qualities according to which we say the events to be, and thought is that in which by speaking they show something or even declare a sentiment, it is necessary then for the parts of every tragedy to be six according to the sort of thing tragedy is. (1449b34–50a9)

The account is complicated, but two things are clear. Action is the primary part of tragedy and involves a putting together of events of which character is the hidden cause. Second, action also involves putting together speeches of which thought or *dianoia* is the hidden cause. Thought seems related to speech in the way character is related to plot. Just as character showed itself only in plot, thought shows itself only in speech. "And whichever things are according to thought should be produced by speech [*logos*]" (1456a36–37). Accordingly, chapter nineteen mentions thought only to move on quickly to *lexis*—that in which thought appears, thus repeating the movement from character to plot in chapter fifteen.

What, then, does Aristotle mean by thought?

> Let the things concerning thought be established as part of those concerning rhetoric, for this is more particular to that way of inquiry. And whichever things are according to thought should be produced by speech/reason [*logos*]. The parts of these are demonstrating, resolving/refuting [*to luein*], and the producing of passions (such as pity, fear, or anger and whichever are like these) and further magnitude and smallnesses. And it is clear that in the events one should make use of the same forms whenever one ought to produce pitiful things, dreadful things, great things or likely things, except that it differs in this way, that the one should be made apparent without teaching [*didaskalia*], while the other should be produced in speech by the one speaking and should come to be with the speech. For what would the task of the one speaking be if things appeared as they should and yet not through speech? (1456a34–b8)

Thought is not what we might call theme but rather what characters say to one another. Accordingly, it is never possible to quote a character in a drama—not even the chorus—in order to say what the drama means. This becomes clear by way of a comparison to the status of thought in rhetoric.[102]

Whether in rhetoric or in poetry, thought is always produced in speech. Aristotle lists the parts of this production: demonstrating, solving (or refutation), producing passions, exaggeration (or making big), and deprecation (or making small). These must be used in tragedy when people speak just as they are used by rhetoricians speaking to produce a certain effect. However, in tragedy they are used without teaching. That is, while the effects of rhetoric are produced in and through speech by one who is speaking, in tragedy the act of speaking is always embedded in some other action. The action of the rhetorician is his speech, which therefore must seem to be for its own sake. This is teaching. Whereas characters in tragedy speak, rhetoricians give speeches. These speeches appear to be pure—perspectiveless *logoi*; in tragedy speeches are always situated in other deeds, and so their meanings are somehow displaced. The thought behind a speech of a candidate for office can be evaluated in terms of the truth of its claims; when we treat a speech this way—in terms of itself—we treat it rhetorically. Or, it can be understood as having motives apart from its claims; when we treat a speech in this way (e.g., seeing its claims as meant to secure a certain block of voters) we treat it dramatically. Thought is always hidden behind *logos*, but in tragedy *logos* is always evidently already a part of the plot. Thought is therefore also transformed by the action in which a speech is embedded. This sort of speech is what Aristotle means by *lexis*.

Once it has been established that in tragedy thought is always embedded in a speech itself embedded in action, the issue for the tragedian becomes how to make the speech fit the situation. He needs something like a science of *lexis*. Aristotle turns to such a science in the second part of chapter nineteen but apparently only to dispense with it.

Of the things concerning *lexis*, the forms [*schêmata*] of *lexis* are one species [*eidos*] of theory/contemplation [*theôria*], which it is for the art of the performer to know and for the one having such an architectonic art: for example, What is a command? and What is a prayer? and a narration/declaration, a threat/ boast, a question and an answer as well as any other such thing. For with the knowledge or ignorance of these, no blame worthy of seriousness [*spoudê*] is brought to the art of poetry. For what should someone assume to have been in error [*hêmartêsthai*] in what Protagoras blames—that, believing himself to pray, he commands, saying "Sing goddess of the wrath . . ."? For he says bidding to do or not is a command. Hence, let it be passed over as being of another [art] and not the art of poetry, being a theoretical matter [*theôrêma*]. (1456b8–19)

Commands, prayers, declarations, threats, questions, and answers—all these seem to constitute a list of the variety of kinds of sentences. Given the absence of punctuation in Greek, many of these sentences are indistinguishable from one another apart from how they are said. The knowledge of how to make such distinctions, then, would not fall only under the art of grammar; it would extend to the sentences as voiced. It would be concerned with their performance.

But why does knowledge of these matters have nothing to do with *poiêtikê*?[103] Aristotle's remark about Protagoras is instructive. Protagoras, the most famous of the sophists, was not only author of the claim that man is the measure of all things, he was also among those who attempted to systematize Greek grammar. Here Aristotle presents him as critical of the first sentence in the most famous poetic work in the Greek language, Homer's *Iliad*. According to Protagoras, Homer uses a command when he ought to have prayed to a god, the mode of *aeide* (sing) being imperative rather than optative. This is itself rather interesting. Does Homer suggest that a prayer is a concealed command? The answer to this question is not so important here as the fact that Protagoras's strict grammar would foreclose the possibility of interesting ambiguity of this sort and with it the possibility of poetry. Protagoras demands univocity because he claims to have an architectonic art of speech. For him, *lexis* is not embedded in *praxis*.[104] Protagoras's grammar, prescriptive rather than descriptive, implies an absolute perspective on the correctness of *lexis* that does not involve understanding speech as embedded in a situation. It is this external knowledge of the *schêmata* of speech that is for Aristotle nonpoetic. A poet works at things from the inside out. While his characters may assume an absolute perspective, he does not. In context, cannot what is grammatically a question indeed be a statement? Homer does not err in this typically tragic way; perhaps Protagoras does.

[20] But must not Aristotle, therefore, avoid separating his account of how things should be said from where they are said? His beginning does not look promising; chapter twenty starts with a list of the parts of speech.

The parts of all *lexis* are as follows: element/letter [*stoicheion*], syllable, connective/binder [*sundesmos*], noun/name/word [*onoma*], verb, joint [*arthron*], case/mode/mood [*ptôsis*], phrase [*logos*]. (1456b20–21)

Aristotle's grammar seems no less formal and atomic than that of Protagoras. At the same time, the list is interesting. These parts are not homogeneous. One notices immediately, for example, that while letters are parts of syllables, and syllables are parts of each of the subsequent parts, *ptôsis* is not an element of anything but a modification of nouns and verbs. And *logos* is a combination of connectives, nouns, verbs, and joints as they are modified by *ptôsis*. The complexity of these relationships becomes clearer if we follow Aristotle in treating each of the parts separately.

The word *stoicheion* has a generic and a specific sense; it means both element and a particular kind of element—a letter. Aristotle begins with it.

> A letter, then, is an undivided sound [*phônê*], although not every one but that from which a sound comes to be put together by nature. For there are also undivided sounds of beasts of which I say [*legô*] none is a letter.(1456b22–25)

While *phônê* means sound, it first means the sound of the human voice and then, by extension, the voices of animals and perhaps inanimate things. Here, Aristotle at first seems to be taking it in its broad sense.[105] If, in addition to human beings, beasts make sounds, then what is the difference between the "rrr" of a man and the same sound voiced by a dog? It is a revealing accident that the manuscripts differ at 1456b23, some reading *sunthetê*—put together or compounded—and some reading *sunetê*—intelligible. Ultimately the only way to distinguish between the sound of a dog and that of a man will be that the latter is a part of an intelligible whole—a *logos*. Only what it will come to be as part of a larger whole distinguishes a human sound from an animal sound. This is our first indication that this account of how to produce *logos* out of its parts might be a concealed analysis of *logos*.

Letters, of course, are not all alike; Aristotle distinguishes three varieties, calling them the parts "of it" (*tautês*), presumably meaning the parts of undivided sound. Some are sounded (vowels), some semisounds (semivowels), and some nonsounds (mutes). Vowels are defined as having audible sound without any *prosbolê* (i.e., either without the addition of anything else or without the application of the tongue). To utter "A" the mouth is opened in a certain way and air gets pushed through; the sound is continuous. A semivowel is an audible sound produced with a *prosbolê*. "R" and "S" are audible by themselves without any addition, and they are continuous. A mute is a con-sonant; it is unsounded even with a *prosbolê* unless it is coupled with something sounded. "K" differs from "T," but the difference is audible only when the two are coupled with something sounded (e.g., KO and TR). While vowels and semivowels are continuous sounds, mutes are discrete. Each time they are made audible they must be coupled with a vowel or semivowel. Mutes are, therefore, another example of an element that can be seen as constitutive of *logos* only retrospectively. They are undivided sounds that have no discernible existence unless they are part of a larger whole. One can see them as parts only by keeping that larger whole in mind. Letters may be parts of syllables, but mutes have no existence apart from syllables. This is only another version of the doubleness of *phônê*—voice and sound. Or, to put the issue slightly differently, why are letters singled out as parts of sound? What about pitch and time?[106] Had Aristotle been thinking of music, his elements would have been different. The division supposedly yielding the independent elements of *lexis* has all the while assumed them to be elements of *lexis*.

From letters, Aristotle turns to syllables.

> A syllable is a sound without significance put together from a mute and something having sound. For GR without the A is a syllable, as well as with the A, i.e., GRA. But to contemplate [*theôrêsai*] the differences of these things also belongs to the art of metrics. (1456b34–38)

Like letters, syllables are presented as prior to that of which they are parts but are essentially defined in terms of the whole of which they are parts. A syllable is *a-sêmos*—nonsignificant. It is defined by comparison to what it is not. Dogs do not utter syllables because it is not in them to utter words. But the GR of a dog may sound very much like the GR of "grammar." Syllables look like building blocks of language; in fact, they are results of its analysis.

Aristotle continues this pattern in the next part of the argument when he turns to connectives (*sundesmoi*). The text is difficult and has been frequently emended.[107]

> A connective is a sound without significance which neither hinders nor makes one significant sound from being put together naturally out of many sounds both at the ends and in the middle, but which it is not appropriate to put on its own at the beginning of a *logos*, for example, *men*, *êtoi*, and *de*. Or [it is] a sound without significance which from many single significant sounds naturally makes one significant sound. (1456b38–57a6)

There seem to be two types of connectives. One does not bind together other significant parts into a significant whole but does not thwart such a connection. These are the various particles in Greek that lend a certain emphasis or modify sounds but do not make or undo the significance of what they modify. However, Aristotle's examples are puzzling. Even if *men* and *de* can somehow be understood as particles that do not bind significant parts together, this seems impossible for *êtoi*. *Men* can be used by itself to express certainty on the part of the speaker, and *de* can be used as an adversative or copulative particle. However they are so frequently used together—*men* meaning "on the one hand" followed by *de* meaning "on the other hand"—that *men* cannot be used by itself without tacitly raising the possibility of a correlative *de* clause to follow. So, Aristotle chooses as an example of a particle that does not bind together significant sounds two words that together constantly perform this function. If *êtoi* is taken not as an example here but as disjoining the examples *men* and *de*, then Aristotle's claim might be that either *men* or *de* is a *sundesmos* but not both together. But *de* alone can serve as a conjunction, and *men* always raises the expectation that something to which it is correlated will follow. If *êtoi* is one of the examples, it is most difficult since, either as disjunctive or comparative, it seems to link two significant sounds together. One might be tempted to emend the passage (Bywater replaces *êtoi* with *dê toi*) were the difficulties of *êtoi* not already present in *men* and *de*. One cannot escape the conclusion that, Aristotle's claim notwithstanding, these are examples of particles that do bind significant sounds together. It is clear that we do not yet know what he is doing.

The second type of connective couples significant sounds into a larger significant sound; "Adam" and "Eve" become "Adam and Eve," but the meanings of "Adam" and "Eve" remain intact. That we are given no examples is just as well since the examples of the first sort would serve here better than they did there. The two types seem alike insofar as neither affects the significance of the initial significant sounds. While there is some confusion about the distinction between the two, what is clear is that just as syllables seemed to be derived from letters but really governed by them with respect to sound, here as yet unspecified "significant sounds" are governing connectives with respect to significance. As binders, connectives are only intelligible in terms of what they bind together. Accordingly, it is extremely difficult to give an account of them before an account of the nouns, verbs, and phrases they bind together.

This proves equally true of joints—*arthra*.

> A joint is sound without significance which makes clear a beginning, end, or division of a *logos*, for example, *amphi*, *peri,* and the rest. Or [it is] a sound without significance which neither hinders nor makes one significant sound out of many sounds and is by nature put at the ends and at the middle. (1457a6–10)

Once again, there seem to be two types. The examples suggest that the first includes prepositions—*amphi* meaning "on both sides of" and *peri* meaning "all around." Prepositions group words together to make them all belong to a phrase, a *logos*. In doing so they set these words apart from those in other phrases. The second type is described in a sentence that is almost identical to the sentence describing the first type of connective. If a joint is meant to be a word that establishes divisions, the point here would seem to be that only given the context would it be possible to see whether a word is dividing or connecting. But all connections are necessarily simultaneously divisions. Uniting two things means first seeing them as two so that one can make them one.

Aristotle seems to present two different "parts" of speech—connectives and joints—that, along with other parts of speech, get put together to make *logoi*. In fact, however, he has identified two functions of speech that are located in the same part. One can distinguish between them only by the function they perform in the larger whole of which they are parts. Aristotle emphasizes this by giving identical definitions to one type of each of the two parts. This is the same ambiguity we first saw within the account of connectives when Aristotle chose as examples for one type of connective words that would have seemed more appropriate to the other. Not only have each of the parts of speech thus far proved intelligible only in terms of the wholes of which they were supposed to be the constitutive elements—letters in terms of syllables, insignificant sounds in terms of significant sounds, connectives in terms of the combinations they effect, it is also the case that parts that look identical apart from the whole they constitute can perform different and even contrary functions once within this whole. In one context *men* can mean "I really mean this." In another, it can mean "On the one hand. . . ."

This ambiguity is not an accidental characteristic of speech. The point of Aristotle's account of connectives and joints in partially identical language is that to connect two things in speech is to present them as separate, and to separate them is to couple them. When I say "either *A* or *B*," I am forcing you to consider *A* and *B* together. When I say *A* and *B* are one, I am forcing you to understand them as apart. Pairing and parting, the double function of all speech, seem at first to work in tandem; in fact, they are simultaneous. This is what makes it possible for a presentation of the constitutive parts of speech to have as its deeper meaning an analysis of the *eidê* of speech. That a connective must be simultaneously a joint is not only the fundamental feature of all *logos*; it is also the fundamental feature of tragedy.

After pairing and parting, Aristotle turns to what are paired and parted—*onomata* (nouns or names, but also adjectives and adverbs).

> An *onoma* is a compound [*sunthetê*], significant sound without time, no part of which is significant in itself; for in doubled [*onomata*] we do not

use [a part] as also itself significant according to itself. For example, in Theodoros [God's gift] the *"doros"* [gift] is not significant. (1457a10–14)

This definition of *onomata*—nouns, adjectives, and adverbs—as compound, significant sounds without time is unintelligible apart from some sense of compound significant sounds with time—verbs. Once again, and with what seems perhaps the most fundamental of parts of speech, we are given not so much an element as something that points beyond itself. At first *onomata* seem to be parts existing independently before the whole of which they are parts and retaining their character within the whole. Instead they seem to be like "doros." It is a masculinized version of *doron*, gift, and so in pointing to a meaning apart from the name, Theodoros, it has an independent existence in itself. Still, as a part within the name, "doros" loses its independent meaning. A mother cannot be thinking etymologically of "god's gift" (theo-doros) every time she scolds little Theodore for tormenting his sister.

In one case, however, this is not so. The name Oedipus puns on "swollen foot," "knows a foot," and "nowhere," and Antigone can be construed as "antibirth." The meaningfulness of these names is "poetic justice"—like a statue of Mitys falling on the murderer of Mitys. Fiction generally and tragedy especially make significant what is not independently significant to show why it cannot be significant. But this is exactly what Aristotle's treatment of *lexis* has done. He treats letters, syllables, and the rest as independently existing parts when in fact they are the results of an analysis of a larger whole—meaningful speech—and would make no sense without it. But Aristotle has treated them as parts only to reveal the whole toward which he is headed—*logos*. Chapter twenty is a prosaic version of the general method of tragedy.

With the introduction of verbs, Aristotle seems to have arrived at a part of speech that really is self-subsistent.

A verb is a compound, significant sound with time no part of which is significant in itself, just as also with *onomata*. For "human being" and "white" do not signify at what time, but "[he] walks" or "[he] has walked" signify in addition present time and that having passed. (1457a14–18)

Verbs seem not to be defined in terms of any subsequent part. However, although *badizei*—"[he] walks"—is a sentence in itself, as a verb in an inflected language, it also implies a third-person singular subject. There is no action without an actor, and so, a verb is in some sense a modification of an *onoma* and unintelligible without being so. At first it looks as though *logos* is built up out of elements. You start with a thing— "human being," add to it a movement—"walks," and end up with *anthrôpos badizei*—"a human being walks." A verb is a modification of a thing that presumes a persistence of the thing through its modification.

This signals an important shift in the discussion of the parts of *lexis*, for Aristotle now turns to *ptôsis*—a mode or modification of an *onoma* or a verb.

> *Ptôsis* belongs to an *onoma* or a verb, sometimes with respect to the signifying of a thing or to a thing and however many such things there are, sometimes with respect to one or many, such as human beings or human being, and sometimes with respect to the things of performance [*hupokritika*], such as a question or a command. For "Did [he] walk?" or "Walk!" is a *ptôsis* of a verb according to these forms [*eidê*]. (1457a18–23)

Ptôsis seems to include modification in case, number, gender, mood, and voice—any alteration through which the original word persists.

Yet this is all a bit too easy. It is not as though words could exist independent of any modification. A noun or verb is never encountered except as in some way modified. A Greek noun is either singular, dual, or plural; it is nominative, accusative, dative, genitive, or vocative. Verbs too appear only in one of their modifications. To look up a Greek verb in a dictionary one looks under the first person, singular, present, progressive form; the verb "to go" will be found entered under "I am going." But this is clearly a convention. Why should this form "be" the verb any more than its other forms? Is "go" any the less present in "the pair of them will have gone" than in "I am going." Not only is any one of its modifications as much the noun or verb as any other, the noun itself never appears in isolation. In the world we never encounter a "man." The man is always walking or running or sitting or reading. Whether doing something or doing nothing, he is modified and not man in himself. Since the noun is never experienced except as modified, there is something inaccurate about taking the noun by itself. To say "the man walks" we must assume there is such a thing as a man apart from walking. As we read the sentence from left to right, we must attach some meaning to the word "man" before we learn that he is walking. But what is he doing before we get to the end of the sentence? In treating him as though he could be doing nothing, we treat him as something he is not. We lie. All *logos* has this form; it lies or overstates to be able to tell the truth. There is therefore a parallel between the structure of tragedy and the structure of *logos*. Tragedy involves unraveling an overstatement by taking it deadly seriously. As we will see, Homer's greatness as a poet consists in having taught the other poets that it was necessary to lie (1460a18–19). The presence in the *Poetics* of the extended analysis of *lexis* in chapters nineteen through twenty-two makes more sense once one sees that *lexis* serves as a metaphor for tragedy.

When Aristotle finally gets to *logos* as compounded of parts some of which are significant and some of which are not, we are able to see that, in fact, he had begun with *logoi* without our realizing it.

> *Logos* is a compound significant sound, some parts of which in themselves signify something, for not every *logos* is mixed together from *onomata* and verbs, for example "the definition of human being," so that it is possible for a *logos* to exist without verbs. Yet it always has a part signifying something, such as "Kleon" in "Kleon walks." And *logos* is doubly one—either signifying one thing or by binding together [*sundesmôi*] from many. For example, the *Iliad* is one by binding together, but the [definition] of human being by signifying one thing. (1457a23–30)

While every *logos* must contain significant sounds, these sounds have only a specious significance prior to having been embedded in *logos*. The true meaning of Kleon is not independent of the various modifications through which he manifests himself. The Athenians no doubt knew who he was when he rose to speak in the debate over what to do with the rebellious Mytilenians, but after he spoke they had reason to think they knew him far better.[108] That "*logos* is doubly one" is therefore no accident. It is one by signifying one thing, but, finally, it can do that only by binding together many things. On one level, Aristotle means that "the definition of human being" is a noun—*horismos*, or "definition"— modified and specified by another noun in the genitive case—*tou anthrôpou*, or "of human being." The whole *logos* thus refers to a single thing. The *Iliad*, on the other hand, collects the various parts of an epic poem under one name. While *ho tou anthrôpou horismos* is a compound sound specifying a single thing, the unity of *Iliad* has to do with many things being called one.

Still, it is interesting that the "definition of human being" literally gives us the unity to which it points—human being—in the genitive case. It gives us a *ptôsis* or modification of human being and so can only signify one thing by presenting one of its various manifestations. Similarly, there is another unity of the *Iliad* according to which it is rather like "Kleon walks." When Homer begins with "Sing goddess of the wrath of Achilles," we do and do not yet understand what this wrath is. Presumably the whole of the *Iliad* is meant to form our understanding of the causes, consequences, and nature of anger. One needs to "understand" what Homer meant by anger to understand the *Iliad*, but one needs to understand the *Iliad* to understand what Homer meant by anger. The *Iliad* is not merely a willful collection of episodes but has a genuine unity. However, for this unity to become manifest, its various parts must be thought together as belonging to one poem. Only when it is assumed can the unity be found. Otherwise there would be no reason to think that the anger of Achilles in the face of Agamemnon's insult had anything to do with the anger of Achilles over the death of Patroklos.

Logos is double not because it effects two different sorts of unifying—parting and pairing—but because it is always simultaneously parting and pairing. Chapter twenty of the *Poetics* is concerned with the elements of *logos*. Although these elements at first seem genuinely independent and self-subsisting, their independence is specious. However, this speciousness is not a simple mistake; the appearance of independence and stability is necessary for the possibility of *logos*. Prescriptive grammar is an illusion necessary to make descriptive grammar clear. It consists in taking the parts of speech to be independent elements when they are the results of analysis of a *logos* that would be altogether unintelligible unless looked at as the product of these parts. It is the nature of *logos*, as it is of tragedy, to treat an *eidos* as though it were a part.

10

Eidê
(1457a31–58a17)

[21]   Aristotle's account of the parts of *lexis* was deceptively simple. As though one could begin with simplest parts and ascend to the more complex, he moved from letters to syllables to words without meaning by themselves to nouns and verbs, and finally, to *logoi*. While at first each stage seemed to be a part of the next, a second look proved it to be dependent on the next stage for its own being. Syllables are distinguishable from animal sounds only insofar as they are parts of words, and words can be words only insofar as they are parts of something significant—a *logos*. The heart of *lexis* is *logos* in its double sense of speech and reason—significant speech.

However, since speech can be significant in a variety of ways, in chapter twenty-one Aristotle turns to the *eidê* of *onomata*—words, now understood in their broadest sense.

> The species [*eidê*] of word [*onomatos*] are the simple—by simple I mean what is not mixed together from things signifying [something], such as earth [*gê*]—and the double. Of the latter, some are mixed together from something signifying and from the non-significant (except not signifying and non-significant in the word), and some are mixed together from things signifying. And there would also be triple and quadruple words and many-fold, such as the many [parts] of "Hermokaïkoxanthos" of the Massiliots. (1457a31–b1)

In chapter twenty *onomata* did not include verbs. Here it seems to mean words in general, including verbs. If so, then either *onoma* here is a metaphorical extension of a species (*eidos*) to include the whole genus (*genos*), or its earlier use was a metaphorical restriction of the genus "word" to one of its species (1457b7–14). In either case one of these

111

analyses is built on a metaphor, which is therefore not only a feature of poetry. Aristotle lets us know from the beginning that his account of the *eidê* of speech is subject to itself.

At first glance, this account of the two *eidê* seems to be merely a digression with little connection to the more important list of species of poetic words that follows it. Given Aristotle's sole example, *gê* , simple words seem relatively straightforward. They seem to be monosyllabic and so necessarily composed of a part that is insignificant apart from the meaning of the word as a whole. Double words would then be multisyllabic with at least one syllable having significance apart from the word. However, this is not what Aristotle has in mind. "Simple" does not mean uncompounded; it means without significant parts. "Double" means compounded of parts, at least one of which has a significance apart from the whole but not retained within the whole. Thus, "*gê*" is simple, but so is "*gaia*." And, while names like "Philadelphia" and "Theodore" and words like "understanding" are clearly double, so too are names like "Carpenter" and "Kane," even though the part having significance in both cases is identical to the whole of which it is the part. "We are going to the Carpenters for dinner" need not mean that we will be eating in a union hall. Accordingly, double words need not be multisyllabic. Aristotle can therefore add triple, quadruple, and many-fold words as an afterthought because they seem to share the essential feature of double words, and so seem not to differ in their *eidos*.

The specific feature of double words emerges more clearly from Aristotle's example. The Massiliots make a compound of the names of three rivers near Phocaea from which Massilia (Marseilles) was founded. Thus Hermos, Kaïkos, and Xanthos combine to form Hermokaïkoxanthos. Presumably this names a place—rather like Three Rivers Stadium. It begins as an obvious compound in which the significance of the parts describes the place, but, as the sound of the word becomes associated with the place, the sound comes to name the place, and the sense of the parts is suppressed. Very few New Yorkers would immediately recognize a connection between themselves and Richard III of England. "New York" is a sound that refers to a middle-Atlantic state or to a city at the mouth of the Hudson River. Neither is new or connected to York. And while Paris may bring to mind beautiful women, it does not automatically remind us of the theft of Helen or the sack of Troy. Still, these significant parts remain buried in the words of which they are parts and are subject to archeological excavation. Therefore, one must wonder whether "double" assumes its importance as an *eidos* of *onoma* not because of the spacial putting together of two otherwise separate elements but because of the residue of an earlier meaning contained within a new meaning. Antigone is a woman, but beneath her name lurks "antibirth." Aristotle presents as though it were spacial, a putting together of parts that, properly speaking, need not be spacial at all. Double words need not even be multisyllabic. Think of Citizen Kane or, what is here more important, *gê*. As a common noun it means earth; as a proper noun it names the female god. When Earth does something or is something, she is a person; however, she is a person who never escapes the significance of her name.[109]

The doubleness, indeed tripleness, of Hermokaïkoxanthos is only a metaphor for the particularly poetic doubleness of which Aristotle is really talking. He begins his account of the *eidê* of words with the distinction between simple and double because poetry depends on the doubleness potentially present in all language, as the list of what "every word is" will make clear.

> Every word is either ordinary/authoritative [*kurion*], foreign [*glôtta*], metaphor, ornament [*kosmos*], made-up [*pepoiêmenon*], lengthened [*epektetamenon*], shortened [*huphêirêmenon*], or altered [*exêllagmenon*]. (1457b1–3)

These terms are mostly adapted from other contexts; the language Aristotle uses in the analysis of language is thus itself metaphorical. Each of the eight terms mentioned, with the exception of *kosmos*, receives explication in the sequel.

Kurion and *glôtta* are considered as a pair.

> I say [*legô*] *kurion* [to be] what everyone uses, but *glôtta* what others use; so that it is apparent that it is possible for the same thing to be both *kurion* and *glôtta*, although not to the same [people]. For to the Cyprians, *sigunon* [spear] is *kurion*, but to us *glôtta*. (1457b3–6)

Since "other" is a relative term, *kurion* and *glôtta* vary depending on its meaning. The word *kurion* itself, while perfectly ordinary to Aristotle, is exotic to us. As foreign (*glôtta* literally means "tongue" and not so literally "dialect"), it calls more attention to itself than would one of its translations—ordinary, authoritative, or sovereign. Aristotle's own example is more significant than is at first apparent. He says that *sigunon* is *kurion* to us but *glôtta* to the Cyprians for whom it means "spear." This seems to be a reference to Herodotus's Inquiries 5.9.

> The Ligyes who live up over Massilia call peddlers *sigunnai*, but the Cyprians call spears [*sigunnai*].

This is the last sentence of a chapter describing a people called the Sigunnai who live north of Thrace. In different places, versions of the word *sigunon* thus mean variously peddler, spear, and a barbarian people. Cyprians would presumably find the Massilian use of *sigunon* exotic even though they had their own perfectly ordinary use of the word. Americans feel a twinge of the exotic when we hear the English say they'll have a look under the bonnet of their automobiles, although the word is ordinary American English. A single word can in this way be both ordinary and strange even to the same people.

Herodotus reports that the Sigunnai dress like the Medes. They explain the similarity of looks by claiming to have been originally a colony of the Medes, although Herodotus cannot begin to understand how this could be. Still, he says, "anything could come to be in a great enough time." The Sigunnai, therefore, interpret common looks—*eidos*—as common origin—*genesis*. An eidetic relation is understood as genetic even though Herodotus admits the connection between the Medes and the Sigunnai, if it ever existed, has been lost in time. So, a manifest but inexplicable spacial sameness is explained by an immanifest temporal sameness.[110] But, that the Sigunnai must postulate this connection to explain their current state means their Medean origins have been imperfectly preserved. And if this is the case, some of what was once *kurion* among the Medes may now be *glôtta* among the Sigunnai. Furthermore, words once ordinary to the Medes may still be ordinary to the Sigunnai, although having different meanings. The introduction of time accounts for how the same word can be both ordinary and strange to the same people. When the Athenians go to the theater to see *Oedipus the King (Oidipous Tyrannos)*, they know that in the era to which the fiction of the play belongs, *tyrannos* simply meant king; in contemporary Athens it means tyrant. They cannot help hearing the latter through the former. *Tyrannos* is thus simultaneously *kurion* and *glôtta* to them.

The split between the ordinary and the foreign or strange is not so clear-cut as it first seemed. While showing us that it is possible for a word to be both and so double, Aristotle alludes to a Herodotean story in which a common *eidos* is explained in terms of a common *genos*. He does this just before introducing an account of metaphor in terms of *eidos* and *genos*.

> Metaphor is the application of a word belonging to something else either from the genus [*genos*] to a species [*eidos*], or from the species to the genus, or from the species to a species, or according to analogy. (1457b6–9)

On the one hand, genus and species are to be taken in the "standard" Aristotelian way; genus is to species as animal is to mammal.[111] Genus is prior in being in the sense that if there are mammals, there will of necessity be animals, but if there are animals, there need not be mammals.[112] On the other hand, Aristotle's account of the parts of speech was built on an intentional confusion of the distinction between eidetic and genetic accounts. In a genetic account, one takes the elements with which one begins as prior in being—they are parts having an independent existence in their own right. Accordingly, one moves from them, not to them. Aristotle seemed to begin with sound as a genus, gradually specifying its forms, but he had already excluded certain sounds on the basis of what he was about to specify. In an eidetic account, these elements have their being only as divisions of the whole of which they are parts. One must seem to move from them to move to them. Thus, because sound never appears except as specified, "species has more being than genus."[113] There are, therefore, two ways of looking at the standard Aristotelian understanding of the relationship between genus and species: one according to which genus is prior, the other according to which species is prior. To see genus as prior means to move from first principles—to see them as governing the being of a thing; to see species as prior means to move to first principles—to see the being of a thing as governing the principles of its intelligibility. The situation is further complicated by the fact that genus and species are relative terms for Aristotle. If the species is the subject of which the genus is the predicate, relative to animal, mammal is a species, and relative to man, it is a genus.[114] A genus is not simply something in terms of which something else is understood but itself must be understood in terms of something else.

In presenting the parts of *logos* as though they were self-subsisting, Aristotle treated predicates as though they were subjects. This was fated to be as soon as he made them the subjects of his inquiry. He had to treat them as subjects to understand them as predicates, which is to say he had to treat them as *eidê* to understand them as *genê*. Aristotle's method of description, therefore, imitates the content of his description, for the confusion of genus and species seems to be a necessity at the heart of *logos*. But Aristotle has also defined metaphor in terms of a confusion of genus and species. There seems to be something essentially metaphorical about language. It demands that we use ordinary words in ways that are, underneath it all, quite strange. Insofar as it is a distinctive feature of language, metaphor will bring this doubleness to light. By making the ordinary strange, it makes poetry possible.

Aristotle first discusses metaphors in which a genus is allowed to stand for a species.

> By from genus to species I mean, for example, "my ship stands here," for to be at anchor is a sort of standing. (1457b9–11)

For something to stay put is the genus of which standing at anchor is a species; Homer seems to have used the broader term poetically to refer to the narrower meaning. Now, this is complicated by the fact that we have no reason to believe that Homer possessed the verb "to stand at anchor"—*hormein*. It occurs in neither the *Iliad* nor the *Odyssey*. Thus, although Homer might have been speaking metaphorically for poetic reasons, he might also have been using the only word available to him. The first Greek to use *poiein* to mean "to make poetry" rather than "to do" need not have done so in a poem. Metaphor is as necessary to ordinary communication as it is to poetry. The sentence "My ship stands here" occurs twice in Homer. At the beginning of the *Odyssey* (I.185) Athena utters it when she comes to Ithaca disguised as a sailor named Mentes. There is, of course, no ship; Athena is lying. At the end of *Odyssey* (XXIV.308), while claiming to be Eperitus, son of Apheidas, Odysseus utters the same sentence to Laertes, his real father. Once again it is a lie. Not only does "stand" stand for something else; so does the whole *logos* in which it stands. Aristotle's example makes its point, but he seems also to have something more in mind.

The second sort of metaphor lets a species stand for the whole genus.

> And from species to genus: "Surely Odysseus has done ten thousand [*muria*] good things." For ten thousand is many and here [*nun*] has been used in place of many. (1457b11–13)

Grammarians later distinguish two meanings of *muria*. When the first syllable is accented, it means "ten thousand"; when the second syllable is accented, it means "countless." While there were no written accents in Aristotle's Greek, there were still two ordinary meanings of the word. Aristotle, therefore, again points to a poetic metaphor that becomes a regular feature of the language. The passage quoted is from the beginning of the *Iliad* (II.272). Tempted by Agamemnon with the possibility of returning home, the Greek army is rushing toward their ships. Odysseus saves the day by ranging through the troops, shaming the nobles and frightening the *demos*. When they are finally reassembled, Thersites, the only man of the people to speak in the *Iliad*, gives a speech in which he pretty much tells the truth about Agamemnon's bad treatment of Achilles. Odysseus beats him and tells him to keep quiet. The content of Thersites' speech is never addressed; he is simply upbraided for speaking ill of his betters. This is the deed referred to in the *Poetics*, a deed unique in Homer and, however interesting and revealing, hardly the paradigm for nobility.

Like his first example, Aristotle's second example of metaphor is used in a *logos* that is itself not what it seems to be. The two examples share a peculiar feature. If metaphor means using a word in a way other than it is usually used, the "usual" would seem to have to be held constant. However, in both cases, the context of the metaphor itself, the *logos* of which it is a part, is used in an unusual way. Furthermore, while a metaphorical use of the language seems to presuppose a nonpoetic, ordinary use, so far Aristotle's own examples of metaphor are very much a part of the ordinary language.

In the third case of metaphor one species stands for another.

And from species to species: for example, "drawing off the soul with bronze" and "cutting with long-edged bronze." For here "to draw off" has expressed [*eirêken*] "to cut," and "to cut" "to draw off." For both are a taking away. (1457b13–16)

The two quotations seem to be from Empedocles' *Katharmoi*.[115] In the first, "drawing off" appears to mean bleeding with a knife, and so "cutting." In the second, "cutting" appears to mean using a bronze vessel to cut the flow of a stream so as to collect liquid, and so "drawing off." This substitution of one for the other is possible, according to Aristotle, because both are species of the genus, taking away, that presumably could be substituted for them in the two phrases. However, once again, although both examples contain the ambiguity necessarily present in metaphor, they also point to the larger ambiguity of their context. The bronze of the first example draws off blood in cutting it. Its drawing off is thus metaphorical. At the same time, before this particular metaphor, the language itself uses the word cutting (*tomê*) metaphorically to mean surgery.[116] Like *catharsis* in the *Poetics*, *katharmoi* can mean either purifications or purgations. It seems to possess both a religious and a medical significance. Now, while purifying oneself religiously may mean dying, this is not the goal of medical purgation. We haven't enough left of Empedocles' poem to be sure, but Aristotle, at least, seems to suggest that the whole of the *Katharmoi* might be systematically ambiguous and so metaphorical.

The final example of metaphor is analogy.

By analogy, I mean when the second stands similarly toward the first as the fourth toward the third. For instead of the second he will say the fourth, or instead of the fourth the second. And sometimes they add instead of what it says what is related to it. I mean, for example, a cup stands similarly toward Dionysus as a shield toward Ares. He will say, therefore, that the cup is the shield of Dionysus and the shield the cup of Ares. Or, old age [stands] toward life as evening toward day; he will therefore say evening to be the old age of day, or, like Empedocles, also old age to be the evening of life, or the sunset of life. For some of the analogies there is no word laid down, yet the similitude will be said none the less. For example, to scatter seed is to sow, while the [scattering] of the flame of the sun is nameless. But this stands similarly toward the sun as does sowing toward the seed, whence is said "sowing the god-made flame." But it is possible to use this manner of metaphor also in a different way, to deny some one of the properties of something addressed with an alien designation, for example, if he should say the shield is the cup not of Ares but without wine. (1457b16–33)

The first case is fairly clear. If men are to women as bucks are to does, it is possible to speak of men metaphorically as bucks. It gets a bit more complicated when the terms of the relationships are interchanged. Bucks are not like men absolutely but only insofar as they are related to does as men are to women. Thus, a man could be metaphorically called a woman's buck and a woman a man's doe. Still, this is not so complicated that Aristotle needs two examples. His second example is not only somewhat superfluous; it is also the analogy underlying the riddle of the Sphinx, and so the Oedipus story. Does tragedy especially have to do with analogic metaphor?

This is suggestive given the account of incomplete analogy that follows immediately. Analogy makes it possible to generate a new and never before experienced being. Seed is scattered by sowing. The flame of the sun is also scattered. We can therefore metaphorically refer to the sowing of the sun's flame. What is most interesting here is the tacit analogy—the one Aristotle suggests but leaves unnamed. The term correlative to "sow" in the analogy first looks to be "sun." But there is clearly something wrong here. It is the activity of scattering flame that ought to parallel sowing. The sun is correlative to the one who sows—the farmer. Aristotle has thus, without saying so, given an account of analogic metaphor in poetry that points back to the way in which in ordinary language terms get generated for things unknown. And the most important of the things unknown are the gods.

Aristotle's final example suggests a way in which analogy can limit itself by containing within itself an account of how the ordinary use of a word differs from its extended use. When a shield is called Ares' wineless cup, we are alerted not only to the similarity between the god of war and the god of the theater, we are also alerted to their differences.

Analogic metaphor does not so much differ from the three previous kinds as build on them. It shows us that metaphor need not be limited to a single word standing for another. That is why the examples Aristotle chooses to illustrate each of the forms of metaphor are taken from contexts themselves metaphorical. Once the principle of analogy has been introduced, a metaphor could be extended indefinitely, its length depending only on the ingenuity of the poet. To say that a king is the father of his people is surely a metaphor. Working out its details in such a way as finally to show its limits—how a king is not the father of his people—would be an extended metaphor of a particularly interesting kind. It would be *Oedipus the King*.

Although the account of metaphor was to be followed by an account of *kosmos*—ornament—nowhere does such an account appear. This might be attributed to the fact that elsewhere (*Rhetoric* 1404b7) Aristotle seems to use the verb *kosmein* to describe all words that are not ordinary or *kuria*. If any poetic word is ornamental, then *kosmos* would apply to every member of the list at the beginning of chapter twenty-one. But why then doesn't Aristotle say that it is the genus of which all the others are species, or, what amounts to the same thing, why doesn't he omit mentioning it and describe the other items on the list? Now, *kosmos* is not simple in its own right. It means ornament, but it also means cosmos, the ordered whole of things. If it means something like ordered whole here, it would be Aristotle's way of pointing to the recurring feature of the account thus far—that, although the "simple" *eidos* of words is used to establish a context that the "double" *eidos* of words can break down, it is nevertheless hard to establish these simple words. They too are what they are by virtue of a context—the larger whole or cosmos in which they play a part. The clarity of simple words is supposed to be the measure of the ambiguity of double words, but that clarity is an illusion. The line separating ordinary and exotic shifts according to the situation. Accordingly, one must first know the situation to know what is ordinary. In leaving out the account of *kosmos*, Aristotle imitates what he means by *kosmos*. Insofar as all words make sense only in light of a larger unstated whole, all words are ornamental, that is to say not ordinary or authoritative. No word is by itself clear. If metaphor is the use of an ordinary word in a strange or exotic way, all *logos* seems to be metaphorical.

All of this is confirmed by the remainder of the chapter. Aristotle gives two examples of made-up words. The first, *ernuges*, is said to mean "horns." It seems to be formed out of *ernê*—branches—and mean something like "branchings." The second, *arêtêr*, is said to mean "priest." It seems to be formed out of *araomai*—"to pray." Neither of these is made up of utterly meaningless parts—traces of meanings remain in them. They are double. But the words in terms of which they are explained are also not simple. The word for horn, *keras*, means the horn of an animal, but it also means horn as a material out of which things are made and the things made themselves—drinking vessels, bows, musical instruments, writing implements, and so forth. "Branchings" are "horns," but "horns" are "bows," and, with a change of accent, the word for bow is the same as the word for life. There seems to be no end to the possible transfers (*meta-phora*) of meaning present in apparently ordinary words. All words are potentially double, for as soon as we invent forks we have made it possible to speak of forks in the road. Or do we name the tools after the roads?

This doubleness emerges as well in Aristotle's treatment of words that are poetic by virtue of being lengthened, shortened, or altered. A word is lengthened when a vowel is lengthened or a syllable added, shortened when part of the word is taken away, and altered when, of the naming, part remains and part is made up. The examples are straightforward, although the first example of lengthening is peculiar. That *poleôs* becomes *poleôs* is a case of a lengthening an epsilon into an eta but also a case of shortening an omega to an omicron. And the lengthening of vowels is frequently compensatory—the result of the omission of a syllable, which Aristotle omits to mention as a species of shortening. As the lengthening and shortening that occur naturally in languages are often the signs of differences in dialect (*glôtta*), what is perceived as lengthening in one place will be perceived as shortening in another. Once again there seems to be no authoritative measure. Poetic lengthening and shortening are not simply for the sake of exotic ornamentation; they are frequently necessitated by the meter of a poetic line and its position in the poem as a whole. Single words are thus subject to an order of a whole larger than themselves. One of Aristotle's examples of shortening is particularly revealing. In the sentence, *mia ginetai amphoterôn ops, ops* is a shortened version of *opsis*.[117] "One sight comes to be from both" seems to be a reference to the way in which from two eyes we come to see one image.[118] The singleness of human sight conceals an underlying doubleness; the same is true of *logos*.

The final section of chapter twenty-one is especially perplexing. It is a reflection on the grammatical gender of words, which seems to be both out of place—Aristotle had not mentioned it in his synopsis—and filled with errors.

Of nouns [words] themselves, some are masculine, some feminine and some in between. Whichever end in N, R, or S, or whichever are a mixture of this (these are Psi and X), are masculine. And whichever [end] in those of the vowels [sonants] that are always long, such as in eta or omega, or, of those lengthened, in A, are feminine. So that those in which masculine and feminine [end] happen to be equal in number, for Psi and X are combined [with S]. No noun ends in a consonant [mute] or in a short vowel. But only three [end] in I—*meli, kommi,* and *peperi*—and five in U. And the in between [end] in these and in N and S. (1458a8–17)

Many nominative feminine nouns end in sigma—*naus, elpis, nemesis,* and so forth. *Mêtêr* (mother) and *nux* (night), to name only two of many, are both feminine. While it seems true that masculine nouns end in nu, rho, and sigma, feminine nouns do not all end in long vowels, and many neuter nouns (those "in between" masculine and feminine) end in alpha. In addition, Aristotle is precise but incorrect about the number of words ending in iota and upsilon.[119] The whole passage is extremely problematic in other ways as well. Aristotle has just finished using *onoma* to mean word. By restricting it to nouns here without telling us what he is doing, he makes it appear as though all words have gender. Furthermore, we now classify Greek nouns according to gender by their stems. This is an attempt to establish something from which all forms of the word derive, although the stem is itself not necessarily a word. By singling out the nominative singular as though it were the word, Aristotle has identified the word with one of its modifications.

These difficulties are hard to account for. While they could be mistakes, it is queer that Aristotle should make such sweeping claims about gender just after he himself had used two words, *opsis* and *polis,* that are feminine in gender and in the nominative singular end in sigma. Something may have dropped out of the text, or we may not have plumbed the depths of the text we have. Still, in a general way, the section is connected to the rest of the chapter. If words were to divide neatly into two *eidê*—simple and double—it would have to be possible for some words to be unambiguous and straightforward in their meanings. These words would be nonmetaphorical, nonexotic, and neither lengthened, shortened, nor altered; they would be ordinary. Chapter twenty-one reveals that, however sensible such an account at first seems, there are no simple words. If the evidence of the rest of the chapter were not enough, the reflection on gender with which it ends points to an additional difficulty. Nouns, at least, are not simply what they are; they all carry another distinction. "Ship" (*naus*) does not only mean "vehicle for transportation over water"; it also carries a gender. It is feminine, and so referred to as "she." Now, one ought not confuse real gender with grammatical gender. Still, grammatical gender is a sign within the conventions of language of a natural, extralinguistic order that affects the meanings of individual words. Just as meter can be the invisible cause of shortening and lengthening, that all nouns must be fit into a gender shapes what those nouns mean. As long as "ship" means not only "vehicle for transportation over water" but also "she," it will not be simple. Any word will stand out when the elements of its doubleness are at odds. Ordinarily nouns ending in "*os*" are masculine, but *nêsos* (island) is feminine. This tension between its grammatical gender and its ending prevents *nêsos* from being simple. Although Aristotle does not speculate here about why nouns have gender, perhaps it has something to do with singling out the nominative case. This emphasizes the noun as subject. As that of which things are predicated, the subject seems to have a being independent of its context. Giving words this being is only a breath away from personifying them. The connection between grammatical "subject" and "subjectivity" is more than a linguistic accident. "Just" is an adjective. By placing an article in front of it, we make it a noun and a potential subject—"the just." As a sign of how we experience beings with this sort of independence (i.e., as persons), in Greek the article has a gender. The just becomes the goddess Justice.[120]

11

Metaphor
(1458a18–59a16)

[22] Both the *Nicomachean Ethics* and the *Politics* understand human beings as rational animals. This duality in our natures seems to lead to a duality of human virtue. Moral virtue is concerned with action—*praxis*; intellectual virtue is concerned with contemplation—*theôria*. But moral virtue is unintelligible without a species of thinking—"it is not possible to be good in the highest sense without prudence."[121] And intellectual virtue is itself a species of action.[122] There is, therefore, less to the split between the moral and intellectual than at first meets the eye. In the *Poetics*, human beings are the most mimetic of animals, and *mimêsis* has its own duality. As mimicry, it is a form of action—a doing; as making a representation, it involves standing back from one's doing, and so reflecting. Yet, as a mimic knows that he is not the person or thing mimicked, mimicry involves some reflection. And representation is, after all, an activity—a doing. Here too, the initial split is not as clear as it first seems. Now, the *Poetics* has from the outset had a dual task—to describe the *eidê* of the art of poetry and the parts out of which a poem is generated. It is a book at once for aspiring poets and for literary critics—an account of doing and an account of reflecting on doing. However, Aristotle never makes it explicit that he is engaged in this double account; he does both at the same time. In writing a book that is simultaneously an account of doing and an account of reflecting, Aristotle is writing an account of those beings who always reflect as they do and do as they reflect—human beings.

The issue can be put in another way. All inquiry requires that we see what is in front of us as different from what it at first seemed to be. For example, inquiring into a book means not taking it at face value; it means doing a certain violence to its initial appearance. The understanding that results from inquiry is thus possible only after an initial displacement of appearances. We must see that something familiar is other than we took it to be. Anticipating this necessity, good writing provides within itself the particular displacement necessary to understand its surface and so eventually the displacement as well. One might say that understanding always involves *poiêsis* plus literary criticism. The best *poiêsis*, therefore, contains its own criticism or analysis. Now, this is a description of Aristotle's account of tragedy thus far. Tragedy, as the paradigm for what is possible in *logos*, is in some sense the paradigm for the unity of the rational animal.

We saw that Aristotle's account of words (*onomata*) turned on the distinction between the ordinary (*kurion*) and the foreign, strange, or exotic (*glôtta*) and furthermore that the two were not ever really separable. Metaphor intentionally combines the two by using the ordinary in a strange or exotic way. Meta-phor is a trans-fer or displacement of the ordinary. That this displacement is the heart of *logos*, is the underlying issue of the discussion of the virtue of *lexis* in chapter twenty-two.

> It is a virtue of *lexis* to be clear and not base. That from ordinary words is thus clearest but base (the poetry of Kleophon is an example and that of Sthenelos), while that having used things of an alien sort [*xenikois*] is august and alters the idiomatic [private—*idiôtikon*]. I mean by alien the foreign [*glôtta*], metaphor, the lengthened and everything opposed to the ordinary. But, were someone to make everything in this way, it would be either an enigma or a barbarism—if out of metaphors, an enigma, but if out of foreign [words] a barbarism. (1458a18–26)

Elsewhere Aristotle links the virtue of *lexis* with the function of *logos*.

> Let a virtue of *lexis* be defined as to be clear. For the sign is that if *logos* is not clear, it will not do its task. (*Rhetoric* 1404b1–4)

Granted that ordinary speech is most clear, it is also *tapeinê*—low, base, abject, or self-effacing. The best *lexis* is a mean between the clarity of the ordinary and the august sound of the alien produced by altering what is *idiôtikon*—private, usual, or prosaic. Aristotle seems to conflate *kurion* as ordinary with *idiôtikon*, but the latter also suggests the private as opposed to the public, and so can refer to something not "common" at all. Aristotle, therefore, points to the danger of the extremes. If every word were foreign, the result would be barbarism; nothing would be understood. And if every word were metaphorical, the result would be enigmatic; again, nothing would be understood.

He, therefore, concludes that a mixture is necessary.

For this is the form of an enigma: while saying things that exist, to join them together in impossible ways. With respect to the putting together of words, this is not possible to do, but with respect to the [putting together] of metaphors it is possible—for example, "I saw a man welding bronze to a man with fire," and such things. But when they are from foreign words, it is a barbarism. These, then, ought somehow to have been mixed. For, on the one hand, the nonidiomatic will make it not base—for example, the foreign, metaphor, *kosmos* and the other species mentioned, and, on the other hand, the ordinary [will make] clarity.(1458a26–34)

Of what is this mixture to be made? The obvious solution is the one with which the section concludes—that the ordinary will be mixed with the nonidiomatic, the one to provide clarity, the other dignity. Yet Aristotle has just finished discussing the dangers of enigma and barbarism—the one linked to metaphor, the other to foreign words. Could the mixture be understood to be of enigma and barbarism? And what would that have to do with the more obvious mixture of the ordinary and the strange?

Since we know from the previous chapter that what is foreign to one is ordinary to another, we have to wonder about what it would mean to say that something is altogether ordinary. Aristotle's use of *idiôtikon* as interchangeable with *kurion* suggests that, when pushed to the extreme, the *kurion* is not prosaic in the sense of ordinary but private in the sense of unintelligible—an enigma. An expression with which I am so comfortable that it seems not at all strange but completely my own is no longer a common medium of exchange. The mixture of the strange and the ordinary is thus not only necessary for poetic *lexis*; it is a necessary condition for the very possibility of *logos*. Anything short of this mixture will be either enigmatic or barbaric. Because it is characteristic of metaphor to mix the strange and the ordinary, metaphor is somehow characteristic of all *logos*.

The two poles of *logos* are the utterly strange and the utterly ordinary. But the utterly ordinary turns out to be as strange as the utterly strange. In both cases speech disappears, either into the meaningless noise of barbarism or into pure meaning where speech is so self-effacing as to become invisible as speech. Aristotle goes on to say that not the least part of putting together the strange and the ordinary involves lengthening, shortening, and altering. This is the simplest way of affecting the "feel" of words to make one aware that they are words without at the same time affecting their sense. When words have clarity as well as a feel of strangeness, we neither lose sight of what they mean nor do we lose sight of the fact that they mean. The task of *logos* is clarity. When it accomplishes this task, it tends to make itself invisible. Ordinary speech is not only base; it is self-effacing, at its most extreme so self-effacing as to make us forget what it is doing.

This is connected to Aristotle's account of the criticisms of the practice of poetic lengthening. Anyone can write poetry if any word can be changed to suit the needs of the situation. An iamb is a metrical foot consisting of a short syllable followed by a long. If any epsilon can be changed to an eta, then any short syllable containing an epsilon can be made long. And if an unlimited number of such changes are permitted, then any syllable can be made long or short at will. It is not hard to write iambs under constraints like these. This comic criticism points to a fundamental issue. That any word can be changed in a given situation does not mean that every word can be changed. Only one or two things can be made strange at a time. The context for this strangeness must be ordinary; it must be taken for granted so that something else can be highlighted. There is thus no *logos* that everywhere calls attention to itself as *logos*—no altogether exotic *logos*. Were such a thing possible, it would be like a drama without content or someone who, although claiming to be an actor, played no part. A certain moderation is thus necessary for poetry.

> And due measure [*metron*] is common to all of the parts. For, using metaphors, foreign words and the other species inappropriately and on purpose, the same thing could be accomplished with respect to the laughable. Let it be observed how much the suitable differs with respect to the insertion of words in the meter [*metron*] in epics. (1458b12–17)

Moderation, or measure, has to be the rule so that one can occasionally be immoderate. The *metron* has to be kept ordinary on the whole if it is to be lengthened or shortened in particular cases. Otherwise lengthening will not be visible as lengthening. That this principle applies to meaning as well as to sound is suggested by Aristotle's own sentence. Because the overall context concerns poetic meter (*metron*), the use of *metron* to mean due measure calls attention to itself as strange.

Aristotle uses a series of examples to show what happens to poetry when the exotic or strange is replaced by the ordinary. First he compares a line from Aeschylus's *Philoctetes* with a parallel line in Euripides' play of the same title.[123] They differ by only one word. Where Aeschylus says "the ulcer which eats (*esthiei*) the flesh of my foot," Euripides says "the ulcer which feasts upon (*thoinatai*) the flesh of my foot." Aristotle prefers Euripides version as less ordinary. But, since "eats" is as metaphorical as "feasts upon," this is a strange example with which to begin. It is perhaps explained by the repeated coupling of ordinary (*kurion*) with customary (*eiôthos*). Metaphors that are so customary as to be taken for granted become ordinary; they are what we would call dead metaphors. Once again, however, there seems to be no absolute difference between the strange and the ordinary.

The examples from Homer that follow are also strange. Aristotle first rewrites a line from the *Odyssey* (IX:515) to show what it would look like written in ordinary language. The Cyclops expresses his surprise at having been blinded by "one who is little (*oligos*), of no account (*outidanos*) and unseemly (*aeikês*)." Aristotle changes this to "one small (*mikros*), weak (*asthenikos*) and unattractive (*aeidês*)." The first is more poetic, although once again the difference between strange and the ordinary is not straightforward. *Oligos* is a perfectly ordinary word that is made strange because it is ordinarily used of a things few in number, not small in size. And even were *aeidês* more ordinary than *aeikês*, it is etymologically so close to *Aïdês*, the poetic form of Hades, that it has its own poetically useful strangeness. In fact, Odysseus replies to the Cyclops's insult by saying that he would like to send him to Hades (*Odyssey* XI:524). In the second example, the line to be rewritten is *Odyssey* XX:259. Aristotle changes "putting down an unseemly (*aeikelion*) stool and a little (*oligên*) table" to "putting down a wretched (*mochthêron*) stool and a small (*micran*) table." Once again, the use of *oligos* for size is unusual, but there are other things yet stranger. In his experiment at making the *Odyssey* prosaic, Aristotle has used two replacements for "unseemly" (*aeikês* or *aeikelion*). He first replaces it by *aeidês*—ugly or unattractive; he then replaces it by *mochthêron*—wretched. The strange word thus looks less precise and clear than the ordinary words because it can mean either ugly or wretched. And yet its imprecision suggests a connection between the wretched and the ugly invisible in the more precise *aeidês* and *mochthêron*. In this case, then, the strange proves more precise than the ordinary. Furthermore, the "word" to be replaced here is really two words—*aeikês* and *aeikelion*. The latter is the poetic version of the former. There are, then, levels of poetic replacement here; *aeikelion* is more poetic than *aeikês*, which is in turn more poetic than *aeidês* or *mochthêron*. But, then, no word is simply poetic; its strangeness is always a function of expectations. Dead metaphors are not so strange as ordinary words used in extraordinary ways. And there are layers of strangeness. In his final example, Aristotle says that "the shore roars" is more poetic than "the shore cries out." Be this as it may, it is worth noting that in the *Iliad* (XVII:265) this metaphor is not simply a description of the sound of the sea; it is part of a simile describing the sound of the Trojan army. With respect to "the shore cries out," it may be poetic, but with respect to the sound of the army, it is ordinary.

All of these examples are meant to point to the relative character of the strange and the ordinary; they are defined in terms of each other. Were it possible to have a *logos* that was fully ordinary, it would make everything clear but itself, since it would be utterly self-effacing. At the same time, a fully nonidiomatic and strange *logos* would be simply unclear, and so would be no *logos* at all. The virtue of *lexis*, the expression of *logos*, is therefore maximum clarity consistent with maximum self-awareness. This requires a strategic disruption of the power of *logos* to mean so as to call attention to that power. This can be accomplished in a variety of ways, for example, by lengthening, shortening, word order, foreign words, and double words (i.e., words with some residue of meaning in them). But the single most important way is metaphor.

> For this alone is not to be taken from another, and is a sign of a good nature; for to metaphorize well is to contemplate what is like [*homoion*]. (1459a6–8)

Metaphor alone involves a transfer of meaning so that something that makes sense on the level of the ordinary, and so is clear, is also situated so that it points to an entirely different reading, and so is strange. It takes a good nature to see the possibility of this connection. Because the strangeness and the ordinariness are located in exactly the same words (think of Aristotle's earlier use of *metron*), each can be maximized at no expense to the other. This is what Aristotle means by saying that to make metaphors well is to see what is like or similar (1459a8). This talent—seeing similarities—cannot be learned because it is the underlying condition of all learning, to be able to see that the ordinary is strange without losing sight of the fact that it is ordinary. At the same time, without some form of it, thinking is not possible at all.[124] If metaphor is most suitable for iambs (1459a10), and iambic meter is especially appropriate for spoken language, and so for drama (1449a19–28), then the language of tragedy will be especially metaphorical. This should come as no surprise, for it is the task of tragedy to present the ordinary in its awful strangeness.

12

Epic and Tragedy: Action in Speech and Speech in Action
(1459a17–62b19)

[23] Chapter twenty-three seems to mark a significant break from what has preceded it. The last sentence of the previous chapter tells us as much.

> Concerning tragedy, then, and imitation in action, let what has been said be sufficient for us. (1459a15–16)

With the completion of Aristotle's account of *lexis*, the long account of tragedy begun in chapter six has been concluded. But it is not sufficient to say, as many commentators do, that Aristotle turns to epic in order to fulfill the promise made at the beginning of chapter six (1449b21–22).[125] Since at that point he also promised a discussion of comedy, we need, at the very least, to wonder why the treatment of epic follows that of tragedy while the treatment of comedy is either omitted or, even if it existed and has been lost, follows the account of epic. Furthermore, we get not so much a discussion of epic as a praise of Homer as the greatest of all poets. Why is tragedy praised as the highest kind of poetry while at the same time an epic poet is singled out as the greatest of poets? Perhaps we can begin to answer these questions by asking another. What is the connection between this account of epic poetry and what immediately precedes it—the analysis of all *logos* as a mixture of the strange and the ordinary?

Aristotle begins in a roundabout way, not making it immediately clear that epic is to be his theme.

> About the arts of description and of imitation in meter, it is clear that, as in tragedy, dramatic plots should be put together and [plots] about one whole and complete action, having beginning, middle and end in order that it may

make the proper pleasure like a single whole animal and the putting together
not be similar to histories in which they make clear, of necessity, not the
making of one action but of one time, whatever happens in it concerning
one or many, each of which holds toward the others as it happened. (1459a17–
24)

Aristotle has not previously referred to the art of description (*diêgêmatikê*),
although at 1449b10–11 he did say that epic was especially distinct from
tragedy in having a simple meter and in being a narrative (*apaggelia*).[126]
It is also unclear whether he means to distinguish an art of description
in meter from an art of nonmetric description, and, if so, whether he
means the discussion in the sequel to apply to both or only to the metric. The former would accord with his previous claim that meter is not
the defining characteristic of poetic imitation (1447b17–20). The latter
would fit with his tacit exclusion of Herodotus's *Inquiries* in the immediate sequel (1459a24–29). Aristotle seems to hint, at least, at an art of
nonmetric description with principles much like those of the art of tragedy, which would be neither epic, on the one hand, nor history on the
other. Would such an art include the sort of prose description of which
the *Poetics* itself is an instance?

Still, epic is Aristotle's first concern. Its plots should be dramatic
(*dramatikos* is used for the only time in the *Poetics*) and thus, like tragedy, be about whole actions, each with a beginning, middle, and end, so
that they can provide the pleasure only possible through the perception
of a whole. In the parallel passage concerning tragedy (1450b34–51a6),
Aristotle had also used the image of an animal as whole. There he had
made a point of the beauty of an animal easily seen at one time (*eusunopton*)
and had compared it to a plot easily remembered (*eumnêmoneuton*), a
spacial whole serving as metaphor for a temporal whole. While the wholeness
of epic is now also likened to the wholeness of an animal, it is not called
beautiful but is rather said to produce its proper pleasure. Unlike history, in which there is no principle of wholeness other than the time in
which events occurred, in epic, events form a whole because they all
belong logically to the same action; their temporal connection is a logical connection. Insofar as historical events are unified, they have been
gathered together because they occurred at a certain time. Now, this will
prove far less true of history than even Aristotle's own example suggests, but the general point is nevertheless important. In "history" the
time defines the action; in tragedy, epic, and nonmetric description, the
action defines the time. At the same time, epic and nonmetric description differ from tragedy. Like animals they are organic wholes, but unlike beautiful animals they are perhaps not "easily seen at one time" or

"easily remembered." They are wholes, the wholeness of which is not apparent at first.

As is ordinary in the *Poetics*, Aristotle's example of the disunity of action in history is strange. Because the battle of Salamis occurred at the same time as the defeat of the Carthaginians in Sicily, the two events might be treated in the same history, but this does not make them part of a single action. Without explicitly saying so, Aristotle is referring to Herodotus's *Inquiries*, where the simultaneity of the two events is mentioned (VII:166). Herodotus says that the defeat of the Persians at Salamis took place on the same day as the defeat of Hamilcar and the Carthaginians by the Syracusans. This is offered as one possible explanation (from the Syracusan point of view) of why Gelon, king of Syracuse, did not come to the aid of the Greeks—he had to worry about an invasion of his own. It follows an alternative explanation according to which Gelon never had any intention of aiding the Greeks, was biding his time to see who would win, and had even made arrangements to make large payments to the Persians should they have won. In thus giving an account of how the two battles were not related (Gelon did not, after all, come to the aid of the Greeks), Herodotus places both of them in a larger context in which they are related. Although Gelon did not send aid to the Greeks, this does not mean he plays no part in their story—their *muthos*. He offered two hundred ships, twenty thousand hoplites, and two thousand horses on the condition that he be given command. Had the Athenians accepted, they might still have won at Salamis, but it would have been a different battle—one, for example, in which they could no longer claim to have supplied more than half the ships in the fleet. The Gelon episode belongs to the story Herodotus tells insofar as it helps to establish the significance of the victory at Salamis as setting the stage for future Athenian hegemony. Only if history were simply a list of things that have happened without any attempt to understand their connection would it fit Aristotle's description here.

Epic and history seem, therefore, to differ in degree rather than in kind. History is more, and most epic poetry less, whole than Aristotle seems to suggest.

> For just as the sea battle at Salamis and the battle against the Carthaginians in Sicily came to be at the same times, although not inclining to the same end, so also in successive times, sometimes something comes to be after another without one end coming to be. But most of the poets do [*drôsi*] this. Hence, as we said already, also in this respect Homer would appear to speak divinely beside the others, in not even attempting to make/poetize the war whole, although it had a beginning, middle and end. (1459a24–29)

In praising Homer as so extraordinary, Aristotle indicates that the poems of ordinary poets are as little wholes as histories. And, as we have seen, histories are more whole than they seem.

Still, having made the distinction, Aristotle uses it to praise Homer.

> For the plot would have tended to be too great and not easily seen together, or, if moderated with respect to greatness, complicated with respect to variety. But, as it stands, taking one part, he has used episodes from many of them, such as the catalogue of ships and other episodes by which he divides the poem. (1459a29–37)

Homer strikes a mean between trying to do too much and so making synopsis impossible and condensing too much and so making the result too complicated. He solves the problem by taking as his subject only a small part of the war and introducing episodes from other parts, apparently digressions but, in fact, connected to a central theme. All of this is connected to the virtue of *lexis* as outlined in chapter twenty-two, which points, in turn, to the structure of *logos* as such. The first sign of this connection occurred at the end of chapter twenty (1457a29), where Aristotle used the *Iliad* as an example of a *logos*. A *logos* was said to be a mixture of significant and insignificant signs to form a significant whole. The *Iliad*, in combining the apparently irrelevant with the relevant, makes a whole that calls attention to itself as a whole. Were all episodes connected unproblematically to one another, the resulting whole would be altogether ordinary. Were all episodes unconnected to one another, the result would be no whole at all. It would be the equivalent of a barbarism and so be altogether strange. Homer's genius consists in mixing these two, the ordinary and the strange, in an appropriate way. There is, therefore, a proportion running through the last part of the *Poetics*: the relevant:the irrelevant::the ordinary:the strange::the significant:the nonsignificant. Aristotle makes the members of each pair first seem distinct from one another, but in each case they prove inseparable. There are no syllables apart from significant words, no utterly ordinary or strange words, and no pure histories or epics. But without assuming there were such things, we would never have come to know that there aren't.

Chapter twenty-three is not really a new beginning; it is an extension of the discussion of *lexis*. That the two discussions at first seem to be unconnected episodes is only a sign of what connects them. Chapters nineteen through twenty-two made clear how even the simplest *logos* necessarily contains the doubleness of the strange and the ordinary outlined by Aristotle in his account of metaphor. Chapter twenty-three begins a description of how this is the case in a *logos* like the *Iliad*, which must be both familiar or clear and strange or unclear to be clear at all.

In general, some disruption of meaning is the indispensable condition for making it clear that there is meaning. A word that did its job without ever calling attention to itself would for its user replace the thing for which it is meant to be the representation. And yet, to call attention to itself, to be less than transparent, is to fail to do its job perfectly. This might be called the tragedy of *logos*. History, even in the pure form presented by Aristotle, is an attempt to connect real events that at first glance stand unconnected. The events are perfectly ordinary, but their connections are not. History attempts to render these strange connections ordinary in the way that all inquiry strives to make the unknown known. Epic, more complicated, presents us with strange events (e.g., Odysseus's slaying of the suitors), but, in Homer at least, the events are connected in apparently ordinary ways. The story is well plotted and plausible. It is the events themselves and their modes of description that are exotic. While history combats strangeness in its subject, epic calls attention to its own strangeness. Poetry generally is a celebration of the strangeness in *logos* so as to produce wonder at what otherwise would be taken for granted—the ordinary. Its goal is not that of simple inquiry—to make the strange ordinary—but to make the ordinary strange. Tragedy, like all poetry, makes the ordinary an object of wonder; however, it also makes its own doing thematic. It begins with something that seems perfectly ordinary but is actually a decayed metaphor, something once strange (e.g., the king as the father of his people). It then treats this metaphor as though it were *kurion*—perfectly ordinary speech. In this way the original strangeness of the metaphor is regenerated. We have to come to see how the king is not a father so as to make visible once again the ground for the original likeness. The once strange and now ordinary must be seen as strange so as to see its true meaning as ordinary. Tragedy is a way of rebarbarizing ourselves in thought so that we can understand what it means to be civilized. It forces us to ask questions like "Why bury dead bodies?" and "Why do we not eat our relatives?"—questions that reveal their importance by tempting us to laugh at their strangeness. Tragedy restores them as questions and at the same time forces us to wonder at the process whereby they have ceased to be questions.

The *Poetics* ends with a reflection on the relationship between tragedy and epic. We have seen that the terms of the discussion of epic are simply variations of the terms of the discussion of *lexis*. The issue in both is the necessary doubleness of *logos*. This explains how Aristotle can make the transition—neither section is simply a digression; however, it does not yet make clear why he concludes the book as he does. By turning to epic Aristotle is able to turn to the virtues of Homer as a poet and so to introduce a great puzzle. Tragedy is clearly a greater form of poetry than epic for Aristotle, but Homer is clearly the greatest of the poets. Presumably the greatest poem would be, in principle, the perfect instance of the greatest form of poetry. Why, then, does the greatest poet not write the greatest poem? If we remember the extended meaning of the word poet, we can expand the question. Why is the greatest doer or actor not the man who does the greatest deed or action? Why has Aristotle separated the poet/doer from the poem/deed at the conclusion of the *Poetics*?

[24] Aristotle begins chapter twenty-four by making clear that, because tragedy and epic share so much, it is legitimate to compare them.

> Yet epic poetry should have the same forms [*eidê*] as tragedy; for [it is] either simple, complex, of character [*êthikê*] or of passion [*pathêtikê*]. And the parts, except song and *opsis*, are the same. For it too needs reversals, recognitions and sufferings [*pathêmata*], as well as to have thoughts and *lexis* beautifully, all of which Homer has used both first and sufficiently. For even of his poems, each combined [*eidê*]—the *Iliad* [combined] the simple and that of passion while the *Odyssey* [combined] the complex (for it has recognition throughout the whole) and that of character; and in addition to these he has surpassed everyone in *lexis* and in thought. (1459b7–16)

If tragedy and epic take the same forms and are both constituted by plot, character, thought, and *lexis*, then it is not surprising that Aristotle should think they can be ranked according to how they fulfill the possibilities of each form by use of their various parts. That tragedy involves song and *opsis*, and epic does not, may be ignored for, although they are parts of tragedy, song and *opsis* are not necessary to its effect. Plays need not be performed; they can be read (1462a12).

However, the argument is not without problems. If *opsis* refers not only to the act of performance but, as previously argued to the *kosmos* of *opsis*, then, at least for the moment, Aristotle will have suppressed a possible crucial difference between tragedy and epic.[127] What is in principle visible provides the standard for the one, but is that true for the other? Second, Aristotle lists the parts that tragedy and epic share in a peculiar way. He mentions only two explicitly—thought and *lexis*. Instead of plot, we get what are elsewhere (1452b9–10) called the parts of plot—reversal, recognition, and suffering. We assume the inclusion of character because Aristotle says that the parts of epic are the same as the parts of tragedy with the exception of song and *opsis*. What is unified in the account of tragedy by the name plot is left to be put together in the account of epic. And character, which in the account of tragedy is called separate but discussed in terms of plot, is not here distinguished from the parts of plot. In tragedy the plot must be a whole by itself. Whatever unity a play has comes from the unity of its action since there is no visible single author of the action; the poet does not appear in his poem. Epic, however, is closer to history. Just as the historian seems to confer a wholeness on the events he relates by relating them together, narration necessarily calls attention to the poet as the principle of the unity of his poem. The narration of qualities of character seems of the same order as the narration of deeds. We hear them from one voice. Homeric characters come equipped with epithets that tell us about them before we see what they do. Indeed, strictly speaking, we never see what they do at all; we only hear Homer tell us about what they did. In tragedy, character may emerge only out of the plot, but the availability of knowledge about characters in epic subtly suppresses the manner in which we come to such knowledge.

The author who is visible in his own work undercuts the power of the deed in the work. Homer, necessarily more visible in the *Iliad* than Sophocles is in the *Oedipus*, therefore has his work cut out for him. This is especially surprising given Aristotle's praise of Homer. Despite the drawbacks of epic, in the *Odyssey* Homer succeeds in combining two *eidê*—complex and that of character—to excel at bringing out character by way of the recognitions in the plot. And in the *Iliad*, he combines the simple *eidos* and that of suffering with the result that he surpasses everybody in the parts that Aristotle had previously connected with these *eidê*—thought and *lexis*.[128]

Aristotle establishes that epic and tragedy are comparable so that he can proceed to what differentiates them. At first he seems to say that they differ primarily in length and in meter (1459b17–20). However, the *Poetics* all but began with a denial that epic poets were defined by the meter they used (1447b13–23), and in chapter seven Aristotle gives the conditions, repeated here, that govern plot as such—not simply in tragedy (1450b25–51a15). In fact, the greater length of epic and its uniformity of meter are important because they point to something else.

> Epic poetry has something quite peculiar to it with regard to the extension of its magnitude on account of the impossibility in tragedy of imitating many parts being acted [*prattomena*] at the same time, but only the performers' part on the stage. But in epic poetry, because it is description, it is possible to make [*poiein*] many parts accomplished at the same time, by which, when proper, the bulk of the poem is increased. (1459b22–28)

Epic has the advantage of being able to present simultaneously occurring events. Tragedy can present only what is happening onstage. Tragedy, of course, includes many reports of actions not presented on the stage, but such reports are always necessarily themselves part of some current action. The messenger must always be before our eyes. Like the definition of the parts of epic, epic itself presents us with many parts without forcing us to put them together into a temporal whole. These accounts are, therefore, not themselves actions. They tell us about movements but do not themselves move. For this reason epic can make a split between the sequence of events in a poem and the sequence of their telling, or between dramatic time and narrative time. In tragedy there can be no such distinction; things happen in the order in which they are told. In epic, then, the order that makes things intelligible is not the same as the order in which they occur. Homer can use flashbacks, or he can cut suddenly away from a battle to what the gods are saying about it and then cut back without having lost a second in the time of the battle. In epic, the eidetic order of the events of the poem is not the same as their genetic order. Tragedy, however, because it must make the two identical, must give the illusion that the temporal sequence is an intelligible sequence. The epic poet is visible as making sense out of things; his voice imposes a unity on the action. The tragic poet is invisible; the events of the poem must make sense of themselves. To the extent that a tragedy is a whole, then, it must give the illusion that events make sense of themselves. Tragedy necessarily describes a world in which fate rules.

In the first chapter of the *Poetics* Aristotle indicated that the distinguishing feature of poetic imitation was time. Imitation in *logos* means imitation in time even when that which is imitated is not itself undergoing any change. A description of an urn moves even though it presumes no movement in that which it describes. Tragedy and epic are imitations of actions—movements. Two sorts of time are thus involved. The putting together of the parts of the imitation—the poet's activity—takes time, and the activity imitated in the poem takes time. Plot makes its appearance in the first sentence of the *Poetics* before any mention of tragedy or dramatic poetry because, if plot is a putting together of actions, poetry always involves plot on at least one of these levels of time. When a poem's subject matter is something itself unfolding in time, both levels will be present. In dramatic poetry the two become one. The movement of doing is made identical to the movement of understanding; acting and thinking are one.

According to Aristotle, the difference between epic and tragedy with regard to meter is twofold. First, it is typical of epic to use one meter throughout, while the meter in tragedy alters. Second, the specific meter used in epic, heroic, is *stasimôtaton* (1459b34)—the most stately, or, etymologically, the most at rest, while the meters appropriate to tragedy are *kinêtika*—in motion. The uniformity of meter in epic points again to a single underlying narrative voice. That the meter is the most stately or unmoving suggests the detachment of the utterance from that which it describes. When the chorus become excited in tragedy, because they are part of the action that they are describing, the meter in which they speak alters. While all meter moves, that of epic tends toward the static; it emphasizes the detachment of the poet from his poem. In tragedy the meter tends toward motion; the poet disappears into his poem. These two tendencies—call them rest and motion—are present in any poem; indeed, they are another manifestation of the doubleness of all *mimêsis* as action and representation. Poetry always involves some togetherness of motion and rest.

There is yet another constraint on tragedy in comparison to epic. Book XXI of the *Iliad* contains an account of Achilles' battle with the river Scamander, which is at the same time the god, Xanthus. There would be no way to present this double being directly in tragedy. To present it at all, the poet would need to pull back from the action to remark on the fact that what human beings call Scamander, the gods call Xanthus. Something like this is done in tragedy when a character gives an account of some action that has occurred offstage.[129] However, this account is always at the same time an action in the sequence of events that constitute the plot of the drama. Strictly speaking, in tragedy there are no parenthetical remarks. This is not the case for epic where narration allows for interspersing (*episodioun*) with unlike (*anomoios*) episodes (1459b30). Tragedy must begin with the *homoion*—the like.[130] The importance of *opsis* is the sign that tragedy must begin with the everyday— what is ordinary (*kurion*) or like. Accordingly, the meter common to tragedy is iambic, and its characteristic figure is metaphor, which makes the ordinary strange by a transfer of meaning. Tragedies fail when they do not escape the like or ordinary, but they must always begin there. As strange as a plot can get, it always begins with ordinary human beings on stage. That tragedies are in principle to be performed places a limit on how fantastic they can become.

Epic, however, is different. Because it is not meant to be seen, it can be indifferent to the distinction between the strange and the ordinary. Its meter is heroic, which Aristotle says is receptive to both foreign words and metaphors (1459b35–36). Things can be strangely described from a distance when one's business is simply description, but such language would sound peculiar in the give-and-take of ordinary conversation. Narrative imitation is in this way odd or extraordinary (*perritê*) compared with other forms of imitation (1459b36–37). Accordingly, it is not unusual for epics to be peopled with strange and marvelous creatures, as cases as diverse as the *Odyssey*, *Divine Comedy*, *Beowulf*, and the *Epic of Gil-*

gamesh suggest. Monsters can be a part of the action in narratives in a way not possible in drama. Thus, whereas tragedy begins necessarily from the ordinary and has to generate something strange out of it, epic can begin with what is already strange. The principle of tragedy is the *homoion*— the like; the principle of epic is the *anomoion*—the unlike. Tragedy, therefore, stands to epic as *kurion* stands to *glôtta*.

Epic poetry uses monsters as images. Monsters, like epic poetry itself, are put together out of discrepant parts. Just as centaurs are impossible combinations of men and horses, and Cyclopes are beings who can speak but are not social, in epics things happening at the same time are put together by stringing them out in an impossibly nontemporal sequence. Tragedies cannot show us the pure elements out of which human beings are composed; they must begin with beings recognizably human, analyze them into their monstrously pure parts, and then use these parts as images. Sophocles cannot show us "anger itself"; instead, he begins with a man, Oedipus, putting him in a situation in which his nature as "the angry man" will show itself in its purity. Thus, while all poetry uses the strange to shed light on the ordinary, tragedy transforms the ordinary into the strange before our eyes. It is in this respect the most self-reflective of the forms of poetry. Understanding what goes on in tragedy would teach one to write epic.

This understanding of epic is especially interesting in light of Aristotle's praise of Homer.

> Homer is worthy of being praised in many other ways, but also because, alone of the poets, he is not ignorant of what he himself ought to do [*poiein*] [or: of what he ought to make himself]. For the poet himself ought least to speak; for he is not an imitator with respect to these things. Indeed, some others exert themselves [*agônizontai*] throughout the whole, but they imitate briefly [*oliga*] and seldom. But he, after a brief [*oliga*] preface, directly introduces a man or a woman or some other character [*allo ti êthos*]—none without characters, but having character. (1460a5–11)

Homer's characters speak for themselves. By not simply describing these characters, he allows them to have character; for were we to know them as we know other objects, they would not be alive for us. We must learn about them through their words and deeds. Were Homer to tell us about them directly, he would be no imitator; his descriptions would have fatally falsified what they were meant to describe. To speak as a poet, then, is not to be a poet. Poets who cannot suppress their own voices compete for attention with their characters. They neither know what to do (*poiein*) nor how to poetize (*poiein*) themselves. Homer is the most dramatic of the epic poets because drama is the only way to imitate the human soul.

Fighting against the prerogative of his own form, he keeps himself out of his own poem.

He also does not indiscriminately introduce wonders. True, the gods are present in the *Iliad* and *Odyssey* on Homer's authority, but in the *Odyssey*, at least, monsters and other wonders are generally narrated by Odysseus—the most notorious of liars (we are thereby invited to see how untrustworthy epic poetry can be).[131] As we have seen, monsters are possible in epic where the action is not limited by what can be seen. Aristotle indicates the importance of this fact in his remark about the variety of characters introduced by Homer—"a man or a woman or some other character." If not man or woman, then what? If Aristotle has nonhuman characters in mind, he must mean gods and monsters. In tragedy, even when the nonhuman appears, it must be anthropomorphic. The Olympians are the gods of tragedy, for they show themselves as men and women. They are never neuter "characters."[132] Epic recalls an earlier age of pre-Olympian gods—cosmic gods who can be said to do things but cannot be seen doing them. So long as we do not envision Achilles fighting the river Scamander, the episode seems like a battle. When we try to imagine what it would actually look like for Achilles to strike a river, the event begins to look either mad or comical. It is no easier to envision that coupling of Ouranos (Sky) and Gaia (Earth) that produced Kronos. All poetry personifies and, therefore, tacitly affirms the centrality of the human experience of things. We fight for our lives in a raging river as though the river were our enemy with a will of its own. We are immersed in a world in which we have vested interests preventing us from being detached observers. Poetry expresses this investment, but anthropocentrism by itself does not necessarily involve reflecting on the centrality of the human. Tragedy, as necessarily bound up with what can be seen, cannot ignore the fact that the locus of intention in the world is human behavior. Accordingly, a tragic poet has no choice but to imitate human action. Homer's superiority consists in having a choice and still resisting the human temptation to leave the human behind. Even his gods and monsters are never without character; they have insides as well as outsides. Aphrodite who is love is also prone to be in love.

Tragedy and epic are distinct in their relationship to the visible. Because it is so bound up with the visible, tragedy can present invisible things only indirectly, thus mimicking our natural access to them. Epic, on the other hand, can present the invisible as though it were visible. The two forms are therefore distinct in their treatment of the wondrous.

While one ought to make [*poiein*] the wondrous [*to thaumaston*] in tragedies, the irrational [*alogon*/unspeakable] is more possible in epic, on account of which the wondrous especially occurs because of not looking at the one acting. For the things concerning the flight of Hektor, were they on stage, would appear laughable—men standing and not pursuing while one man signals, shaking his head—but in epic it is not noticed. (1460a11–17)

The reference is to *Iliad* XXII, where Achilles chases a frightened Hektor before killing him. Achilles' shake of the head is supposed to be what keeps the Greeks from closing in on Hektor. We can take that for granted because Homer tells us it is the case; however, given the amount of ground covered in Achilles' pursuit of Hektor, it is not so clear that the Greeks could even have seen a movement of Achilles' head let alone interpreted it correctly. At the least he would have had to repeat it a number of times to the various segments of the army he passed by during the chase. Either Homer ignores limitations of space—the sign could never have been seen at so great a distance, or he ignores limitations of time—the sign would have had to be repeated. He thus makes it seem that something unfolds in space and time that could never have existed in space and time. This sort of wondrous event, the irrational (*alogon*), is less possible in tragedy where the cosmos of the visible governs, although it is in some sense clearly not unspeakable (*alogon*).

Epic concentrates our attention on the result of an action rather than on the means by which it comes to be. We are told that Achilles pursued Hektor, and, because the details of the pursuit as presented are rather elaborate, we are not likely to ask whether they cohere. Because we know that he pursued Hektor, we tend to assume whatever was necessary for the pursuit to be possible. Homer is the master at taking advantage of this tendency.

The wondrous is pleasant, and the sign of this is that in narrating everyone adds things so as to be gratifying. Homer has even taught the others that [or: how] they should speak falsely; this is paralogism. For human beings think that whenever, one thing being the case, something else is, or whenever, one thing coming to be, another comes to be, if the latter is, then also the former is or comes to be. But this is false. Hence, were the first false— but, supposing it to be the case, it is necessary for another to be or come to be—one ought to add [the second]. For on account of knowing this to be true, our soul misreasons [*paralogizetai*] that the first is also. (1460a17–25)

We all add things when we tell stories, but what sort do we add? According to Aristotle, listeners are gratified by wonders. But a story is most wondrous when it contains events that arise contrary to expectation and yet still not by chance but for some purpose.[133] So what we add to stories must in the end fit with the conclusion of the story. Stories start with the punch line and then add appropriate details, but in the telling, the details seem to come before the punch line. Homer was an astute psychologist for he knew that our soul tends to provide plots and scenarios for what it finds before it. It knows that if *A* is true *B* will also be true; confronted with the presence of *B*, it tends to assume the prior existence of *A* to account for the existence of *B*. Homer teaches the poets to take advantage of the fact that our soul regularly breaks the law of the excluded middle; he teaches them to use our tendency to speak falsely to ourselves out of a desire for the truth. Poets are mythologizers; their plots (*muthoi*) gratify us by appealing to our natural tendency to want to explain what is before us. That "all human beings by nature desire to be in a state of knowing" (*Metaphysics* 980a22) does not, however, mean that all men by nature desire to learn. Loose ends make us uncomfortable; having them tied up gratifies us. But they must be plausibly tied up. Thus, impossible likelihoods are preferable to unbelievable possibilities (1460a26–27). That certain things seem likely means that it makes sense that they should occur. The necessary, understood as the intelligible, is thus in the end the governing principle of likelihood. However, the necessary, in its universality, is impossible.

Poetry begins with the fact and provides a likely story to account for its being a fact. But, in presenting such an account as plausible, a poet invites "our soul" to forget that it is a likely story. We take the story to be a genuine account of the coming to be of something rather than an account of the way in which such a thing, because of what it is, is likely to have come to be. We take an eidetic account to be a genetic account. Poets cannot help tempting us in this way. They cannot tell us the truth, for to be a poet is to speak falsely. Homer simply teaches them to know what they are doing. Paralogism is that which is contrary to reason. Oddly enough, reasoning requires it.

Chapter twenty-four, which began with an explicit likening of tragedy and epic, ends by tacitly differentiating them. Not only should poets prefer impossible likelihoods to unbelievable possibilities, they should also avoid making speeches (*logoi*) out of irrational—*alogon* (perhaps unspoken)—parts. Best of all to have nothing irrational; second best to keep it outside the plot (*mutheuma*). Aristotle uses three examples here— all from tragedy. It was irrational to suppose that Oedipus, who became king because Laius had died, would never have heard of the manner of Laius's death. But since this happened (or didn't happen) before the play begins, we at least are not confronted with it directly. So long as the irrational remains unspoken, a poet can get away with it. Accordingly, Aristotle criticizes the speech in which the *paidagogos* of Sophocles'

Electra (680–763) announces the death of Orestes. He does not say why the speech is so irrational. However it is interesting that, as part of the plan to deceive Clytemnestra and Aegisthus, the speech is meant to be false, and that, even though false, its account of the victory of an Athenian in the chariot race at the Pythian games would have been appealing to an Athenian audience. (Aristotle's final example is from a play that is not extant.) When he gets around to excusing irrationality in a plot, Aristotle returns to epic. The sleeping Odysseus is put ashore at Ithaca with everything given to him in Phaeacia and never awakens. Aristotle says that a baser poet could not have gotten away with this; Homer makes the absurdity pleasant by obliterating it with other good things. Although Aristotle does not acknowledge it, Sophocles does something like this in the speech of the *paidagogos* in the *Electra*. Still, strictly speaking there are no idle parts (1460b3) in tragedy; each word is a part of the action. In epic it is always possible to introduce a parenthesis. The irrational can thus enter without doing violence to the rationality of the plot. Characters about to try to kill each other cannot become overly brilliant in their language without straining credulity. Nevertheless a poet might describe such a contest in language more brilliant than either of its participants would use. Indeed, this fits the case of the *paidagogos* in the *Electra*. He waxes poetic, and the excess of his language becomes an element of the plot. Within the play, his speech is meant to cover up the fact that Orestes did not really die. To the audience it is supposed to emphasize the fact of his lie.

Tragedy and epic are both imitations of action and both involve systematic lying. Aristotle first calls our attention to their similarity and then makes clear their difference. It is more difficult to lie in tragedy than epic because wonders and irrationalities are more difficult to introduce without calling forth the reaction that they shouldn't have been there in the first place. A narrative voice makes it easier to cover up irrationalities, and so to include them. Aristotle says "over brilliant diction"—*lian lampra lexis*—is frequently used for this sort of cover-up. The phrase, an example of what it is about, suggests that Aristotle might be hiding an irrationality of his own. However different tragedy and epic are, lying remains the principle of all poetry because the poet must necessarily present an analysis of something as though it were a causal account. The more plausible and seamless the plot, the more thorough this underlying deception. *Mimêsis* aims at being indistinguishable from that which it represents. But then the least deceptive poem would not be the one that succeeds in covering up its irrationality so much as the one that successfully reveals it. There is good lying and bad, roughly corresponding to good and bad poetry. It is difficult to place epic and tragedy neatly

within this distinction. In tragedy the voice of the poet disappears behind the voices of his characters, and the imitation approaches being
indistinguishable from its object; tragedy is truer to its object but falser
to itself as imitation. In epic the narrative voice remains throughout as
a reminder of the distance between the poet and the poem; it is truer to
itself but falser to its object. In poetry, lies must seem true (likely impossibilities are preferable to unbelievable possibilities), and the truth
must be presented through lies. It is no wonder then, that before concluding the *Poetics* with a final ranking of epic and tragedy, Aristotle
turns in chapter twenty-five to the question of good and bad lying.

[25] Poetry frequently seems to contain things unacceptable by the standards
of ordinary life. To defend a particular instance of poetry, therefore, means
either to show that it only appears to contain these things or to show
how and why ordinary standards do not apply. Aristotle begins with a
general statement of the problem.

> Concerning problems and solutions [*luseis*], both of how many and of what
> sort of species [*eidê*] they consist, would become apparent by contemplating
> [*theôrousin*] [them] in the following way. For, since the poet is an imitator
> [*mimêtês*] just as if he were a painter of animals or some other maker of
> images, it is necessary [for him] always to imitate one of three beings in
> number; for [it is necessary for him to imitate] either such as it was or is,
> or such as they say [it to be] or as it seems, or such as it should be. And
> these are reported in a *lexis* in which there are foreign words [*glôttai*], metaphors
> and modifications [*pathê*] of *lexis*. For we allow these things to the poets.
> (1460b6–13)

Chapter twenty-five seems to divide roughly in two. Aristotle first treats
the species (*eidê*) of error (*hamartia*, 1460b17) in poetry (1460b6–32)
and then gives a list of specific problems and their resolutions (*luseis*)
(1460b32–61b25). His language recalls the account of tragic plot, which
is based on an error the results of which unravel (*luein*) by the end of
the play. Aristotle now suggests that reading poetry often involves recognizing an error which we, by contemplating (or as spectators—*theôrousin*),
resolve or unravel. Our activity as interpreters of difficulties within poetry
is thus implicitly likened to the action that occurs within tragedy.

At the same time, poets, earlier likened to painters (*grapheis*, 1448a5),
are here explicitly likened to *zôgraphoi*—painters of animals. Poets are
imitators of moving things. These imitations, unlike those of the painters, also move; however, their movement is deceiving, for it tends to
conceal the extent to which the poets' own order has replaced the order
of the movement imitated. Because it is an imitation in time, poetry seems

to be an imitation of the temporal. However, like painting, in the end it is an imitation that stays put. Poetry is more philosophical than history because the story line of poetry must come to a point. The line of analysis of this point, for both the poet and the spectator, extends over time, but the point is atemporal.

If contemplation is itself a movement in time, it is subject to the same representation as other actions. Aristotle makes two suggestions—that poetry, like painting, produces imitations that are in the end at rest, and that the act of interpreting, like the action of a tragedy, extends over time. It will therefore have a beginning, middle, and end, and the beginning will only truly make sense in terms of the end. At the same time, to begin at all will require treating one's beginning as though it were independent of the end. Thus, although at first it seems that the poet is at rest and the object of his poetry is in motion, in fact it is the poet who is in motion and the object of his poetry at rest. Tragedy is the highest form of poetry for Aristotle because it takes as its object the action of understanding action. Accordingly, it makes us wonder about the status of the poet at rest as well as making us wonder about our own status as spectators. Tragedy, therefore, provides an example of the interpretation all poetry requires. Just as the *lusis* of tragedy reveals the problematic character of its *desis*, all poetry has to be treated as a problem that demands a *lusis*. Chapter twenty-five at first seems something of a digression, but, by turning to poetic problems and various ways of resolving them, Aristotle is giving us a lesson in how to read poetry.

Poetry is of necessity ambiguous, not only in what it says but also in how it says it. Any poetic speech may be a claim about how things are or were (i.e., a claim about the true being of things). Or, it may be a claim about what seems to be the case or what people say (i.e., about the conventional being of things). Or, it may be a claim about how things ought to be (i.e., about the good). Assessing the truth of any claim will depend on first determining to which of the three orders it belongs. When a poet has one of his characters swear by Zeus, it may be a sign of the poet's belief in Zeus, but it also may simply be an indication of the fact that men believe in Zeus. And, finally, Zeus might represent an understanding of perfection not existing but nonetheless by which we may take our bearings. Even were it possible to decide this issue by quoting the text, Zeus could be a foreign word or a metaphor.

The difficulty in interpreting poetry is reflected in the two species of poetic error.

In addition to this, the same rightness does not belong to the art of politics and the art of poetry, nor to any other art and the art of poetry. But error [*hamartia*] belonging to the art of poetry itself is twofold—on the one hand with respect to itself and on the other hand with respect to the accidental. For if he has intended to imitate, but was incapable,[134] the error belongs to itself. However, if he has intended what is not right, and a horse has at once thrown both right legs forward, or an error with respect to a particular art, such as with respect to medicine or another art, or any impossibilities whatsoever, [the error] does not belong to itself. (1460b13–21)

Politics is for Aristotle the architectonic art; it is also most sovereign (*kuriôtatê*) or, as the word is used in the *Poetics*, most ordinary.[135] The same rightness does not belong to politics and poetics because the sovereign art, like the ordinary word, is not double in nature. It succeeds when it does its job and fails when it does not. Like the other arts, the art of poetry fails when it does not accomplish what it intends, but, unlike them, it does not always intend to succeed. As poetic errors are sometimes intentional, poets may sometimes say false things without blame. Aristotle's example is interesting. For purposes of his own, a poet may intend a falsehood and so might well represent a horse as running by thrusting both of his right limbs forward at once. While this does not seem the most natural way for a horse to run, when pacing they do run this way. Does Aristotle use a false example for his own purposes to indicate that poets sometimes use falsity for their own purposes? But what purposes justify falsity?

If he has made impossible things, he has erred, but it is right if he achieves its end (for the end has been said), if in this way he makes this or another part more astounding. The pursuit of Hektor is an example. If, however, it is either more, or not less, possible for the end to exist also according to the art concerning these things, then he has not rightly erred. For one ought, if it is possible, generally to err in no respect. Yet of what is the error— of things according to art or according to something else accidental? For it is less if he did not know that a female deer does not have horns than if he painted/wrote [*egrapsen*] non-imitatively. (1460b23–32)

There are, then, two species of error in connection with poetry, but only one is, properly speaking, poetic. Poets and their characters frequently say things that are in error according to the arts specifically concerned with these things. This often occurs in poetry when characters say things that are immoral or false. But this is not yet poetic error since what they say may plausibly seem true or right to men of the sort that these characters are meant to imitate. It is possible to imitate truly what is in itself false. Similarly, poets themselves may say false things when they deem it necessary for a larger effect. Aristotle's own example—horses pacing—seemed at first to fit this description. In fact, since horses can run by first moving their left legs forward together and then their right, the fact of the example rather than its content served as the genuine example. Aristotle used a false example to show that "poets" often use falsity to serve their own ends. His second example shows how complicated this is. Someone who doesn't know that female deer do not have horns but correctly imitates what he thinks them to be is less in error than someone who fails accurately to imitate his own notion of female deer. Aristotle uses the verb *graphein*, which means both to paint or draw and to write, for this imitative activity. We don't know whether he does this intentionally (had he used *zôgraphein* again, there would have been no ambiguity) and so means to say that there is no meaningful difference between poetry and painting with respect to this error in imitation, or unintentionally, in which case he could mean this example to apply only to painting. Since the issue throughout this section is poetry, it seems likely that the ambiguity is intended. Painters and poets, and presumably imitators as such, can err in three ways: intentionally for some further purpose, unintentionally through ignorance of what they are imitating, or untintentionally because of lack of skill. Aristotle's example shows how difficult it is for an interpreter to tell the difference. Intentional and unintentional error can be distinguished only if we know the poet's intention, but since this is known only from his poem—his deed—it looks as though we have to interpret the intention on the basis of the poem and the poem on the basis of the intention. In theory this is a circle; in practice it involves looking to the text surrounding each instance of error for indications that the error was intended and then moving back to the error to wonder why it might have been intended. When, at the end of chapter twenty-one (1458a9), Aristotle claimed that only masculine nouns end in sigma six lines after having used the feminine noun *polis* (1458a3), we have at least a hint that his error was intentional. Unintentional error due to lack of knowledge is equally difficult to distinguish from unintentional error due to lack of skill. Once again, one must look to the text as a whole to get clear about the character of the part. When due to ignorance, a particular error will be connected in rational ways to the remainder of the whole of which it is a part, but not when due to lack of skill. This principle of interpretation is not new. That the whole must be looked to to interpret the significance of the part, which in turn must be understood to grasp the whole, was the principle underlying Aristotle's analysis of *logos* as a whole.

While all of this may make some sense of how to distinguish intentional from unintentional error, it does not yet shed light on why one might intend to err. Best of all, says Aristotle, is not to err, but sometimes error is necessary to make a part more astounding. Error, like foreign words, stands out from what is authoritative or ordinary (*kurion*). Of course, if a poem were all error, just as if it were all foreign words, nothing would be astounding. It may be hard to find a needle in a haystack, but it is impossible to find a needle in a stack of needles. Error startles only given the expectation of truth. But if, as Aristotle says, in general poets should not err, when error is present, it will stand out. A text once taken at face value will now be seen as a problem with conflicting elements to be reconciled. In erring deliberately a poet will be able to determine just how a text will emerge as problematic. Error leads to contradiction and contradiction to wonder. For Aristotle, philosophy begins in wonder, and lovers of stories (*philomuthoi*) are in a way philosophers.[136] Philosophy is not possible apart from a willingness to wonder about the seemingly ordinary. Poetry uses various means of bringing out the strange in the ordinary. An extraordinary story about the origins of life is necessary so that the extraordinary character of ordinary life can come to sight. In amazing us with stories about the extraordinary origins of the day-to-day, myths remind us of how little we really understand the day-to-day. They induce knowledge of ignorance. *Mimêsis* lies behind knowledge of ignorance since only by representing something to ourselves can we single it out as an object of inquiry. Something like poetry is therefore necessary to the activity of philosophy, which is to say, to the activity of thought. There is a poetic element essential to all thinking since to think about something one must place it in the foreground, using everything else as background. This single-mindedness is in one sense an error for to understand the things in the background they would have to be placed in the foreground. Still, this error is necessary. Not everything can be in the foreground at once. Aristotle's account of poetry seems to share with Socratic philosophy a recognition of the necessity to begin in error.

We may have to begin in error; however, to begin at all means that we do not want to end in error.[137] In making the ordinary seem strange, poetry threatens to turn us into lovers of being dazzled. We begin by taking our ordinary world for granted. Poetry awakens us to its wonders—to begin with, the wonder that the world is at all. It may provide us with a story, a *muthos*, of the origins of the world or of the gods by which we swear—"First of all Chaos came to be, after this broadbreasted earth. . . ." Then, however, we risk simply becoming complacent on a higher level. The gods that once gave voice to our sense of the strangeness of the world become common coin. We now take them for granted. It is, therefore, not enough to leave matters at producing a sense of the strange; metaphors quickly die and become *kurion*. Thinking first requires that the ordinary be made strange, for there is no learning without knowledge of ignorance. But the strange must then be understood as ordinary—it must be analyzed. Although philosophy has a poetic element, it is not the same as poetry. The problems to which philosophy seeks solutions would be invisible without poetry, but poetry does not by itself provide solutions. This must be kept in mind to understand the problems and resolutions to which Aristotle turns in the remainder of chapter twenty-five.

The first of the problems is the charge that the poet has said something untrue (1460b32–33). Aristotle suggests three solutions; in different ways all deny the charge by claiming that something else was really the object of imitation. In connection with the first solution, Aristotle cites Sophocles' remark to the effect that he made men such as they ought to be while Euripides made them as they are. This shifts the object of imitation from what is to what ought to be. Second, the object of imitation might be what men say (e.g., about the gods). Third, the object of imitation might be what was rather than what is. Aristotle's example here is taken from *Iliad* X:152. Odysseus and Nestor come to awaken Diomedes for a nighttime council concerning a reconnaissance of the Trojan camp. Diomedes' men sleep with their spears upright, butt end in the ground. Apparently, in the fourth century this is no longer accepted military procedure, although the fact that it is still done in Illyria is an indication that it may have been done elsewhere in the past. This error is therefore only an error if one assumes that the current way of doing things is the only way of doing things. In fact, something like this is true of all three of Aristotle's solutions. Only if we assumed no disproportion between what is and what ought to be (i.e., only were we perfectly self-satisfied and complacent) would the representation of men as they ought to be seem contradictory. And only if we expected what "men say" to be unproblematic would we find it odd that ordinary conventions seem false. Aristotle groups these first three *luseis* together because they address one problem. Of course, poets do not always know, let alone tell, the truth. However, when they seem to speak falsely, we ought to ask whether it is not because they violate our most taken-for-granted customs. Whenever we find ourselves blaming (*epitiman*) them for not telling the truth, as a practical principle, it is a good idea to wonder whether they have touched one of those beliefs so powerful in us that we do not even know we hold them for we are not even aware of alternatives to them. The good, the past, and the notion that what men say is after all only conventional are each correctives for this sort of complacency.

Another species of problem has to do with whether something has been said or done beautifully or nobly (*kalôs*).

Concerning whether something has been said or done by someone beautifully or not beautifully, not only must the thing done or said itself be inquired into, looking at whether it is good [*spoudaion*] or base [*phaulon*], but also at the one acting or speaking—toward whom, when, in what way, or for the sake of what, for example in order that a greater good come to be or in order that a greater evil be avoided. (1461a4–9)

A speech or deed is always attached to a person; its beauty will therefore depend on its appropriateness to that person in a particular context. This is just to say that all poetry is in some measure dialogic. When a villain says base things, he only says what is fitting. The character is ignoble, not the poetry. And when a Iago says noble things, the poetry would be ugly were it not for the fact that it is his vice to seem perfectly just while being altogether evil. Beautiful speech suits not only the noble man but also the man who is meant to seem noble. This is the fourth *lusis*—that beautiful poetry does not consist in imitating only the beautiful. To show itself, the beautiful needs a context not itself simply beautiful. To represent this context the poet must sometimes depict, but does not necessarily endorse, the ugly or base. Aristotle thus warns us not to identify the poet with his poem. One cannot quote a line from a poem and attribute it to a poet. It is not the poet, Sophocles, but the chorus of Colonians who say "Not to be born surpasses every *logos*, but once one has come to light to go there quickly from where one has come is by far the second best."[138] Sophocles cannot be judged by the truth or beauty of this utterance but only by whether it is appropriate for the chorus to say in the context. Once again, the interpretation of the part requires an understanding of the whole. And once again we have to be wary of thinking that we have found an error when we have simply not been paying enough attention.

The rest of the solutions of chapter twenty-five are of problems emerging in connection with *lexis*. If a line does not seem to make sense, perhaps we are not understanding it correctly. Sometimes, because a word is foreign, it is taken in a sense other than was intended. Aristotle gives three examples of this fifth *lusis*. At the beginning of the *Iliad* (I:50) Apollo, in his anger at the Greeks, sends a plague (I:61); his "arrow" first strikes down *ouréas* and dogs, afterward aiming at the men themselves. Now *ouréas* ought to be the accusative plural of "mules," but it is hard to see what the point would be in singling out mules for Apollo's wrath. Therefore Aristotle suggests that *ouréas* be taken as a foreign form of the accusative plural of *ouros*—guard. While Aristotle's general intent seems clear and sound, the particular example is curious. If the guards are stricken first, we still have to wonder why the dogs go with them. And even were that problem solved, it would be odd that the plague strikes the Greeks themselves after it strikes their guards. Are the guards not to be understood as Greeks or as men? Aristotle's "solution" has made a modest problem more difficult. *Oureus* occurs only once again in Homer (*Iliad* X:84) where it is equally ambiguous. Strangely enough, this second occurrence brings us back to the nighttime reconnaissance of Odysseus and Diomedes, which is also the location of Aristotle's second example. At *Iliad* X:313–16 the Trojans select Dolon for their nighttime reconnaissance. He is said to be ill-shaped but swift of foot, but if his form (*eidos*) is so bad, how can he run so fast? Aristotle's solution is that in Crete having a good *eidos* can simply mean having a good face.[139] Being ugly would not slow Dolon down. Aristotle's final example is again from the *Iliad* (IX:202–4). An embassy has been sent by Agamemnon to offer Achilles inducements to return to the army. When they arrive, Achilles tells Patroklos to mix the wine *zôroteron*. It seems to mean to make the wine more lively by making it stronger (i.e., less mixed with water), but unmixed wine is ordinarily connected to drunkenness and debauchery. Since that seems inappropriate here, Aristotle suggests that a foreign meaning of *zôroteron*, "more quickly," would restore the decorum of the situation. Although this example seems less plausible than the second, the general point is sound. Where a poem is unclear or the language seems inappropriate, it is always possible that a word from another time or place is being given a meaning it did not originally have. On the other hand, the ambiguity could also be intentional. When Sophocles calls Oedipus a *tyrannos*, he uses the word in its old sense, "king," but he knows full well that, when heard, it will also bring to mind its new sense, "tyrant." A good deal would be missed if we were to resolve this "problem" by concluding that Oedipus is a *tyrannos* only in the old sense.

Sometimes problems of *lexis* are due to metaphors read literally; this is the sixth *lusis*. Aristotle's first example is problematic because he seems to be working from a different text of the *Iliad*.

> But it has been said metaphorically—for example, "then all gods and men slept through the night," while at the same time he says "and yet when at the Trojan plain he gazed . . . the din of flutes and pipes." For "all" has been said metaphorically instead of many, for "all" is a "much." (1461a16–20)

This is difficult to understand since the two quotations appear nowhere near each other in the text we have of the *Iliad*. The first is almost the same as the first lines of Book II. Zeus, the only one awake among gods and men, decides to send Agamemnon a dream telling him that if he attacks the Trojans at once he will take their city. It is a lie, a part of a larger plan designed to increase Achilles' honor. The second quotation is from the beginning Book X (roughly lines 11 and 13). Book X opens with Agamemnon said to be the only one of the Greeks awake. He is gazing at the Trojan camp and wondering at the many fires and the sounds. To solve the problem in Aristotle's text one must create a problem to be solved in Homer's text. It is generally assumed that Aristotle has confused the beginning of Book II with the beginning of Book X, or more charitably, that he had before him a text in which Book X began as Book II now begins.[140] If we grant this, then the problem to be solved is that the book begins by saying that Agamemnon is the only god or man who is awake but ten lines later describes all sorts of activity in the Trojan camp. Aristotle's solution is to say that in this case "all" is a metaphor for "many"— a species standing for a genus.

However, this problem in Homer and its offspring in Aristotle both admit of alternative solutions. Aristotle has repeatedly used examples either from or in some way pointing to *Iliad* Book X. Now, Book X as a whole is rather problematic. Agamemnon sends Odysseus and Diomedes on a reconnaissance of the Trojan camp in the course of which they capture Dolon and promise that they will free him if he tells them what they want to know. When he does, they kill him. Before returning to their camp, they take time out to slaughter some sleeping Thracians. This presentation of Odysseus and Diomedes as unnecessarily brutal is a problem of a much higher order than those explicitly mentioned by Aristotle.[141] Understanding the *Iliad* would mean finding a *lusis* for this problem. Now, if all gods and men other than Agamemnon are asleep, but the Trojans are not asleep, the simple *lusis* to Aristotle's original problem is that the Trojans are not men. This seems absurd. And yet, if Aristotle did not mix up the beginnings of Books II and X but intended us to think of the two "at the same time," he might have intended us to compare the wakeful Agamemnon in Book X to the wakeful Zeus in Book II. For Zeus, the death of the Greeks is only an instrument to further the glory of Achilles. He doesn't think twice about the morality of sending a misleading dream to Agamemnon; he lies to further a greater end. Odysseus and Diomedes do not treat Trojans any better than Zeus had treated Greeks. They lie to Dolon to further their own purposes. In both cases men are treated as mere instruments. Therefore one ought to be careful not to accept at face value the words of beings having purposes of their own. This is no less true of poets than of gods and wily heroes.

Aristotle goes out of his way to call attention to Book X of the *Iliad* for several reasons. If the harshness of the activity of Odysseus and Diomedes is connected to Zeus's attitude toward human beings, Aristotle would seem subtly to have suggested that, for the Greeks in Book X, gods are to men as Greeks are to Trojans. That Trojans are not considered human is the result of the long war; this is the "solution" for the problem of *Iliad* Book X.[142] At the same time, by connecting Books II and X, Aristotle teaches us to be suspicious of those who have plans—whether gods or men. Zeus and Odysseus tell plausible but false stories. To understand the true intent of these stories we need to be suspicious. This advice applies not just to gods and heroes; it also applies to poets and authors generally. The greatest of mistakes is to assume that their apparent ends are always their real ends.

In chapter twenty-five Aristotle gives examples of how to resolve textual difficulties. Of necessity, each example also teaches us to see difficulties we otherwise might have missed. As a whole, the chapter is an exercise in how to read skeptically. This holds true in the remaining forms of *lusis*, the seventh of which is *prosôidia*—intonation. The accents, which in our Greek texts indicate tonal variation, were not yet written in Aristotle's time. Accordingly, words written the same were sometimes sounded differently, the difference in pronunciation indicating difference in meaning. Aristotle quotes the phrase *didomen de hoi*. His first example is more significant than it first appears. In our text of the *Iliad didomen de toi* occurs at XXI:297, where the gods promise Achilles victory over Hektor. Aristotle's treatment of the same problem in *On Sophistical Refutations* (166b1–9) seems to indicate that his text had *didomen de hoi* at II:15, once again in connection with the dream Zeus sends to Agamemnon promising victory over the Trojans. If the accent is on the first syllable, *didomen* is the present indicative—"we give"; if on the second syllable, it is the present infinitive used as an imperative—"give." If we read the present indicative, Zeus would have lied; if we read the infinitive, Zeus would have told the dream what to say but would not himself be promising Agamemnon anything. Zeus would have slid out from the moral difficulty since how Agamemnon interprets his dreams is his own business.[143] However real the difference between the two readings, the lesson to be learned is skepticism in the face of the promises of the gods. Even the gods cannot speak univocally.

Aristotle's second example of a solution by way of *prosôidia* turns on whether *ou* is read as aspirated and with a circumflex or as unaspirated and enclitic. In the former case the phrase in which it is found (*Iliad* XXIII:327) would mean something like "part of which is rotted by rain"; in the latter case it would mean "which is not rotted by rain." In certain contexts, intonation is thus so important that it cannot only alter but completely reverse the meaning of a sentence. This is also the effect of his eighth form of *lusis*, division, which includes determining where words begin and end and what we would call punctuation. In Aristotle's time Greek is unpunctuated and there are no spaces between words. It also includes ambiguous constructions that would not even be revealed by punctuation in English. In each case, the sense of the whole is the only way to arrive at the appropriate divisions. But, even having made the divisions, the ambiguity remains, and may be exploited by the poet. Aristotle's example is from Empedocles (fragment 35).

> Suddenly the things having learned before to be immortal grew mortal and things pure before having been mixed. (1461a24–25)

The context seems to be the combining and separating powers of love and strife. The difficulty is that "before" (*prin*) can be taken either with "things pure" or with "having been mixed." If the former, the meaning is that things that had been pure before came to be mixed. If the latter, the meaning is that pure things were previously mixed. The two meanings are clearly at odds, yet it is curious that, had Empedocles meant both readings to hold, he would have claimed that, on the one hand, pure things are the stuff out of which mixtures are made, while, on the other, pure things are distilled out of mixtures. The first would be genetic— the second eidetic. Empedocles would have written a cosmology much as Aristotle wrote his account of the parts of speech in which the relationship of parts to whole is double. The whole is put together out of parts that get their being as parts only from the whole that they constitute. This reminds us of the *lusis* under discussion in which the sense of the whole is the only way to determine how to divide a *logos*. We cannot divide properly without knowing what the whole means, and we cannot know what the whole means without dividing properly.

Aristotle names the ninth solution *amphibolia*—ambiguity. His example once again returns us to *Iliad* X (ll. 252–53). Odysseus tells Diomedes that they had better leave since the night is more (*pleô*) than two-thirds gone, and there remains only a third. But if more than two-thirds is gone how can there be a full third left? Aristotle's solution is that *pleô* is ambiguous. It can mean "more," but it can also mean "the greater part of." If the greater part of two-thirds of the night has passed, then more than a third remains.

A word may be used in a customary or idiomatic way. This is Aristotle's tenth solution. Just as it is customary still to call wine that has been diluted wine, poets can refer to greaves of tin even though greaves are always made of a mixture of copper and tin. And just as it is customary to call iron workers coppersmiths, Ganymede can be called a winebearer for Zeus even though the gods drink no wine. There are idioms of ordinary language, and there are poetic idioms built by analogy to those of ordinary language. Aristotle's examples are interesting because they show how the startling idioms of poetry call attention to their analogues in ordinary language, analogues so common as not to seem problematic at all. Aristotle again "solves" poetic problems in such a way as to make us aware that all language is far more problematic than we are ordinarily aware. His examples once more come from the *Iliad*, the first from XXI:592. When Agenor casts his spear, it bounces off Achilles' "greaves of new wrought tin." It is interesting first because, although Aristotle's solution requires that we let tin stand for a mixture of tin and copper (i.e., bronze), the spear that is deflected is called bronze (l.594). Aristotle's solution has thus created a new textual problem: why is bronze called tin and then two lines later called bronze? The larger context of the example is also of interest. Just as Agenor is about to lose this fight with Achilles, Apollo spirits him away and takes his place so that Achilles will pursue him. Not only are we confronted with another example of the duplicity of the gods; we are also given a lesson in the danger of this sort of solution. In certain situations the difference between an ironsmith and a bronzesmith might be as crucial as the difference between the man Agenor and the look-alike god who takes his place. Aristotle's second example is from *Iliad* XX:234. Aeneas has given Achilles' genealogy and is in the middle of giving his own. Both heroes are mixtures of the divine and the human. Aeneas breaks off by saying that the words of mortals are tangled or distorted. And when he is about to lose the battle that follows, Aeneas too is spirited off by his mother, Aphrodite. Aristotle's examples repeatedly call attention to the intentional duplicity of both gods and men.

When a word seems to signify something inconsistent, one has to look for a way in which it can be made significant. Aristotle refers again to a problem in the battle between Achilles and Aeneas at *Iliad* XX:272. The line quoted says that the spear of Aeneas was stopped by the gold layer of Achilles' shield after penetrating two other layers. This seems impossible since, as decorative, gold would always be placed on the outside of the shield. Aristotle says we have to inquire into the various ways by which to make sense of this peculiar claim. He does not, however, himself solve this problem of the surface and the depth. Instead he discusses the need to take care not to think we have found inconsistencies in texts when we find that they disagree with certain of our own presuppositions. If we assume that Antigone insists on burying her brother Polyneices so that his shade will be able to go to Hades, we will not understand why it is that she is so intent on getting caught for her contravention of Creon's decree. In fact, although in other plays it might be perfectly sensible to assume that burial has something to do with going to Hades, nowhere does Sophocles' Antigone use this justification for her action. In warning us to seek a sensible meaning for any apparent contradiction, Aristotle warns us not to fall into the trap of so assuming that we know what an author must have meant that we feel no need to look at what he actually said. If we assume that Job is a Jew and so a participant in the covenant with God, we will understand him in one way. If, however, we notice that he is nowhere said to be a Jew, we will understand him in another manner. A poetic problem is frequently no more than a contradiction generated when an error (*harmartêma*, 1461b8) we bring to the text is at odds with what is actually there. A good poet, anticipating our erroneous assumptions, will use them against us to make us aware in the end of what we have assumed without knowing it.

Aristotle concludes this section with a summary of the species of poetic problems. Earlier the species had been two—problems proper and accidental to the poem itself. Here, Aristotle seems to further divide the problems proper to the poem itself. The first is the impossible (*to adunaton*); this may be legitimately introduced either out of a necessity in the poem itself, or as a paradigm of what is better, or as an example of ordinary opinion. The second, the irrational things (*t'aloga*), may be introduced in connection with what men say or as an example of the way what is unlikely is likely to come to be at one time or another. The third, things said inconsistently (*ta hupenantiôs eirêmena*), has to be examined just like arguments to see if the opposition is real or only apparent. When a poet seems to contradict either his own words elsewhere or what a prudent man would think, it is necessary to ask whether in both cases the same thing is at issue, and in the same relationship, and similarly. When Aristotle says that the censure of irrationality and wickedness is appropriate if there is no necessity for the irrationality and no use made of it, he seems to indicate a fourth species of problem—wickedness (*mochthêria*).

This list of the species of problems is especially interesting given the conclusion of chapter twenty-five.

> Censures then are borne by five species—either as impossibilities, as irrationalities, as harms, as inconsistencies or as against what is right according to an art. But solutions must be sought from the number of those mentioned. And there are twelve. (1461b22–25)

This is curious. Aristotle, who had just listed four species of problems, now says there are five. Impossibilities, irrationalities, and inconsistencies appear on both lists, but harms (*blabara*) have not been previously mentioned—unless we take them to be the same as the wickedness mentioned earlier. The last species was treated earlier in the chapter (1460b19–21), but so were many other things; it seems strange to single it out here. In addition, Aristotle's final remark is very puzzling. He says that twelve solutions have been mentioned. We found eleven. Others have found other numbers, sometimes forcing things a little to confirm Aristotle's claim that there are twelve.[144] The text can be juggled in a variety of ways, but the problem admits of no easy solution. So Aristotle has given us an example of an error—contrary to his explicit claim, the species of problems do not easily number five and their solutions do not easily number twelve. We notice this discrepancy and struggle with it to make things come out right. In the process we come to understand how problems we thought to differ might be the same and those thought to be the same might differ. This is how a text generates wonder. Aristotle makes the otherwise ordinary seem strange and so pulls us into the text. The contradiction forces us to think through his examples with greater care. The intention of chapter twenty-five is to show how apparent contradiction is the engine of all interpretation. We have to think about the events of the *Iliad* because they do not seem to add up; the harshness of Odysseus and Diomedes in Book X seems gratuitous. What was true on the simplest level of *logos*—that a strategic disruption of meaning is necessary for any meaning at all—is also true on the highest level of *logos*. This is what Aristotle really means by a poetic *lusis*; it is, by the way, number twelve.

[26] If chapter twenty-five was meant to be a lesson in the questions one must raise to resolve apparent problems, chapter twenty-six presents us with such a problem and its resolution. How can tragedy be superior to epic if "they say" the audience for tragedy is the vulgar, while the audience for epic is the *epieikeis*—the good or equitable?

> One might raise the question whether epic or tragic imitation is better. For if the less vulgar is better, and such is always the one with a view to better spectators, it is very clear that the vulgar is the one imitating everything. For, as though there will be no perceiving lest he himself embellish, they make a lot of movement, like the base flautists who roll around when they have to imitate the discus and, when playing Scylla, drag the leader of the chorus around. Tragedy, then, is such as those earlier performers considered those of them later; for Mynniskus used to call Callipides an ape because he exaggerated so much, and such was the opinion also about Pindarus. But as these hold toward those, the whole art holds toward epic. The one, they say, to exist with a view to *epieikeis* spectators who require no gestures at all, but tragedy with a view to the base. If it is vulgar, it is clear that it would be worse. (1461b26–62a4)

Tragedy seems to stand to epic as exaggerated movements in tragedy stand to less elaborate movements. Epic seems finer because it is more subtle; tragedy seems vulgar because it is grosser. An imitation that shows us everything leaves nothing for us to do. As requiring less of its audi-

ence, tragedy is more vulgar. If this is correct, how can Aristotle maintain that tragedy is the highest form of poetry?

Aristotle addresses this difficulty first by distinguishing between the
art of poetry and the art of performance (*hupokritikê*). Excess of gesture
and of movement belongs to the latter, not the former. That it is possible to produce a dreadful version of *Hamlet* is not something for which
Shakespeare ought to be held responsible. The tragedy is no more the
performance than the public recitation of a rhapsode is the epic poem.
Such movement need not detract from tragedy. Although sometimes base,
movement need not always be so. Sexually explicit imitation has its appeal,
but not all dance is so crudely mimetic. In any case, tragedy produces
its effect independent of performance. Like epic, it can be read apart
from any performance. Thus, while the audience of tragedy does include
the vulgar, it does not exclude the *epieikeis*. Only if tragedy were to
sacrifice the better audience for the worse, would it follow that it is an
inferior form of poetry, but, as read, tragedy has all the possibilities of
epic and, as performed, it adds the considerable pleasures of spectacle
(*opsis*) and music. Because tragedy has, in addition to its own peculiar
charms, everything present in epic, it seems superior to epic.

Aristotle never says that tragedy does not appeal to spectators who
are common. It is apparently superior to epic because it is simultaneously
vulgar and not. But tragedy's success in combining the *phaulon* (the base)
with the *epieikes* (the good, meet, or equitable) is simply another version of the combination of the ordinary and the strange characteristic of
logos in general and metaphor in particular. It is a way of combining
"what men customarily say" with "what ought to be" so as to reveal "what
is." Aristotle had said that exotic or strange language was most appropriate to epic, and here he makes clear that this has to do with its subject matter. Epic is concerned with the noble—what men ought to be
rather than with what is or what men say. In both its form and its content it is strange. We have known since chapter three (1448a25–28) that
tragedy is like epic in its content and like comedy in its form. Comedy
is, of course, an imitation of the *phaulon* (1449a32–33) and uses a meter,
iambic, appropriate to its content (1448b30–32). In epic and in comedy
there is an agreement of form and content; in tragedy, however, they
are at odds. While the language most appropriate to epic is strange, and
ordinary language is found in comedy, metaphor suits tragedy, for it
transforms the ordinary into the strange. It is as though Aristotle had
anticipated Nietzsche's famous definition of tragedy to correct it; tragedy is Apollinian content and Dionysian form. All of this must be taken
with a grain of salt. Homer may be an epic poet, but he is the most dramatic
of epic poets, and his poems certainly contain metaphors. In praising
him for so frequently using dialogue, Aristotle also implies that epic can

borrow a form more popular—more vulgar—than chapter twenty-six seems to indicate. And tragedy is far from using only iambic meter; the chorus seldom sings in iambs and is frequently more dark and strange in its language than anything in Homer.

Yet if there are epic elements of tragedy and tragic elements of epic, what is the point of Aristotle's conclusion that tragedy is superior to epic? Aristotle's final comparison of the two provides a hint. Tragedy is superior to epic insofar as it serves the same end in a shorter length, and whatever is more concentrated, without losing any of its content, is more pleasant.[145] As a sign of this Aristotle remarks that

> from any sort of [epic] imitation whatever many tragedies come to be, so that if, they make one plot, either it will appear cut short by being shown briefly or watered down by following the appropriate length. (1462b5–7)

An epic that contains the unity present in tragedy will either appear too long or, if its length is appropriate, it will seem truncated. There is a long tradition of understanding the *Poetics* as a truncated work of which the "second book" on comedy has been lost.[146] The ultimate ground for this tradition is Aristotle's remark at 1449b21 that "we will speak later concerning the art of imitation in hexameters and concerning comedy." Now, Aristotle has just praised Homer for teaching the poets how to lie and, at the very least, may plan to fulfill his promise about comedy in a nonconventional way.[147] We will return to the question of comedy, but, for the moment, let us assume that the *Poetics* as we have it is complete. Even so it seems truncated. Aristotle has written a book in his own voice, not in dialogue, which has as its initial goal to arouse wonder, the goal of poetry, in us about the nature of *poiêtikê* and which seems to be cut short. Aristotle has written a species of epic poem in which he praises tragedy as the highest kind of poetry. No wonder he was so intent on giving the highest praise to an epic poet even though tragedy was the highest form of poetry. Commentators have frequently seen that the *Poetics* as a whole, and chapter twenty–six in particular, represent an argument with Plato.[148] In Book III of the *Republic*, Plato's Socrates praises simple narrative over dialogic imitation (392c–98b). The *Poetics* concludes with a praise of dramatic poetry over simple narration. This apparent argument between Plato and Aristotle over the best form of poetry conceals a deeper agreement about the nature of philosophy. The *Poetics* concludes with this issue.

In both epic poems and philosophical treatises we hear the author's voice directly. Presumably what he means is what he says; his intentions are clear. In tragedies and philosophical dialogues characters speak, but we nowhere hear the author's voice directly. The author's intention is hidden. The doubleness of *logos* as necessarily at once ordinary and strange, straightforward and elusive, underlies the tension between epic and tragedy. Epic poems and treatises seem to speak straight to us. Although tragedies and dialogues involve speech in our presence, they seem not to speak to us at all. However, as Aristotle points out, Homer taught the poets that it was necessary to speak falsehoods (1460a18–19). Underlying all of chapter twenty-five was one fundamental problem: How is it possible to tell when an author has erred intentionally and when unintentionally? If poets are liars, how can we tell when they are lying to us and when not? And if we cannot differentiate intentional and unintentional error, then isn't the straightforwardness of epics and treatises illusory? Aristotle and Homer are no more visible in their writings than are Plato and Sophocles. Just as the intention of a character in a play is available to us only through his actions, the intention of an author is available to us only through his *logos*. The true superiority of tragedy to epic consists in making visible the necessary invisibility of the author, but neither epic nor tragedy is ordinary or straightforward.

If we know that we can never know what an author intends, doesn't that relieve us of any obligation to make the attempt? Or, put differently, doesn't the necessary invisibility of the author have the effect of removing the ordinary or authoritative (*kurion*) element from *logos*. *Logos* that need mean nothing can mean anything. Under these conditions, interpretation would cease to be a seeking, a *philo-sophia*, and become simply an act of will. Any interpretation of a text would be on a par with any other although it is not at all clear why one would bother to interpret in the first place.

In chapters nineteen through twenty-six of the *Poetics*, Aristotle attempts to find the mean between two initially plausible, but finally impossible, understandings of *logos*. According to one view, while language can be prettified in various ways, the underlying truth of *logos* is the ordinary and authoritative—*to kurion*. Such language is simple and straightforward. It is not charged with ambiguity, and its intentions are clear. If this were not the case, poetic language would be impossible because poetic language, as constituted by not being ordinary, is essentially derivative. On the other hand, Aristotle's account of the problem of intentional versus unintentional lying, and consequently of the invisibility of the intention of the author in any particular case, makes it seem as though, taken by itself, no *logos* is authoritative or straightforward. Still, in chapter twenty-five, Aristotle gives a series of examples meant to show how to distinguish between intentional and unintentional error by thinking through the whole of which the error is a part so as to show how it adds up. This procedure recalls Aristotle's own account of the parts of speech in terms of the whole that they constitute. As a result, something like an authoritative reading becomes possible as a goal of interpretation rather than as a beginning point. This is what has been at stake from the outset of the *Poetics* in Aristotle's distinction between the eidetic and the genetic. A genetic account treats the elements of understanding as self-subsisting parts. It makes an appeal to these parts as *kurion*, authoritative. An eidetic account, while aiming at the authoritative, acknowledges the partiality of its beginning points. Aristotle concludes the *Poetics* with a reminder that he has been concerned with "tragedy and epic, both their *eidê* and their parts" (1462b16–17). Parts that seem to have an independence from the whole that they constitute are in fact discernible as distinct parts only in terms of the whole that they constitute. While they must be treated as distinct for any inquiry of the whole to begin, their distinctness is a noble lie.

On the one hand, *logos* does not serve up meaning to us on a platter. On the other hand, it does not allow us to invent meaning at will. The *Poetics* is an account of the way in which *logos* combines these two truths—the ordinary and the exotic—to pull us into a problem and force us to seek a solution. All *logos* does this. Poetry does it self-consciously—its goal is to arouse wonder. Tragedy makes this most human of processes itself thematic and so an object of wonder. The *Poetics* is an analysis of the doubleness of wonder as what puzzles us and seems strange because it holds out some authoritative meaning as a goal. This doubleness is the fundamental feature of *logos*, *praxis*, and *mimêsis*.

The invisibility of the author makes the necessity for inquiry manifest; by bracketing the authority of what is said, it is an invitation to philosophize. The visibility of the author makes the possibility of inquiry manifest; by presenting the appearance, and so affirming the possibility, of authority, it too is an invitation to philosophize. If the proper goal of poetry as poetry is to generate wonder, because tragedy treats the highest things in such a way as to undermine our conventional understanding of them while making invisible the wisdom of the poet in seeing beyond the conventional, it is the highest form of poetry. Yet Aristotle leaves no doubt that for philosophy the author must be both visible and invisible. In seeming to disagree with Plato on the question of poetry, he agrees on the question of philosophy. Plato seems to praise the straightforwardness of narration, and so epic poetry, but does so in a dialogue and thereby conceals himself. Aristotle seems to praise the indirection of tragedy, and so dialogue, but does so in a simple narrative, which is at the same time a defective "epic," and thereby reveals his own voice. Both misrepresent themselves and, in so doing, acknowledge the need for a mixture. For an overly dogmatic age, the cure is Plato. For an overly skeptical age, the cure is Aristotle. But about the perennial need for duplicity as a cure, the two speak as one.

Notes

1. See, Karl Marx, *Werke, Schriften bis 1844*, Erster Teil, Ergänzungsband (Berlin: Dietz Verlag, 1968), pp. 534ff. and Celeste Schenck, "All of a Piece: Women's Poetry and Autobiography," in *Life/Lines: Theorizing Women's Autobiography*, B. Brodzki and C. Schenck, eds. (Ithaca, NY: Cornell University Press, 1988) pp. 281–85.

2. See Friedrich Nietzsche, *Die Geburt der Tragödie*, Section 14 in *Werke in Drei Bänden* (Munich: Carl Hanser Verlag, 1966) and Sigmund Freud, *Abriss der Psychoanalyse und Das Unbehagen in der Kultur* (Frankfurt: Fischer Bücherei, 1970), pp. 125–29.

3. Consider G.W.F Hegel, *Phänomenologie des Geistes* VII.B.c. (Hamburg: Felix Meiner Verlag, 1952).

4. All quotations from the *Poetics* are taken from the edition of D.W. Lucas (Oxford: Clarendon Press, 1986). Translations are my own.

5. While Aristotle does make the distinction between making (*poiêsis*) and acting (*praxis*) at *Nicomachean Ethics* 1140a1–4, he justifies himself by way of an appeal to exoteric speeches (*exôterikoi logoi*). Their difference on one level does not preclude their sameness on another.

6. This is not unlike what occurs in tragedy. See *Poetics* 1448b10–20.

7. Arabic numbers in square brackets correspond to the chapters of the *Poetics* under discussion in the commentary.

8. I was once a participant in a mock trial, the goal of which was to determine how a real jury would respond to the arguments the defense had prepared. At the conclusion of the trial we were quizzed about our reasons for voting as we had. Many jurors spoke of how they had come to be convinced by the straightforward honesty of the defendant even though they knew that all the participants in the "trial" were actors. This is the irony of all drama; the more real it is, the less real it is.

9. See *Metaphysics* 1074b34–35.

161

10. See Plato *Ion* 530d–32b, *Symposium* 223c–d, and *Apology of Socrates* 22a–c.

11. For example, S.H. Butcher (*Aristotle's Theory of Poetry and Fine Art*, London: Macmillan, 1902, p. 7) translates the beginning of the first sentence as follows: "I propose to treat of Poetry in itself and of its various kinds. . . ." Telford (*Poetics*, translated and edited by Kenneth A. Telford, Lanham, MD.: University Press of America, 1961, p. 1 and pp. 59–68) translates correctly but does not see how important it is that Aristotle is speaking of the *eidê* of the art of poetry as opposed to the *eidê* of poetry. Else (*Aristotle's Poetics: The Argument*, Cambridge, MA: Harvard University Press, 1967, pp. 2–6) sees that Aristotle is concerned with the *eidê* of the art and that he then goes on to discuss the various forms of making poetry by way of a discussion of the various forms of poem made, but Else rejects too quickly the possibility that, albeit without being explicit, Aristotle is referring to the art of poetry as one of the species of the art of making or doing generally. Thus we would be speaking of the art of doing or acting as such, the most important species of which will turn out to be the making of poetry.

12. See Plato's *Ion* 535e.

13. Aristotle goes out of his way to indicate the adverbial use of the accusative case in the last words of the sentence—*kai mê ton auton tropon*, or "and not the same way"—which here refer to how the imitation is made.

14. The word for habit, *sunêtheia*, also means intimacy or even sexual intercourse. Some generation is done with the finished product in mind; this is generation through *technê*. Some generation is the result of actions that lead to a product but are not consciously for the sake of that product. Sexual procreation is the most important example of such making. It is fair to say that the two meanings of *mimêsis*, mimicry and representation, are analagous respectively to erotic and artful making.

15. See *Rhetoric* 1404a21, where Aristotle calls *phônê* most mimetic of all of our parts.

16. We would call it *synecdoche* when the species thus stands for the genus, but see *Poetics* 1457b6–13.

17. *Tais erêmenais* literally means "with those [the arts] having been said." Aristotle frequently uses ordinary idioms that, when read literally, are suggestive. In this case the arts mentioned are clearly the list beginning with epic poetry and ending with the art of the *kithera*. Their common medium is sound. Arts "having been said" would on the other hand presumably refer especially to those arts that produce their effects through voice.

18. Compare Plato's *Republic* 595c–97c and *Ion* 537d–42b.

19. *Melos* can also mean tune (i.e., the music to which lyrics are set). However, there is no question that without further clarification it brings with it the notion of music set to words.

20. See Plato's *Gorgias* 502c where *logos* is said to be what remains after *poiêsis* is stripped of *melos*, *rhuthmos*, and *metros*.

21. For an interpretation the importance of time in differentiating between

the plastic arts and poetry see Lessing's *Laokoön* (London: Oxford University Press, 1965).

22. See Socrates' double account of the relation of pleasure and pain at *Phaedo* 60b–c. He first says they are inseparable and then says that if Aesop had thought to make a myth about them, he would have said that a god yoked them together. The first account is analytic or eidetic, the second poetic or genetic. The poetic account first treats things as separate to show that they are inseparable.

23. For only a few examples compare 1453a5, 1453a23, and 1451a20, also the use of *phaulos* and *spoudaios* throughout chapter five with their use in the final sentence, and the long account of pity and fear in chapter fourteen concerned with the nature of voluntary action with the brief remarks at the end (1454a10ff.) concerning whether the poets produced their plots wittingly or unwittingly.

24. See chapter one.

25. It is in the accusative case and so agrees with "those acting," which is also accusative. However, as the subject of the infinitive it would have to be accusative in any event and therefore could refer to "those imitating," who are also acting.

26. See Seth Benardete, "On Greek Tragedy," in *Current Developments in the Arts and Sciences, The Great Ideas Today 1980* (Chicago: Encyclopaedia Britannica, 1980), pp. 135–40, as well as Michael Davis, *Ancient Tragedy and the Origins of Modern Science* (Carbondale: Southern Illinois University Press, 1988), chapter 2.

27. Aristotle is aware that Homer is not really so easy to categorize. For example, the wonders of Books IX–XII of the *Odyssey*—lotus eaters, Cyclopes, Circe's enchantments, Hades, the sirens, Scylla and Charybdis, Calypso's offer of immortality—are all related by Odysseus. Homer therefore casts some doubt on their authenticity; by concealing Odysseus's motives he introduces a dramatic element into his poem. See 1448b35–36 and 1460a5–11.

28. For a discussion of this difficult text, see the D.W. Lucas edition of the *Poetics*, pp. 66–67.

29. See note 27.

30. See Leo Strauss, *Socrates and Aristophanes* (New York: Basic Books, 1966), p. 43.

31. Else's explanation of what would otherwise be a *men solitarium* at 1448b5 seems to be correct. Until 1448b24 Aristotle is discussing the causes of *poiêtikê* generally or as a whole. Thereafter the discussion splits into an account of what causes specific differences within the genus.

32. The otherwise extraneous reference to meter seems intended to reveal a similar split between action and reflection within rhythm itself.

33. Compare with 1448a1–5.

34. Interestingly enough the two are not the same; apparently the noble do not always do noble things, and the noble things are not always done by noble men.

35. At 1449a9–14 Aristotle suggests another origin of comedy and tragedy out of phallic songs and dithyrambs. As Lucas points out (*Poetics*, p. 80), dithyrambs do not seem to fit Aristotle's account of the dignified origins of tragedy. However, Aristotle himself undermines that account with his turn to Homer as the father of both comedy and tragedy. Aristotle's separation of comedy and tragedy at the outset seems to depend on a first *mimêsis*, which was like pure mimicry and not at all reflective. Thus the first poets would be altogether unselfconscious—their "poems" the pure products of their characters. However, as all *mimêsis* is already in some measure reflective, it should come as no surprise that this pure origin proves to be a fiction. The second less pure account of the origin of tragedy is meant to be a sign of this.

36. Of the *Margites* we possess only fragments. It was a poem written in a mixture of hexameter and iambic about an extremely dumb hero who "knew many things but knew everything badly." For example, Margites was supposed not to have known whether his father or his mother gave birth to him.

37. Compare 1447a13–16.

38. See Lucas, p. 97; Telford, p. 81; and Else, p. 224.

39. See Benardete, "On Greek Tragedy," pp. 127–35.

40. It is also not immediately clear why the action imitated must be complete or perfect.

41. In all of Aristotle's works nothing has been so debated as the meaning of catharsis in his definition of tragedy. "A great historic discussion has centred round this phrase. No passage, probably, in ancient literature has been so frequently handled by commentators, critics, and poets, by men who knew Greek, and by men who knew no Greek" (Butcher, p. 243). "The Cooper-Gudeman Bibliography and its continuation by M.T. Herrik (AJP 52 [1931] 168–74) list 147 books, dissertations, and articles since 1856 whose titles clearly indicate that they deal specifically with catharsis; and to that figure one must add of course all the major editions of the *Poetics* and many of the general books on the *Politics* and Aristotle" (Else, p. 226). Both Butcher (pp. 241–73) and Else (pp. 221–32), as well as D.W. Lucas (pp. 273–90) and Stephen Halliwell (*Aristotle's Poetics*, Chapel Hill: University of North Carolina Press, 1986, pp. 350–56) have extended and useful discussions of the various contending meanings proposed for catharsis and for pity and fear in the *Poetics*. Apart from the scholarly debate, it is of considerably more interest that the issue has been discussed by men like Pierre Corneille ("Discours de la Tragédie" in *Théâtre complet*, Vol. 1, Paris: Garnier, 1971, pp. 33-56), Jean Racine (Preface to *Phèdre*, Paris: Larousse, 1965), Gotthold Ephraim Lessing (*Hamburgische Dramaturgie*, Nrs. 73–83 in *Werke*, Bände 6 and 7, Leipzig: Bibliographische Institut, 1911), John Milton (Preface to *Samson Agonistes* in *Poetical Works*, New York: American News Company, no date), Voltaire ("Remarques sur les Discours de Corneille" in Vol. 28 of *Oeuvres Complètes*, Paris: L.-T. Cellot. 1821, pp. 23–51), Goethe (*Nachlese zu Aristotelische Poetik* in *Goethe the Critic*, introduction and notes by G.F. Semos, revised and completed by C.V. Bock, Manchester: Manchester University Press, 1960, pp. 60–63), Dr. Johnson (in *James Boswell's Life of Samuel Johnson, LLD.*, Oxford: Clarendon Press, 1934, 1950), and Nietzsche (*Die Geburt der Tragödie*), as well as others equally impressive.

42. Else (p. 225) points out that although the contemporary debate traces itself back to Jakob Bernays's "medical" interpretation of catharsis as purgation (*Grundzüge der verlorene Abhandlungen des Aristoteles über Wirkung der Tragödie*, Breslau: Trewendt, 1857), such an interpretation was anticipated as early as the Renaissance.

43. See Davis, *Ancient Tragedy and the Origins of Modern Science*, pp. 115–16.

44. See Seth Benardete, *Socrates' Second Sailing* (Chicago: University of Chicago Press, 1989), pp. 153–56.

45. See Benardete, *Socrates' Second Sailing*, pp. 215–23.

46. See Davis, "Courage and Impotence in Shakespeare's Macbeth" in *Essays from The Sarah Lawrence Faculty*, 4/2 (1979), pp. 1–29.

47. See Davis, *Ancient Tragedy and the Origins of Modern Science*, pp. 14–33.

48. It is interesting that the question of whether the evil is deserved or not does not arise in the case of fear (i.e., in my own case).

49. The sentence could also mean that when they make (*poiountai*) a tragedy, poets are necessarily acting (*prattontes*), although it is not clear what this would have to do with *opsis* as a part of tragedy.

50. Compare 1455a22–29.

51. See 1462a12–13.

52. There is some ambiguity about the order in which character (*êthos*) and thought (*dianoia*) are introduced.

> But since imitation is of action, and it is acted by those acting, for whom it is necessary to be of certain sorts with respect to both character and thought, for it is through these that we claim actions to be of certain sorts, thought and character being by nature two causes of actions, and with respect to these also all are fortunate and unfortunate. (1449b36–50a3)

Aristotle seems to go out of his way to make the order interchangeable here. These two "causes of action" (clearly at the root of moral and intellectual virtue in the *Nicomachean Ethics*) are obviously closely related to the putting together of incidents to form an action.

53. This is why it is never really possible to speak of any text as simply self-referential. We may not understand exactly how texts refer to reality, but it is nevertheless reality, not Homer, which determines the relation of love to anger.

54. For example, as much as it might solve certain difficulties, time cannot be turned back. While this seems altogether obvious, it proves to have enormous significance for human life. In this connection see Aeschylus's *Libation Bearers* 363–79, Shakespeare's *Macbeth* III:ii, as well as Davis, "Courage and Impotence in Shakespeare's *Macbeth*," pp. 22–24.

55. Either to *opsin* (accusative singular) or *opseis* (nominative and accusative plural).

56. Even when dismissing *opsis* as the least important of the parts of tragedy, Aristotle refers to it as *psychogogic*—soul-leading (1450b16–17).

57. See Davis, *Ancient Tragedy and the Origins of Modern Science*, chapter two.

58. Among the things we need to keep in mind is Aristotle's introduction of chapter seven as following "after" the things discussed in chapter six. Chapter seven is apparently a middle. Also, consider Aristotle's use of nominal sentences in the passage. Middles are, strictly speaking, not said to be at all; the verb "to be" is used to connect ends with what comes before but is absent in connection with what comes after. Consider also the way in which the terms used for beginning, middle, and end (*archê*, *meson*, and *teleutê*) all have nonspacial meanings—first principle, mean, extremity. Thus, although Aristotle says he is not speaking here about wholes that have no magnitude, it is not immediately clear why that would have to be the case.

59. It is interesting in this connection that *heteron* seems originally to have had the sense of the comparative of "one."

60. If we follow Aristotle's use of *eidos* to mean part, then only when *eidos* retains its orignial meaning as "looks" can the whole of which it is a part be beautiful.

61. As Else points out (p. 227), when theater is limited to daylight viewing, there is an obvious limitation on the length of a continuous performance.

62. See Nietzsche's *Die Geburt der Tragödie*, sections 7, 11, and 12.

63. Aristotle adds that Homer may have this ability "either by art or by nature." Here, at least, he does not settle the issue of whether Homer needs to know what he is doing to do it.

64. The pun on Odysseus's name is present from the very outset of the *Odyssey* (I:62); it is explained only in Book XIX.

65. Furthermore, Aristotle's other example could have been used equally well as paradigmatic of who Odysseus is. A man who stops short of killing his son to avoid going to war has something in common with a man who prefers home to immortality.

66. Poetry is in this way like rhythm and music. It is not possible to look at single note in a melody apart from what precedes and follows it.

67. See Seth Benardete, "A Reading of Sophocles' *Antigone*: I," Interpretation, 4/3 (Spring 1975), pp. 156–57, as well as "Sophocles' *Oedipus Tyrannus*," in *Ancients and Moderns: Essays on the Tradition of Political Philosophy in Honor of Leo Strauss*, Joseph Cropsey, ed. (New York: Basic Books 1964) pp. 6–7.

68. We are given only the dative of the title here—*Anthei*. The nominative could be either *Antheus*, a proper name, or *Anthos*, flower.

69. See Lucas, p. 123.

70. See Lucas, p. 123.

71. It is frequently thought that lines 1451b33–52a1 belong to chapter eight (Lucas, p. 125; Else, pp. 324–25)

72. It is not unimportant that it is really a privation of a privation of knowledge. Ignorance contains within it the potentiality for recognition.

73. One is tempted to say that this is when the perspective of the spectator and that of the character are one; however, nowhere does Aristotle indicate that

when recognition and reversal coincide what is discovered by the character within the play is the same as what is discovered by the audience.

74. It is surely no accident that the moment at which Oedipus learns who he is should be so fuzzy. Directly after the messenger tells him he is not the son of Polybus, Oedipus seems as concerned that Jocasta will think him ill born as he is that he is in fact the son of Laius (1062–63).

75. Nietzsche, *Die Geburt der Tragödie*, Section 7.

76. See Ronna Burger's "Nemesis," *Graduate Faculty Philosophy Journal*, 13/1 (1987), pp. 69–74.

77. The *epieikeis* are not to be shown moving from good fortune (*eutuchia*) to ill fortune (*dustuchia*). The wicked (*mochthêroi*) are not to be shown moving from lack of fortune (*atuchia*) to good fortune. The change from *dustuchia* to *atuchia* suggests that since the wicked do not deserve good fortune they cannot have misfortune. They are not deprived of anything that they deserve.

78. It does not affect the matter that Aristotle may very well have been wrong about Euripides. See, for example, Lucas, p. 147. In the plays we possess of Euripides there seem to be a greater proportion of happy endings. Of course his use of the *deus ex machina* (in the *Iphigeneia among the Taurians*, *Helen*, etc.) could be understood to point to the unhappiness of the endings were it not for this rather artificial divine intervention.

79. This is what Lessing means when he calls painting imitation of bodies with their visible properties and parts contiguous in space and poetry imitation of actions with their parts following upon one another. Paintings can of course imitate actions but only by hinting at past and future through what is present (*Laokoön*, XVI).

80. See Seth Benardete, *Sophocles' Oedipus Tyrannus*, pp. 1–15.

81. In Plato this is the significance of Socratic philosophy as a second sailing.

82. See *Nicomachean Ethics* 1112a16–18.

83. At 1448a6 Aristotle seems to use *homoioi* to mean like us.

84. I read *hêmas* here; were one to accept *hêmeis*, the line would read, "Since tragedy is an imitation of those better than we, good image-makers should be imitated." Even so, it is not clear that we are not also to imitate the painters.

85. See 1454b32, 1455b9, and 1455b21. In no other place is the verb used in this way. This has led to various attempts to emend the text. See Lucas, pp. 25, 27, 168–69, and 181–82; and Else, pp. 508–10 and 515–16.

86. In this way, without realizing it, we have already shared the perspective of Pentheus within the play. See Benardete, "On Greek Tragedy," pp. 135–40.

87. It is so natural that we find it curious, for example, that Orestes conceals himself for so long from Electra at the beginning of Aeschylus's *Libation Bearers*.

88. See Euripides' *Electra* 487–549.

89. See *Libation Bearers* 219–34 and *Iphigeneia among the Taurians* 800–30.

90. On the necessary components of a real mystery novel see A. A. Milne's introduction to his *The Red House Mystery* (New York: E.P. Dutton, 1965, pp. vii–x).

91. See Sophocles' *Electra* 23–76.

92. See *Oedipus at Colonus* 36–80 and 118–37 together with Seth Benardete's "On Greek Tragedy," pp. 112–16.

93. This is a difficult sentence. If *logous* is taken to mean something like arguments or story, then the principle in question could be that the poet should set forth his arguments in general terms. But then what does *pepoiêmenous* mean? Butcher (p. 63) and others take it to refer to plots handed down through tradition as opposed to those made by the poet himself. Lucas (p. 179) thinks that common sense calls for such a distinction here. However, the Greek text makes this very hard. Not only does *pepoiêmenos* nowhere have this meaning in the *Poetics*, that it is masculine plural accusative here is hard to put together with this reading. It seems more likely, given the previous passage, that Artistotle is making a distinction between *logoi*/speeches and men who have been made up—characters.

94. See *Antigone* 223–77 with Benardete's "A Reading of Sophocles' *Antigone*: I," pp. 177–82.

95. See *Philoctetes* 745–46.

96. It is a nice touch that in order to show how hard it is in any account to separate the general and the particular, Artistotle should use Poseidon as his example. An Olympian god is perhaps the example for the Greeks of something simultaneously particular and universal, a being who is at once a person and stands for a quality or nature.

97. See note 85.

98. Compare this with Plato's *Ion* 535e.

99. See, for example, Lucas, pp. 184–88 and Else, pp. 522–40.

100. As Seth Benardete has pointed out, the *Prometheus* is therefore concerned with the limit case of tragedy. Prometheus knows what he will undergo but has not experienced it. The play is therefore concerned with the difference between knowledge accompanied by experience and knowledge unaccompanied by experience. It is concerned with the meaning of *pathei mathos*—learning by suffering.

101. There remain difficulties with the omission of song, however. Aristotle will begin chapter twenty with the elements or letters of *lexis* as fundamental divisions of voice or sound. Letters are one division of sound; musical notes are another. Aristotle's division will, therefore, not be as presuppositionless as he first makes it seem.

102. Aristotle may or may not intend a reference to his *Rhetoric*. As that books contains at least six possible references to the *Poetics* (1372a1, 1404a38, 1404b7, 1404b28, 1405a5, and 1419b5), it is unclear which is referring to which. One of them had to be written first. Still the reference to rhetoric is a nice way of indicating that this discussion of thought is incomplete apart from a discussion of rhetoric and perhaps of its antistrophe, dialectic (*Rhetoric* 1354a1). The effect of Artistotle's neat division of the sciences is ordinarily that something important to the object of the science is left out. The things treated by the sciences are less precise than the sciences that treat them. In this case, there is more to *dianoia* than comes to light in the art of poetry.

103. One would think that the intonation of a sentence when voiced would not be different from melody. It is hard to see why one would belong to *poiêtikê* but the other not.

104. Plato has Protagoras claim that he can answer Socrates' question about the teachability of virtue speaking either in *mythos* or in *logos*. That he considers this choice a question of convenience means that he thinks the form of his answer is indifferent to its content. He thinks that any answer is fully translatable into *logos* (*Protagoras* 320c).

105. In this very first definition Artistotle has already used two versions of what he will later identify as a metaphor (1457b6–9). The first is a metaphorical use of a genus, *stoicheion* as element, to stand for a species, *stoicheion* as letter. The second is a metaphorical use of a species, *phônê* as voice, to stand for a genus, *phônê* as sound. It is important to see that his account is from the outset metaphorical.

106. Aristotle concludes the discussion of letters by saying that they differ on the basis of the arrangement and placement of the mouth, rough and smooth aspiration, length, and pitch. But the pitch of letters (acute, grave, or intermediate) is not the pitch of melody. One is governed by the needs of intelligibility, the other by the needs of a musical wholeness. Artistotle's casual remark that for the details one would turn to the *theôria* of metrics seems to call for nothing less than a science putting together the true and the beautiful.

107. See Lucas, pp. 201–2.

108. See Thucydides' *History Book* III, 36–50.

109. See, for example, Sophocles' *Antigone* 337–41 and Aeschylus's *Eumenides* 1–5.

110. See Seth Benardete, *Herodotean Inquiries*, pp. 131–32.

111. See, for example, *Metaphysics* 1024a29–b10, *Categories* 2b, and *Topics*, Book IV.

112. *Categories* 14b–15a.

113. *Categories* 2b.

114. *Categories* 2b and *Topics* 122a.

115. The two are, respectively, fragments 138 and 143.

116. The language of medicine is frequently the same as the language of war. Cautery and burning are alternative meanings for the word *kausis*.

117. ΟΠΣ seems a sensible emendation for the ΟΗΣ of the text.

118. Compare *A Midsummer Night's Dream* IV.1, where Hermia says "Methinks I see these things with parted eye, when everything seems double."

119. See Lucas, p. 207.

120. Greek also has a neuter gender, which Artistotle describes here as "in between." It is defined in terms of masculine and feminine, and so subordinate to them. It is interesting that for neuter nouns nominative and accusative forms, subject and direct object, are the same, The neuter "gender" clearly indicates a resistance within the language to this personification. *He Dikê* is not *to dikaion*. For the personification of Justice, see Aeschylus's *Libation Bearers* 946–51.

121. *Nicomachean Ethics* 1277b30.

122. See *Politics* 1325b17–23 and *Nicomachean Ethics* 1177a14–22.

123. Neither play is extant.

124. See 1448b15–17.

125. See, for example, Lucas, p. 213; Telford, p. 11; and Else, p. 570.

126. At *Republic* 392d, Socrates uses the word *diêgêsis* to stand as the genus of everything said by the poets and tellers of tales (*muthologoi*).

127. See chapter six above as well as 1449b33 and 55a22–29.

128. See chapter eight above as well as 1455b32–56a3.

129. See, for example, Sophocles' *Trachiniae*, 1–25.

130. Compare 1458a5, 1453a5 and 1454a24.

131. Books IX–XII of the *Odyssey*—Odysseus's account of his adventures—include the episodes of the lotus eaters, the Cyclopes, Aeolus and his bag of winds, the Laestrygonian giants, Circe the enchantress, the descent into Hades, the Sirens, Scylla and Charybdis, and the cattle of the island of the sun.

132. While it is true that pre-Olympian gods appear in tragedy (e.g., Oceanus in Aeschylus's *Prometheus Bound*), they do so only anthropomorphically. Oceanus shows himself as a man—not as ocean, thus sharing, for the sake of appearing on stage, the distinctive feature of the Olympian gods.

133. See 1452a1–11 and chapter seven.

134. The text reads *adunamian*. Either something has dropped out (see Lucas, pp. 43 and 235; and Butcher, p. 98) and the sense is something like "he chose to imitate and had an inability," or the text we have stands, but *adunamia* would have to bear the otherwise unexampled meaning, "impossibility."

135. See *Nicomachean Ethics* 1094a27–28, although, as usual, one can never simply quote Artistotle. What he means in one context gets revised in another. See, for example, *Nicomachean Ethics* 1141a19–23.

136. See *Metaphysics* 982b11–20.

137. See *Metaphysics* 983a11–21.

138. *Oedipus at Colonus* 1224–227.

139. We do the same thing when we admire someone's good looks; indeed *eidos* is formed from the verb to see, and at first means something like "looks."

140. See Lucas, p. 242.

141. Although at 1461b20–21 he does mention the unnecessary vileness of Menelaus in Euripides' *Orestes* as a problem.

142. This is confirmed by Artistotle's second example of a metaphorical solution. He quotes *Iliad* XVIII:489 to the effect that the Bear alone has no part of the bath of Ocean. That is, alone among the constellations, the Bear never sets. However, this is not true. Aristotle solves the difficulty by saying that it is the "only" one means that it is the most notable of those that do not set. The best is thus allowed to stand metaphorically for the whole class. This has its own dangers. When the perfection of the class is identified with the class, imperfect members of the class become doubtful members. When Dolon of the bad looks (*eidos*) can be ruled out of the species (*eidos*), he can be treated as animal.

143. For a discussion of this difficulty see Lucas, pp. 242–43.

144. See, for example, Telford, pp. 49–53 and Lucas, p. 251.

145. Aristotle remarks that if one were to stretch out the *Oedipus* to the epic

length of the *Iliad*, the dilution would be clear. This is especially interesting as it suggests the two might be about the same thing—anger.

146. For the evidence see Lucas, pp. xiii–xiv.

147. Even if there was originally a second book, however, it seems clear from the last lines of chapter twenty-six that Artistotle means the discussion of tragedy and epic to have been concluded.

> Concerning tragedy and epic, then, both of their species and their parts, both how many they are and how they differ, and some causes of the well and the not well [made], and concerning censures and resolutions, let so much have been said. (1462b16–19)

148. See, for example, Else, pp. 636–42 and Halliwell, pp. 1–41.

Bibliography

Aeschylus. *Agamemnon, Libation Bearers, Eumenides, Fragments.* Cambridge, MA: Loeb Classical Library, 1983.

———. *Suppliant Maidens, Persians, Prometheus, Seven Against Thebes.* Cambridge, MA: Loeb Classical Library, 1988.

Aristophanes. *Comoediae.* 2 vols. Oxford: Clarendon Press, 1988.

Aristotle. *"Art" of Rhetoric.* Cambridge, MA: Loeb Classical Library, 1982.

———. *Categories, On Interpretation, Prior Analytics.* Cambridge, MA: Loeb Classical Library, 1973.

———. *Metaphysics.* Oxford: Clarendon Press, 1963.

———. *Nicomachean Ethics.* Cambridge, MA: Loeb Classical Library, 1968.

———. *Poetics.* New York: Everyman Library, 1963.

———. *Poetics.* Translated and edited by Kenneth A. Telford. Lanham, MD: University Press of America, 1961.

———. *Poetics.* Edited by D.W. Lucas. Oxford: Clarendon Press, 1986.

———. *Politics.* Cambridge, MA: Loeb Classical Library, 1972.

———. *Politics.* Translated by Carnes Lord. Chicago: University of Chicago Press, 1985.

———. *Politics.* Edited by W.L. Newman. Oxford: Clarendon Press, 1950.

———. *Posterior Analytics, Topics.* Cambridge, MA: Loeb Classical Library, 1960.

Belfiore, E. "Aristotle's Concept of *Praxis* in the *Poetics.*" *Classical Journal* 79 (1984):110–14.

Benardete, Seth. "A Reading of Sophocles' *Antigone.*" *Interpretation* 4/ 3 (Spring 1975):148–96; 5/1 (Summer 1975):1–55; and 5/2 (Winter 1975):148–84.

———. *Herodotean Inquiries.* The Hague: Martinus Nijhoff, 1969.

———. "On Greek Tragedy." In *Current Developments in the Arts and Sciences, The Great Ideas Today 1980*, pp. 102–43. Chicago: Encyclopaedia Britannica, 1980.

———. *Socrates' Second Sailing.* Chicago: University of Chicago Press, 1989.

———. "Sophocles' *Oedipus Tyrannus.*" In *Ancients and Moderns: Essays on the Tradition of Political Philosophy in Honor of Leo Strauss*, edited by Joseph Cropsey, pp. 1–15. New York: Basic Books, 1964.

Bernays, Jakob. *Grundzüge der verlorene Abhandlungen des Aristoteles über Wirkung der Tragödie.* Breslau: Trewendt, 1857.

Berns, Laurence. "Aristotle's *Poetics.*" In *Ancients and Moderns: Essays on the Tradition of Political Philosophy in Honor of Leo Strauss*, edited by Joseph Cropsey, pp. 70–87. New York: Basic Books, 1964.

Boswell, James. *Life of Samuel Johnson, LLD.* Oxford: Clarendon Press, 1950, 1934.

Brecht, Bertolt. *Brecht on Theater.* Edited and translated by John Willett. New York: Hill and Wang, 1977.

Burger, Ronna. "Mirror of Nature: The Misunderstanding of *Mimesis.*" Unpublished typescript.

———. "Nemesis." *Graduate Faculty Philosophy Journal.* 13/1 (1987):69–74.

———. "To See with Parted Eye: Irony and Dramatic *Mimêsis* in the Greek Tragedies." Unpublished typescript.

Butcher, S.H. *Aristotle's Theory of Poetry and Fine Art.* London: Macmillan, 1902.

Butterworth, C.E. *Averroes' Three Short Commentaries on Aristotle's* Topics,

Rhetoric *and* Poetics. Albany: State University of New York Press, 1977.

Bywater, Ingram. *Aristotle on the Art of Poetry*. Oxford: Clarendon Press, 1909.

Cantor, Paul A. "Aristotle and the History of Tragedy." Unpublished typescript.

Cooper, Lane. *Aristotle on the Art of Poetry*. Boston: Ginn, 1913.

———. *The* Poetics *of Aristotle: Its Meaning and Influence*. New York: Longman's Green, 1927.

Corneille, Pierre. "Discours de la Tragédie." In *Théâtre complet*, Vol. 1, pp. 33–56. Paris: Garnier, 1971.

Dahiyat, I.M. *Avicenna's Commentary on the Poetics of Aristotle*. Leiden: Brill, 1974.

Davis, Michael. *Ancient Tragedy and the Origins of Modern Science*. Carbondale: Southern Illinois University Press, 1988.

———. "Aristotle's Reflections on Revolution." *Graduate Faculty Philosophy Journal*, 11 (1986):49–64.

———. "Cannibalism and Nature." *MHTIE*, 4/1 (1989): 33–50.

———. "Courage and Impotence in Shakespeare's *Macbeth*." *Essays from The Sarah Lawrence Faculty*, 4/2 (1979):1–29.

———. "*Politics* and Poetry: Aristotle's *Politics* Books VII and VIII." *Interpretation*, 19/2 (1991–92):157–68.

Derrida, Jacques. *Dissemination*. Chicago: The University of Chicago Press, 1981.

———. "La mythologie blanche: la métaphore dans le texte philosophique." In *Marges de la Philosophie*, pp. 247–324. Paris: Minuit, 1972.

Else, Gerald. *Aristotle's Poetics: The Argument*. Cambridge, MA: Harvard University Press, 1967.

Euripides. *Fabulae* I–III. Oxford: Clarendon Press, 1989, 1988, 1986.

Freud, Sigmund. *Abriss der Psychoanalyse und das Unbehagen in der Kultur*. Frankfurt: Fischer Bücherei, 1970.

Goethe, J.W. von. "Nachlese zu Aristotelische Poetik." In *Goethe the Critic*, introduction and notes by G.F. Semos, revised and completed by C.V. Bock, pp. 60–63. Manchester: Manchester University Press, 1960.

Halliwell, Stephen. *Aristotle's Poetics*. Chapel Hill: University of North Carolina Press, 1986.

Hegel, G.W.F. *Ästhetik*. Frankfurt: Europäische Verlagsanstalt, 1955.

———. *Phänomenologie des Geistes*. Hamburg: Felix Meiner Verlag, 1952.

Herodotus. *Historiae*. 2 vols. Oxford: Clarendon Press, 1990, 1988.

Hesiod, the Homeric Hymns and Homerica. Cambridge, MA: Loeb Classical Library, 1970.

Homer. *Iliad*. Cambridge, MA: Loeb Classical Library, 1967.

———. *Odyssey*. Cambridge, MA: Loeb Classical Library, 1974.

Horace. *Satires, Epistles and Ars Poetica*, Cambridge, MA: Loeb Classical Library, 1932.

Kaufmann, Walter. *Tragedy and Philosophy*. Garden City, NY: Doubleday Anchor, 1969.

Lessing, G.E. *Hamburgische Dramaturgie*. In *Werke*, Bände 6 and 7. Leipzig: Bibliographische Institut, 1911.

———. *Laokoön*. London: Oxford University Press, 1965.

Lord, Carnes. *Education and Culture in the Political Thought of Aristotle*. Ithaca, NY: Cornell University Press, 1982.

Marx, Karl. *Werke, Schriften bis 1844*. Erster Teil, Ergänzungsband. Berlin: Dietz Verlag, 1968.

Milne, A.A. *The Red House Mystery*. New York: E.P. Dutton, 1965.

Milton, John. *Poetical Works*. New York: American News Company, no date.

Newman, John Henry. *Poetry, With Reference to Aristotle's Poetics*. Boston: Ginn, 1894.

Nietzsche, Friedrich. *Die Geburt der Tragödie*. In *Werke in Drei Bänden*. Munich: Carl Hanser Verlag, 1966.

Olson, Elder. *Aristotle's "Poetics" and English Literature*. Chicago: University of Chicago Press, 1965.

Plato. *Opera*. Edited by John Burnet, 5 vols. 1900–15. Oxford: Clarendon Press, 1977.

Racine, Jean. *Phèdre*. Paris: Larousse, 1965.

Rymer, Thomas. *The Tragedies of the Last Age Consider'd and Examin'd*. New York: Garland Publishing, 1974.

Schenck, Celeste. "All of a Piece: Women's Poetry and Autobiography." In *Life/Lines: Theorizing Women's Autobiography*, edited by B. Brodzki and C. Schenck, pp. 281–285. Ithaca, NY: Cornell University Press, 1988.

Shakespeare. *The Works of William Shakespeare*. Edited by Charles Knight. Boston: Estes and Lauriat, 1878.

Sophocles. *Fabulae*. Oxford: Clarendon Press, 1990.

Strauss, Leo. *The City and Man*. Chicago: Rand McNally, 1964.

———. *Socrates and Aristophanes*. New York: Basic Books, 1966.

Thucydides. *Historiae*. 2 vols. Oxford: Clarendon Press, 1990, 1988.

Trilling, Lionel. "Freud and Literature." In *Criticism: The Foundations of Modern Literary Judgment*, edited by M. Schorer, J. Miles, and G. McKenzie. New York: Harcourt Brace, 1948.

Voltaire. "Remarques sur les Discours de Corneille." In Vol. 28 of *Oeuvres Complètes*, pp. 23–51. Paris: L.-T. Cellot. 1821.

Zuckerkandl, Victor. "On *Mimêsis*." Typescript of lecture given at St. John's College, 1955.

Index

Achilles, xvi–xviii, 40, 80, 140
acting, xvi, 17
action, 16, 100; as blundering, 96;
  doubleness of, xv, 20, 26–27, 29,
  89, 99; as imitation of action,
  xviii, 9; and poetry, xv, 53–54; as
  theme of the *Poetics*, xiv–xv; *see
  also praxis*
actor(s), perspective of, 65, 166n73
Aeschylus, 29, 59; *Agamemnon*, 68;
  Eumenides, 169n109; *Libation
  Bearers*, 68–69, 81, 85, 165n54,
  167n89, 169n120; *Prometheus
  Bound*, 92, 168n100, 170n132
Agathon, 59–60
Ajax, 40, 80
Alcibiades, 59, 60
allo, 50, 51, 53, 56, 65
anagnôizô, 68, 88; *see also* recognition
andreia, xvi–xviii
Apollinian, xiv
archê, 50, 55, 56, 91, 129, 166n58
Aristophanes, 24; *Birds*, 7; *Clouds*,
  12, 22, 59; *Frogs*, 59; *Knights*, 59
Aristotle: humor of, 51; mode of
  writing of, 162n17, 163n23,
  166n58, 170n135; *Categories*,

169n111–13; *Metaphysics*, xv, 62,
  141, 161n9, 169n111, 170n136–
  37; *Nicomachean Ethics*, xv, xvi,
  xvii, 4, 53, 71, 95, 123, 161n5,
  165n52, 167n82, 169n121–22,
  170n35; *Poetics. See Poetics*;
  Politics, xvi, 4, 27, 95, 123,
  169n122; *Rhetoric*, 38, 162n15,
  168n102; *On Sophistical Refutations*, 152; *Topics*, 169n111,
  169n114
arthra, 76, 105–6
audience, 156–57
author, 158–60
authoritative. *See kurion*; ordinary
autonomy, 15

beautiful. *See kaon*
beginning. *See archê*
Benardete, Seth, 163n26, 164n39,
  165n44–45, 166n67, 167n80,
  167n86, 168n92, 168n94,
  168n100, 169n110
Boswell, James, 164n41
brutality, as a problem of *Iliad* X,
  151–52
Burger, Ronna, 167n76
Butcher, S.H., 162n11, 164n41,
  168n93, 170n134

179

About the Author

Michael Davis has taught philosophy at Sarah Lawrence College since 1977. He is the author of *Ancient Tragedy and the Origins of Modern Science* (Carbondale: Southern Illinois University Press, 1988) as well as numerous essays on Plato, Aristotle, and Shakespeare. He is currently working on a collection of essays on Aristotle's *Politics* and a book on Rousseau's *Reveries of a Solitary Walker*.